had met as old tried fr[iends?]
momentprevious all stiffness had slipped away.
e had met with as much ease as if old re
ther I wither. That wonderful confidence I had
him, and he in me, that we had made no
pretences, said nothing for talking sake, but
just lived & acted truly. If I had
disregarded proprieties, and when he said will
you walk up with me, had left Miss Guild
and gone with him, when he had said, sit
under the trees here! pick some flowers, ha
sat down & forgotten time, had wandered
round the grounds & through the greenhouses,
should have felt that all was natural & norm
if I had met the family, or any one else! I
seemed to belong to him & he to me. — I kn
full well that my confidence and joy are buil
on a very fragile foundation. He may like
and have said & done all that he has,
without ever dreaming of anything more than a
simple, sincere friendliness, but I had schoole
my heart to feel that all was hopelessly ov
it is not over, and no power of mine could
keep my soul in bonds longer. It had been

MORE THAN COMMON
POWERS OF PERCEPTION

ELIZABETH ROGERS MASON CABOT, 1834–1920
COURTESY OF THE MASSACHUSETTS HISTORICAL SOCIETY

MORE THAN COMMON
POWERS OF PERCEPTION

The Diary of

Elizabeth Rogers Mason Cabot

EDITED BY P. A. M. TAYLOR

BEACON PRESS   BOSTON

Beacon Press
25 Beacon Street
Boston, Massachusetts 02108-2892

Beacon Press books
are published under the auspices of
the Unitarian Universalist Association of Congregations.

98 97 96 95 94 93 92 91   8 7 6 5 4 3 2 1

Text design by Linda Koegel

Diary entries for February–March 1885 and the years 1890 and
1898–1906 are courtesy of the Schlesinger Library, Radcliffe College.

Library of Congress Cataloging-in-Publication Data

Cabot, Elizabeth Rogers Mason, 1834–1920.
    More than common powers of perception : the diary of Elizabeth
Rogers Mason Cabot / edited by P. A. M. Taylor.
        p.   cm.
    Includes bibliographical references and index.
    ISBN 0-8070-5104-7
    1. Cabot, Elizabeth Rogers Mason, 1834–1920—Diaries.
2. Boston (Mass.)—Social life and customs.   3. Brookline
(Mass.)—Social life and customs.   4. Upper classes—
Massachusetts—Boston—History—19th century.   5. Upper
classes—Massachusetts—Brookline—History—19th century.
6. Boston (Mass.)—Biography.   7. Brookline (Mass.)—
Biography.   8. Women—Massachusetts—Boston—Diaries.
9. Women—Massachusetts—Brookline—Diaries.   I. Taylor,
P. A. M.   II. Title.
F73.44.G333   1990
974.4'6103'092—dc20   90-52582
                                                        CIP

To the Memory of
Norman and Trissie Tyack
with Gratitude and Affection

CONTENTS

LIST OF ILLUSTRATIONS

The illustrations follow page 144

Elizabeth Rogers Mason Cabot's diary is divided between two libraries. The major part was acquired in 1985–86 by the Massachusetts
Historical Society and forms part of the Paine Papers. Its thirty-five
volumes span, though with gaps, the years 1844–1896.[1] The collection also includes thirteen boxes of Mason and Cabot family letters
and nine volumes of the diary of Elizabeth's mother, Hannah Rogers
Mason, 1853–1872. Elizabeth's dairy does not treat all these years at
uniform depth. Childhood entries are brief. From her early teens to
her marriage in 1860, she writes in great detail, with color and
warmth. After that, entries become briefer and more purely factual.
Most of the exceptions concern her long tours and that most critical
episode, the operation performed in 1881 on her youngest daughter.

The minor part is to be found in the Arthur and Elizabeth
Schlesinger Library on the History of Women in America, Radcliffe
College. Use of the five manuscript volumes is made easier by the
existence of a two-volume typed copy, complete and very accurate.
All this material was acquired in 1981. The diary begins in 1861,
and what has been said above, of the years that follow, remains true.
But in one or other collection, every year is to some extent treated,

even if in no more than two, three, six, or ten pages. Even more interesting, the Schlesinger volumes prolong the diary by ten years, that is, to the middle of 1906. That means past Walter's death, though still fourteen years short of Elizabeth's own.[2]

Let it be said at this point that the editor is deeply grateful to the directors and staffs of these two libraries for permission to print the passages in this edition and for help while working.

The editor's prime task has been to provide examples of Elizabeth's styles of writing, to represent all stages of her life, to demonstrate the range of her interests and feelings. Much good writing has had to be sacrificed, especially from her European tours and her American vacations. He has had to attempt this in a volume which can present less than one-eighth of the total diary.

The exact chronological order of entries has been preserved. With a very few exceptions, when Elizabeth treats two or more topics that can be separated, each entry has been reproduced complete. A few illegible words have been indicated by [?] or by a guess inserted within the brackets. The form of dating has been standardized. The place of writing has been indicated whenever there can be any doubt. More controversially, in the hope of helping the reader, the very few spelling mistakes Elizabeth made have been corrected, and her punctuation, highly erratic even when she was not writing under strong emotion, has been reduced to a modern order.

If they are to understand to the full a record of nineteenth-century private life, readers need further help. So I have provided simple explanatory notes to the text.[3] In the introduction, I stress time, place, and class, seeking to define the distance that separates us from this woman of the past. I then suggest some of the ways in which the diary confirms or modifies what has been written in recent women's history, and in doing so I sometimes cite diary entries not included in the edition and call on family letters. Finally, I insist that Elizabeth was an individual, not just a representative figure, a woman whose interests and feelings are accessible to us if we use our imagination. Readers must be clear that this is not a monograph but an edition, so the evidence can be limited, the focus narrow. What matters most are Elizabeth's own words.

If Elizabeth was a person, so too am I, and readers are entitled to be told enough about me to enable them to assess both the qualifications and the handicaps I bring to my task. I am not a woman, not a Bostonian, not an American, and not a member of any country's upper class. My English ancestors can best be described by that useful term "labor aristocracy." My more immediate relations have been white-collar workers, my father a display specialist, in a small department store, who won international awards in the 1920s. No member of my family has ever kept a servant; none has ever worked as one. None of them before me went to a university. None was ever unemployed. I myself attended a school rather like Mrs. Lowell's in the diary, then a small boys' high school, then Cambridge. Apart from about four years of military service, my whole adult life has been spent in academic work, teaching most kinds of history until 1962—when I took up my first appointment specializing in the United States—and doing so (if short periods are counted) in four countries. It was not until I had turned fifty that I began to study Boston, and only much later did I take more than incidental notice of women's history. Perhaps my greatest asset is that of being elderly. Elizabeth died a few weeks after I was born. My parents' and grandparents' recollections went far back into her lifetime. Despite the differences of nationality, place, and class, a scholar who was already at the end of his teens when World War II broke out perhaps can understand Elizabeth better than any who grew up in the 1950s or 1960s. He can remember how a childhood illness, nowadays cured with a few tablets or injections, then entailed weeks in bed. More important, however much he has abandoned in daily practice, he can at least remember the weight of a body of religion, morality, and convention incomprehensible to those twenty or thirty years younger except by strenuous study pursued against the grain of personal experience and preference. I do not share all Elizabeth's values and tastes, but at least, when faced with the record of her doubts, self-questioning, and agonizing, I do not wonder what the fuss was all about.

Thanks have already been expressed to the Massachusetts Historical Society and the Schlesinger Library: Peter Drummey and Eva Moseley should be singled out. Thanks are also due to the director and staff of the Boston Athenaeum, especially Jill Erickson and Sally Pierce; Alan Seaburg at Andover-Harvard Theological Library; Lorna Condon, Society for the Preservation of New England Antiquities; Philip Bergen, Bostonian Society; Karen Shafts, Print Department, Boston Public Library; Robert Sullivan, Brookline Public Library; the librarian and staff of the Brynmor Jones Library, University of Hull; Andrew Watt, who searched in the microfilm of part of the 1860 federal census; Astrid White, who typed the last two drafts; and Barbara Miller Solomon, who saved me from an important mistake.

MORE THAN COMMON

POWERS OF PERCEPTION

When Elizabeth Rogers Mason Cabot died, she was a very old woman. She had been born during Jackson's presidency, had begun her diary during Tyler's, had married toward the end of Buchanan's, and had closed her writing before Roosevelt had handed over to Taft. To understand the past, to establish accurately the distance between it and ourselves, always demands a powerful effort of imagination. For most people, the difficulty is probably greatest when a quite recent past is involved. For times more remote, castles and monasteries, armor and heraldry, the use in the records of Latin or an archaic vernacular, proclaim the distance in unmistakable terms. For a time only a century or a century and a half ago, even in the area of technology and material environment, and still more in that of ideas, there may exist enough similarities to deceive.

Elizabeth grew up with the railroad. When she went to Walpole, New Hampshire, for the summer of 1844, the train took her no further than Nashua. Three years later, it carried her to Fitchburg. In 1848, she traveled by stage only the last fourteen miles; and in her diary she could argue about the merits of the construction that was tearing up ground in Walpole itself. In July 1854, the journey from

Boston took only four hours. Within the city, public transport was at first the omnibus, then the horse-drawn streetcar, with electric power applied only when she was in her fifties. Hackney carriages could be hired on the streets, livery stables were numerous, but families like the Masons had vehicles of their own.

When, in 1852, Elizabeth went to Europe for the first time, she crossed the Atlantic in a wooden paddle wheeler only 266 feet long, 2,226 gross tons. Thirty-four years and three tours later, she returned in an iron steamship driven by a propeller, though one still only 431 feet in length and 5,517 tons gross.[1] But she could cross direct from Boston, and even in 1852 the journey took only eleven days. In Britain and Europe, she could go by train, in 1852–53, from Liverpool to London, from Strasbourg to Paris, and from Berlin to Paris via Brussels, though not from Trieste to Vienna or from Naples to Rome. Yet much more of Europe was easily accessible, for just as stagecoaches permitted journeys beyond railhead in New England, so they supplemented the trains in Europe, even crossing Alpine passes. People as prosperous as the Masons could do better, hiring carriage and driver for considerable distances and several days.[2] Less widely used nowadays, steamboats could be found, not only on Long Island Sound, on the Hudson and Lake Champlain, and on the open sea between Boston, Maine, and the Maritimes, but on the English Channel, on the Mediterranean and the Adriatic, on Swiss lakes, on the Danube, Rhine, Rhone, and Seine. As for the Thames, Hawthorne records finding, at the Tower of London, boats departing every ten minutes for Chelsea, taking forty minutes on the journey, at least as frequent as, and much faster than, a modern bus.[3] Although travel agents and travelers' checks had yet to appear, Hawthorne shows us how easy it was to carry letters of credit from Baring's, to establish a bank account (sometimes at a British or an American bank) in a European city, to draw on this by check, and even to use the same bank for frequent lounging, reading guidebooks and American newspapers, and collecting mail.[4]

Communications, indeed, were better than a modern reader might expect. During her first European tour, Elizabeth received, in Paris, news of Daniel Webster's death within two and a half weeks.[5] When she took her second tour, the Atlantic cable was operating successfully. Even at the earlier date, most places that could interest her, both in Europe and in the United States, were linked by the telegraph, a demonstration of which she attended in her very first year of diary keeping.[6]

When the diary ended, Boston had attained nearly its present shape and contained almost 600,000 people. But when it began, the city was still small, the Mill Pond filled in and some of the South End reclaimed, but the Back Bay still marsh, separated from the Charles River by the often-mentioned Mill Dam. East Boston, and much of South Boston, remained undeveloped, and Roxbury, West Roxbury, Dorchester, Brighton, and Charlestown had not yet been annexed.[7]

Domestic technology made many advances during Elizabeth's lifetime. When she was in her twenties, an upper-class home was likely to have piped water, gas lighting, furnace heat on two or three floors, and a water closet connected to a main sewer, but one not free from problems.[8] In the country, however, a water supply was hard to guarantee—purity still more. Indoor summer temperature could not be controlled. A failure in the supply of ice at Walpole was a grave inconvenience.[9] Much later in the century, old Mrs. Cabot installed an elevator at Beverly Farms, and soon houses had electric light and telephones.[10]

Elizabeth wrote little about her clothes. Dressmakers, no doubt, made her garments but we find her trimming her own hats, and in October 1859 friends came to admire her $78 sewing machine. She became an adult when the clumsy and dangerous crinoline was in fashion—the tragedy she records in her social circle was not unique. Two decades of the bustle followed, cumbersome only at the back. By the 1890s, greater simplicity—and to modern eyes more grace—was achieved.[11] Elizabeth did not use her wealth to collect Paris gowns, but any European tour led her to buy shawls, furs, lace, and gloves, and once an elegant riding habit was sent from England to her winter residence in southwestern France.[12]

Bulky garments, the wearing of layer on layer, frequent changes according to time of day and social engagement, and the lack of any system of speedy laundering or dry cleaning all combined, especially in Europe, to produce what Hawthorne called "our mountain of luggage."[13] When Elizabeth and her family were in England in 1885, they had seven trunks. By the time they reached Liverpool, a year later, to take ship for America, they had fifteen; and the last-minute arrival of purchases from London, Paris, and Florence made it necessary to buy and pack more.[14] Even for their summer at Walpole in 1854, the Masons took "12 trunks, 3 bags, and baskets and bundles innumerable."[15] For a short visit from Walpole to Newport, in the same year, Elizabeth took a big trunk, though she turned it into something of a joke, recording it as a concession to life at a fashionable resort.[16]

Nowhere is historical distance more striking than in health and medical technology. Anesthesia arrived as Elizabeth reached her teens, but lack of antiseptic precautions made any internal surgery hazardous for another thirty years. The diary contains a full record of an operation, performed in London in 1881, and the mixture of old conditions and new is interesting. It took place, not in a hospital, but in a rented house. Elizabeth's description confirms a contemporary photograph, with surgeons in ordinary clothes with sleeves rolled up, no gowns or masks, but with a young assistant using a carbolic spray. The team of surgeons displayed speed and skill; one of them took the trouble to explain the procedures in advance; and care after surgery was notably thorough and humane—though we have to remember that the patient was a child and that the parents were rich.[17] As for illness, medical science remained primitive, and in the environment lurked many dangers. Typhoid was widespread and a killer. There were outbreaks of measles, scarlet fever, diphtheria, and, until late in the century, smallpox. Tuberculosis killed hundreds of young adults each year. Infant mortality was one in six even at the end of the nineteenth century—summer was particularly dangerous—and at the end of the eighteenth Elizabeth's father had been the third of his parents' sons to bear the names William Powell.[18] Childhood ailments, therefore, gave rise to keen anxiety; and, as history and fiction combine to tell us, little could be done except home care, by relations or private nurses, including sitting up all night with the sufferer, while nature did or did not effect a cure.[19]

Elizabeth was devoted to music, and here too the question of distance is involved. She could hear, obviously, only what had been written; in the 1850s that excluded much of Verdi and Wagner, all of Massenet, Tchaikowsky, Puccini, and Janacek. But there were also practical limitations concerning the past. She could hear Haydn and some of Handel, but the latter's operas, and most earlier music, would simply not have been performed in her day.[20]

Establishing distance means far more. Ideas, attitudes, practices, conventions, turns of phrase, all are involved. A few minor points can be made first. During Elizabeth's childhood, New Year was celebrated more seriously than Christmas, though for the latter small items were put into children's stockings and a special dinner was eaten. Christmas, however, grew more and more fashionable, and not only when the family was in Europe. The turning point in the diary seems to have been the winter of 1871–72, when presents were given at Christmas, not at New Year. Dinner was still an afternoon meal, though it was becoming later during the 1850s. Tea drinking was an evening ceremony that attracted callers.[21]

When Elizabeth was young, upper-class girls were bound by rules of etiquette that to the modern mind seem arbitrary and complex.[22] At sixteen, she worried when Mr. Quincy changed his plans, leaving his son Josiah to escort her by train to the family's country home; very soon, at Quincy, she was wondering how much time she could spend, with propriety, in the young man's company. Four years later, she remarked that it was perfectly proper for two young women to enter the Public Library since a female member of the staff was always present. She worried about boarding a train, on her way to skating on a suburban pond, among a crowd of young men, unless she had a relation or close friend as an escort. Very annoying to her was the convention that she could not ride horseback alone with a young man. A third person, not always easy to find at short notice, had to join them.[23] Yet there were degrees of severity. She could go with her cousin Powell Parkman in his sleigh. Some relaxation was thought proper when on vacation. But even then breaches of decorum were not wholly overlooked, for Elizabeth was told of a man who conversed with a young woman outside a Newport hotel, with his hat on and a lighted cigar in his mouth.[24]

Bostonians, indeed, were proud of their deportment, but they were expected to display moral probity and mental cultivation as well as good manners. Theodore Lyman was skeptical about New Yorkers' pretensions to gentility.[25] Nathaniel Hawthorne thought that the coarse and stolid Englishmen could scarcely qualify as gentlemen whatever their formal rank, and his view of upper-class English-women was even more disparaging.[26]

Elizabeth's world, too, was far removed from our own in its use of language. One very obvious example is the extent to which religious terminology was employed in diaries and letters, even by those who had in part lapsed from Unitarianism. Other examples—a few selected so as to put readers on their guard—are changes in the use of single words since the middle of the nineteenth century. When a child was described, or described itself, as "cunning," that meant, not scheming or dishonest, but attractive in a suitably childish way, much what "cute" would mean to a later age. If a child was pronounced "bright," that was an estimate of health and cheerfulness, not intelligence. "Gay" still meant high spirited. "Intercourse" meant any social dealings between persons. Elizabeth never used the words "make love," but they meant paying court to a young woman, in verbal and formal fashion, but with enough persistence to be notice-able. Josiah Quincy's remark had an exceedingly limited meaning when he told Elizabeth that he had been "intimate" with many women he admired, without being able to shake off his love for her.[27] One more example is a little less obvious. In 1856, despairing of finding anything more suitable, Elizabeth bought as a wedding present a volume of Longfellow's poems. She admitted that it was a doubtful choice, one that many people would think too "blue."[28] She did not mean, of course, that anyone thought the eminent and high-minded author guilty of salacious descriptions or music-hall jokes. Nor did she suggest that Longfellow was thought excessively melancholy, "blue" as in popular songs of the 1920s and 1930s. The connection is with "bluestocking." The gift might seem excessively, tiresomely, pretentiously intellectual.

I

Elizabeth Rogers Mason took for granted many of the appurtenances of wealth: carriage and horses, lavish gifts, a room of her own, a dress allowance of $500 a year when that sum was a respectable wage for a semiskilled worker with a family to support. We need to examine a little more closely the economic foundations and the life-style of Boston's rich and to place within that framework the Masons and their friends.

Her father can be placed exactly. He died at the end of 1867, when Elizabeth and her husband were in Europe; so her brother, as executor, found it necessary to write her at length about the will. Unlike other rich Bostonians, Mr. Mason had not been in foreign trade, or wholesaling, or textiles, or railroads. He had been a fairly prominent lawyer, but his wealth had come mostly by inheritance of real estate, his father having been one of the Mount Vernon proprietors. At his death, he was worth $1,450,000; after small legacies had been taken care of and $200,000 set aside in trust for the widow, Elizabeth and her brother shared the fortune equally. He predicted that she would receive $600,000 and that she could safely spend $14,000 during 1868. She thought this an underestimate, and he relaxed the limit to $18,000. More important, he pointed out that later, when formalities and legal fees would have come to an end, she would have $30,000 or even $40,000 a year.[29]

Not only was Elizabeth rich: she mixed with successful and prosperous people. Uncle David Sears was a millionaire. Aunt Parkman and the parents of some of her friends were worth $100,000 or more. When her husband's father, Samuel Cabot, died in 1863, he left his widow $150,000 and two estates.[30] Walter Cabot himself, as far as we can tell, made no money of his own. Elizabeth's brother, William Powell Mason, Jr., however, became a corporation director and manager of estates and was soon a millionaire; his home, 211 Commonwealth Avenue, was a showplace.[31] Of Elizabeth's children, Henry Bromfield married Anna M. Codman; Ruth, Robert Treat Paine II; Elise, Ralph Emerson Forbes; Walter Mason, Katharine H. Hixon; and Mabel, Ellery Sedgwick. Among her friends' husbands were the names Appleton, Codman, Coolidge, Eliot, Lyman, Minot, Revere, Saltonstall, and Sturgis—men not only prosperous but also recognized as members of leading families. *all Brahmins*

The Masons regularly occupied three homes, though one of them *her parents* seems to have been rented. Seen from the front, 63 Mount Vernon Street was a not particularly impressive row house, occupied from 1848. Yet in 1852 a ball could be given there, with dancing from room to room, and six years later seventy people came to hear a concert. The architect's plan provides the answer.[32] The house was less than thirty feet wide, but it was nearly eighty deep. There were cellars. The "basement" was at street level, with a vestibule, a huge half-oval hall with a staircase, a library whose windows were in the bow front, smaller spaces whose use is uncertain (though a penciled note suggests that one was a water closet), a kitchen twenty-five feet long, pantries, and a backstairs. The principal rooms were on the floor above, beside a broad hall. On the staircase side were rooms about ten feet wide; but most of the floor was occupied by three rooms in line— front parlor, "center room," and dining room—and when doors were thrown open an almost unbroken space was obtained. The "center room" was sixteen feet in height and, lacking windows, was lit by a big oval skylight, forming the bottom of a well that went through the whole height of the house. A similar skylight formed the top of the stairway. There were two floors of bedrooms (at least ten of them, the biggest as much as twenty-seven feet by eighteen) and dressing rooms. A few of the smaller rooms had windows on the well, so probably there was some means of ventilation, not only of lighting. Only the backstairs went as far as the attic. It is not clear whether that space housed servants; for with so many rooms, and a small family, they could easily have occupied the back of the bedroom floors. The country places were less monumental, but were certainly not cramped. Boggy Meadow, at Walpole, had a piazza, a large drawing room, parlor, library, dining room, kitchen, and ten bedrooms, though some of those were for servants. Blue Hill, not exactly located but close to Canton, had a piazza, hall, parlor, study, dining room, kitchen, laundry, four bedrooms, two dressing rooms, bathroom, day and night nurseries, and servants' quarters.[33]

Within about a decade of her marriage, Elizabeth was almost equally well housed. Choices were not easy, as can be seen in the letter she wrote from Rome in 1868, to Lizzie (Mrs. J. Elliot) Cabot, Walter's sister-in-law. For some years, Elizabeth and Walter had had a house on Cedar Street and had used Blue Hill, or borrowed Cabot homes, during the summer. Now, with a fortune, the time had come to organize a more settled way of life. Blue Hill seemed too far from Boston to serve as a principal home, though Walter hoped to live in the country the year round. Brookline did not seem rural enough. Something on the North Shore was desirable, during the summer heat. She had to take account of the fact that servants did not like full-time rural life. Moreover, knowing that she herself was prone to worry, she wanted to avoid too complex a plan.[34]

It took several years to make decisions and put them into effect. Elizabeth's brother took over Boggy Meadow. Blue Hill and the Cedar Street and Mount Vernon Street houses were sold, Mrs. Mason moving to Beacon Street for the brief remainder of her life. Elizabeth and Walter built a house on Heath Street, Brookline, Walter planting hundreds of trees and shrubs from England, and somewhere near owning a farm with a tenant, his principal interest being cows. The house was big enough for a garden party and for a musical entertainment for eighty or ninety guests.[35] Then they bought a summer place at Manchester-by-the-Sea, a house that Elizabeth, according to her mood, found big enough for comfort or small enough not to take seriously.

In all this, they were following the changing habits of their class, and it is time to generalize about the upper-class way of life. When Elizabeth was a child, half of Boston's rich lived on six streets.[36] The concentration was convenient. Unannounced calls wasted little time. Messages could readily be sent. Tradesmen called to take orders and deliver goods. By the standards of Victorian England, such houses were run with small staffs, though certainly they were supplemented by casual help. In 1860, the Masons had no more than one man-servant and four women, though the servants' ages denoted long experience.[37] By the 1890s, one in five of Boston's rich lived beyond city limits, though more than a thousand could still be found on Beacon Hill in the Back Bay or—a few—in Roxbury Highlands. Those who settled in Brookline—though some Cabots had been there a long time—were choosing what came to be written about as "the wealthiest town in the world, and the best governed." By the time her diary ended, Elizabeth's neighbors on Heath Street were Mrs. Henry F. Dana, Augustus Lowell, William C. Cox, Mrs. J. Sullivan Warren (a relation), J. Randolph Coolidge, Theodore Lyman, and Louis and Francis Cabot. Names equally distinguished could be found on neighboring Warren and Clyde streets, and the Country Club was very close. We find Elizabeth worrying—and the episode is well documented elsewhere—about proposals for street improvements, which would have transformed an area very near the estates into a middle-class suburb.[38]

We have already seen some of the restrictions imposed by the state of technology, even on the rich; but, in many aspects, their life was comfortable. Boarding schools were not yet fashionable, and it was from Boston Latin or local private schools that upper-class boys proceeded, almost automatically, to Harvard College and some of them also to law or medical school. Groups of friends might share all these experiences, go together on a long tour of Europe, then enlist together in the Union Army, usually separated into different units, but occasionally perishing on the same battlefield. Some went into family firms, some into other kinds of business, others into professions; a few led a leisured gentlemanly life, with a little voluntary public service. Often they maintained their connection with Harvard, serving on its Board of Overseers, fundraising, donating buildings, attending reunions of their class, or founding small clubs with college contemporaries as fellow members.[39]

The year 1851 saw the founding of the Somerset Club, first of the city's clubs of high prestige, with its own building. But until late in the century a quite different kind of club was more important: one that met for dinner in regular rotation in members' homes or, like the Saturday Club, in a private room at "Mr. Parker's," that is, in a hotel.[40] Similarly, although Boston had several theaters, the biggest of them seating 3,000 and putting on all kinds of entertainment from grand opera to Blondin on his tightrope, much of the city's music and drama continued to be private and sometimes amateur. Performances were sometimes in small rented halls but often in houses (with elegantly printed programs), and Walter Cabot's parents had a small private theater, joined by a conservatory to their main Brookline house.[41] Nor was all this the total of Boston's high culture. There were several daily newspapers and serious periodicals. There were bookshops selling English and European books along with American. The Handel and Haydn Society flourished. Eminent citizens were likely to be members of the Boston Athenaeum, in those days an art gallery as well as a great library.

Whether people of leisure or holding jobs, such Bostonians took lengthy vacations, in hotels, rented houses, or second homes of their own. Such families as the Cabots often borrowed each other's homes. Bar Harbor was not developed until the 1880s, but our families could be found at Newport, in the White Mountains, and a little later in the Adirondacks (though for a time this was for men only, with canoes and guides), but above all along the North Shore, from Nahant to Magnolia. Theodore Lyman, visiting old Mrs. Cabot at Beverly Farms while on leave from the Army of the Potomac, found in the district "a perfect nest of our acquaintance."[42] Luxury hotels, and a few of the grander houses, put on dances and concerts, even enticing visiting opera stars. But most vacation life was much simpler, a matter of tea parties, visits from house to house, carriage drives and boating, picnics, bathing, and walks to admire a rocky coast or to see the sun rise from the Blue Hills, with much reading, sewing, and gossip in rooms or on piazzas.

Tours of Europe might last for several years. Bostonians went as far as Vienna and Berlin, Naples and Madrid. They traveled the Rhineland, visited the English Lake District, spent winters at Pau near the Pyrenees. In the principal cities, they occupied big apartments on the most fashionable streets. They did not think of themselves as tourists, for in Rome William Wetmore Story could provide introductions, in London the American minister might be visited, and, when a group of Bostonians including Elizabeth watched Louis Napoleon's entry into Paris, several of them had already met him.[43] It remains true, though, that most of the people met were other Americans, often relations and close friends. They had been seen off at the docks by members of their circle, they were welcomed by them on their return, and of a young man who dropped in while she was sewing with a friend Elizabeth could remark, "I last saw him in the dome of St. Peter's."[44] A handful of Bostonians were more adventurous, going as far as Greece, the Holy Land, and Egypt, and in 1845 Elizabeth's cousin Powell Parkman returned from what was no doubt business rather than vacation, in Manila and Canton.[45]

II

I am introducing a woman, but Boston's women, however high their rank, inhabited a man's world. In politics, business, churches, and charity organizations, the key decisions were in men's hands. Women were prominent in missionary societies, in temperance agitation, in work for the poor and for the abolition of slavery. By the 1870s, a few of them sat on Boston's School Committee, by the 1880s on unpaid state boards dealing with prisons, education, and health. Some joined suffrage organizations and demonstrated for their cause from the galleries of the State House. They might work with male supporters behind the scenes. Never did they write party programs, attend conventions or caucuses, march in processions, or consume the dinners so frequent in Boston's political life. Never did they take part in City Council or General Court debates.

Closer study, however, will show that, at least at the top of the social structure, women's constraints were not in all respects over-whelming, and certainly that is true in schooling and later intel-lectual activity. Elizabeth began her education with a teacher who visited her home, then in a small class at a friend's house. The woman who ran the only formal school that Elizabeth attended was tech-nically unqualified, led to her work by the need to earn money in widowhood. But Mrs. Lowell had a powerful mind and high prin-ciples. She wrote textbooks and translated one, in mathematics, from German, adapted French plays for private performance, and as-sembled anthologies. When she left that school, Elizabeth claimed to be able to read Sallust with ease.[46] A few years later, after giving up her school because of poor health, Mrs. Lowell presented "readings," which Elizabeth attended with delight: carefully arranged passages from famous writers, from St. Francis of Sales, Jeremy Taylor, and the Cambridge Platonists, through Goethe, Humboldt, and Cole-ridge, to Emerson and Carlyle, Kingsley and Ruskin, with a per-sonal commentary that encouraged discussion.[47] Elizabeth also took individual lessons, in French from 1845, in Italian from 1850, in German from 1857, though she gives us no evidence of wide reading in any of those languages. She attended the Lowell Lectures and heard such eminent visitors as Thackeray. With an English woman, Mrs. Hodges, she undertook a course in history, geography, and biog-raphy. Modern readers may find the syllabus arid—but only until they reflect on what was being taught in men's colleges at the time. Elizabeth went far beyond recitation from one or two texts. She was required to keep more than a single discipline in mind. She had to concern herself with England, France, and, to some extent, central Europe. She had to search for information, at home, at the Public Library, or at the Athenaeum.[48]

Beyond all this, with one or another of her closest friends she met regularly for serious reading: Thoreau, or Ruskin, or Wordsworth's *Excursion*. She heard sermons that were carefully composed (and as a school exercise Mrs. Lowell required summaries), even if, for her, they lacked the power to inspire.[49] At home and on vacation, lawyers, businessmen, and college students were among the family's visitors, with conversation far beyond the chatter of the ballroom.

Elizabeth thought seriously and wrote well, but she knew that something was lacking. She was given less disciplined work than the young men of her circle experienced in their long years in school and college. There was no prospect of career or public service to provide incentive, for if a woman remained single her options would be to remain a dependent in her family, to teach (usually at the lowest levels), or—for a very few—to write articles and books. Young men had wider opportunities, more experience of mixing with able friends and colleagues, and far greater material rewards. Nor did anyone question their capacity to benefit from their education. Attending a Harvard commencement, Elizabeth concluded that the young men seemed not nearly grateful enough for their good luck.[50]

Writers of women's history have shown us how important in a young woman's life was a circle of female relations and friends. Perhaps Elizabeth felt all the more need of her small circle of neighbors, from having no sister of her own. In the diary, Lizzie Ticknor, Mary Quincy, and Annie Webber appear in the very first year, Jenny Revere in 1845, Susie Welles in 1846, Loulie Gardner in 1850, Nellie Hooper in 1855. They were in and out of one another's homes, for tea, reading, sewing, conversation, or seeking company for walks and rides. Often they met on the North Shore. Sometimes one of them visited Walpole.

Alone, with members of her family, or with these friends, Elizabeth played no modern games, for lawn tennis, golf, and cycling became fashionable much later. But a good deal of exercise, and much company, came with walking, horseback riding, skating, sometimes bathing, and even rowing. From the age of eleven, Elizabeth was devoted to opera. In 1855, she went to *La Favorita* and *Lucrezia Borgia* twice each in a short season. The great bel canto operas of Rossini, Donizetti, and Bellini were almost new. Elizabeth compared performances, charted the rise and fall of singers, and lavished more space on their costume than she ever devoted to her own. What is more, Elizabeth and her friends organized clubs to perform German and Italian music. They attempted Haydn and Mozart masses. As soloists, at home or in concerts arranged by their music masters, they struggled with their favorite arias. Tina Shelton, no very close friend but acknowledged to be the most talented of these amateur singers, was once heard in a duet with Brignoli, a visiting opera star.[51]

These girls were not just fellow performers but intimate friends. They gossiped about other friends, confided in one another, and talked far into the night.[52] When separated, they exchanged letters, but long separations were few, usually because of European tours. The tone of their letters was warm. In one, undated, Annie Webber wrote, "You know dear Lillie I love you like my own sister, and when I think of *home* you always seem to form a part of it."[53] As Mary Quincy left for Europe in 1855, she wrote, "I cannot believe, my dear little friend, that we are to be separated for so long a time, but be assured that however long that time may be, you will find no change in my true affection for you." In a letter from Basle she told Elizabeth, "I kissed your dear letter when I found it waiting for me here—the voiceless message that told so much." On this the diary comments, "It is a dreamy thing for me, receiving a friend's thoughts and love, sealed up when warm from the heart."[54] That friendship survived Elizabeth's rejection of her friend's brother as a suitor. Jenny Revere can be the last example. One of her letters, written in the saloon of an Atlantic steamship, speculated about Mary Quincy's preferences in men. Another contained a careful discussion—for letters could be serious and even religious in tone—of the difference between true and self-seeking love; and that was in a letter congratulating Elizabeth on *not* marrying Josiah Quincy.[55]

These young women often expressed the fear that the almost inevitable engagement and marriage would put an end to such friendships. "We quit the raft of common interests and pursuits in which we have been floating," as the diary puts it, "and embark in our own little boats."[56] In a letter commenting on Susie Welles's engagement, Elizabeth admitted, "It is very selfish, but I cannot help a few hot tears, they will soon dry, and then I shall try to think only of your happiness." Susie was more optimistic: "I do so long for one of your warm kisses, for I shall never be one of those who love *any* of their dear friends one whit the less for this."[57] There is evidence that some of the friendships did last—certainly those with Annie Webber, Jenny Revere, and Loulie Gardner, Jenny writing as late as 1898 and, among much else, mentioning Susie Welles, now Sturgis.[58] Nor was marriage a barrier to the making of new friendships. Marian Hovey, first met in the 1850s, became a close friend in the 1870s and 1880s.[59]

Even more important, Lizzie Cabot became very close from the time of Elizabeth's engagement. At that time, she wrote an appraisal of Walter's character. She showed deep sympathy, more than twenty years later, at the time of Mabel's operation, when, incidentally, she was caring for some of Elizabeth's children. As late as Christmas 1899 we find Elizabeth responding, "We have fared along the road of life together for so many years now that we know that our love is truer and warmer and needs no telling."[60] Fortunately, then, some agreed with Elizabeth that "a woman needs a woman's affection, however much a husband's love may be to her."[61]

It remains true that, however much expected and hoped for, engagements were disturbing. The friends discussed bouquets and valentines, especially when senders were anonymous. Rumors of attachments circulated by letter or word of mouth, and reputable ladies like Mrs. Mason and Aunt Parkman seem sometimes to have been guilty of promoting them. More than once, Elizabeth found herself a victim. The atmosphere became highly charged, "a whole world becoming engaged," and she herself "ever in excitement."[62] Preparations for weddings, presents, and the ceremonies themselves were often described.

One generalization needs to be made before I comment further on Elizabeth's own experiences. It is simply to stress how separately young men and young women were brought up, so much so that suitors were far less close than female friends and engaged couples almost strangers one to another. Watching a fencing match, Elizabeth remarked how seldom one could see "the manly side" of men, so often met at parties and dances.[63] Yet the conventions of the day did not depend on severe parental pressure or on rigorous chaperonage. The circle of eligibles was quite small, parents knew the other family, and a code could be taken for granted regardless of a young man's personal characteristics. The women themselves knew men's reputations: Elizabeth accepts a hearsay judgment of Paul Revere's high principles but comments on the charm of William Howe, whose character "may be poor."[64] Young men and women, too, were conscious of informal, unorganized oversight, for it was surely that consideration that caused Elizabeth annoyance and embarrassment when, in serious conversation with Josiah Quincy on Boston Common, she was observed by a lady, tactful enough to pretend not to recognize them, but not necessarily self-sacrificing enough to remain silent about what she had seen.[65]

In her early twenties, Elizabeth sometimes accepted the probability of single life. More commonly, she looked toward marriage and felt left behind as friends were committing themselves. In fact, in addition to the man she married at twenty-six, she took three men seriously, and at least five others either had proposed or had to be viewed as at least unwelcome suitors. Many possible situations existed, and it is unfortunate that a recent study of courtship confines itself so completely to the relations approved or existing between engaged men and women.[66] Men could be admired without any closer attraction existing on either side. Men who seemed to be serious might be brushed aside without regret. Others might be rejected as suitors, but with considerable regret at the pain inflicted, and a sense of loss of what could have been a valued friendship. Josiah Quincy's suit worried Elizabeth for more than two years, for at one and the same time she admired his intellect and principles, was repelled by the coldness of his manner, and deplored her own inability to respond.[67] On the other hand, a woman's love for a man did not necessarily influence him, and she was expected not to show her feelings until his declaration "gave her the right." Elizabeth thought this "the false propriety of the world" and argued in the diary that her love for Walter Cabot expressed "the purest and best part of her nature," which she was not ashamed to lay before God.[68] To make matters more complicated, rejected suitors, sometimes more than one at a time, were likely to be encountered later in society.[69] On the other hand, if a rival engaged a young man's affections, she was all too likely to be one of the young woman's close friends.

After nearly two years of increasingly disturbed feelings, all attempts to reach a state of resignation proving fruitless, Elizabeth was proposed to by Walter—at first by letter—and after a six-month engagement they were married during the summer of 1860. This rather brief engagement—for there were no financial difficulties and no family opposition on either side—is not very much described in the diary. Walter visited her most days, while trying to launch a career in Boston yet living with his parents at Brookline. There were many calls on other branches of the Cabot family. Churchgoing, visits to art galleries, walks and drives, and a fancy-dress ball are all mentioned, a mixture of public and private activities that gave them some opportunity of getting to know one another, beyond the superficial encounters of routine social life.[70]

III

Elizabeth distinguished among the young women closest to her: "Every friend has a sphere . . . to Jenny I look for warm sympathy . . . to Susie . . . for stedfast looking to God and duty, with cheerfulness and affection." Mary Quincy could help her in her struggles, because she had gone through similar experiences, when others were too good to understand.[71] This reminds us—if we need reminding—that Elizabeth too was an individual, not merely an inhabitant of a city and a member of a class at a certain period of history. At the age of fourteen she provided a verbal self-portrait, with a few faults, outweighed by intelligence and other good qualities; fortunately, she also helped us bring her photograph to life, by telling us that her hair was dark brown, her complexion having "a good deal of color," and her eyes dark blue.[72] So, although separation of person and social setting must be somewhat arbitrary, we turn to her family relationships, her experience of illness and depression, her religion, and her opinions about the status of her sex.

Elizabeth felt responsibility for her two slightly younger brothers, exposed as they were to what she vaguely understood to be the temptations of young men. Although she worried about her adequacy in this relationship, in fact she seems to have shown and received deep affection, though she saw more of William Powell than of Edward Bromfield, who died in an accident in the Civil War.[73] About her parents, her feelings were more mixed. Her mother's eyesight was very poor, and often she was ill and depressed. Elizabeth tried to sympathize, read to her, and took more and more responsibility for the household. She left school out of a sense of duty. She doubted whether she could bring herself to marry while her mother lived. When she did become engaged, she chose a house close enough for daily visiting. She felt guilty after deciding on a European tour. Yet, however strong her affection, however positive her sense of duty, Elizabeth felt the conflict between the restraints of home and her own need to develop. More than that, she found confidential conversation impossible and envied friends whose mothers were more accessible.[74] She admired her father's intelligence. But, although she thought she understood why he kept himself aloof, she knew that convention, inability to express feeling, and criticism of other people's behavior were dominant at home. She wanted to break through, to throw her arms around her parents and declare her love. She could not do it, though she was not sure whether to blame the atmosphere of home life or some deeper defect within herself.[75] To some extent, she used Aunt Parkman as a substitute, and at one time she was visiting her on West Street nearly every day.[76]

We have seen some of Elizabeth's wider interests, but our list is not yet complete. At the age of twenty-one, she joined Federal Street, a conservative Unitarian church whose minister was Ezra Stiles Gannett. She did so with no expression of fervor but with the hope of personal improvement. She began to teach young children in Sunday school, though she doubted whether she could ever establish warm relations with them. Soon she developed doubts, first as to the Old Testament she was expected to expound, then as to the value of the Lord's Supper and the evidence for the ministry of Christ. Reading Theodore Parker seems to have confirmed, not initiated, her views.[77] Yet no one can read her diary and letters, and the letters she received from her close friends, without admitting that she and her circle continued to express themselves in religious terms. She and they assumed the existence of a God who not only ruled the universe but cared for individuals. She assumed the existence of an afterlife in which personal relationships would continue. Her diary entries are sometimes prayers. She taught her children to pray. Often she went to church, and great preachers moved her, whether Charles Spurgeon, Henry Whitney Bellows, or Phillips Brooks.[78] She retained scruples, too, about the use of Sunday, preferring, in Normandy, to visit a ruined castle rather than attend a race meeting.[79]

Only intermittently did she display interest in public questions.

She approved—contrary to her father—Dr. Gannett's reluctant opposition to the enforcing of the Fugitive Slave Act and his acceptance of the possibility of disunion.[80] She felt the weight of suffering in the Civil War without debating its issues. She took an inconspicuous part in relief and patriotic organizations. Without emphasis in the diary, she spent some time at the Home for Aged Colored Women and in the Children's Aid Society. More positively, but rather late in life, she became interested in the higher education of women.

Although she once attended a suffrage meeting, she joined no organization of that kind, nor does she name any leader of a women's movement. This does not mean, however, that she lacked opinions. She did not doubt that men differed from women in temperament as well as by education and experience. But she rejected any view of female inferiority, despite the prevalence of this opinion all around her. She was sure that the world overrated the male qualities of enterprise, vigor, and courage, qualities that made for success in career and public life. She admired women for their patience, disinterestedness, endurance, and capacity for sympathy, and she thought that, as civilization advanced, "delicacy" would be recognized as superior to "force," the "passive" virtues to the "showy" ones. She concluded that women were "higher, purer, nearer the perfect image." In the short run, she argued that the qualities of the two sexes were complementary, that each had elements of inferiority and superiority, and that, therefore, in marriage there could be an overall equality, women's opinions and wishes being taken seriously, without men laying down the law.[81]

These were views of her teens and early twenties. Elizabeth then made a happy marriage. But to say that is not to deny the presence of hardships and problems.

Among the letters congratulating her upon her engagement was one from Lizzie Cabot, commenting thus on Walter: "You must let me say that no woman ever trusted her happiness in more gentle, faithful, unselfish hands, and that it is a great satisfaction to know that he is now to receive the love and sympathy he never fails to give to other people, and to reap richly what he has sown." Elizabeth herself recognized not only his manliness but his intellectual quality, his sensitivity, and his reserve.[82]

In some respects, however, Walter remains a shadowy figure. He had been thoroughly trained in France as an engineer. Very soon after his engagement, he published an announcement of handling problems of factory heating and ventilation and drainage of mines, and his qualifications were attested by John Murray Forbes, a Lowell, a Crowninshield, and a Bigelow. But little came of this, and if any occupational description is in order, it is that of gentleman farmer.[83] We cannot know whether his inactive life was due to frequent bouts of illness or to lack of incentive when his wife was so rich. One thing is clear. Although he was given no *Transcript* obituary, although even the Brookline papers took little account of his death, and although the huge Cabot genealogy contains no portrait, he impressed himself on people close to him and won, and retained, the devotion of a woman of intelligence and force of character, who had long doubted her capacity for emotional response.[84] The diary provides abundant evidence, and so do the letters they exchanged in the rare periods of their separation. Elizabeth accepted what in earlier years she might have resented, such expressions as "Dearest little wife." Compared with the diary, the style of her letters is relaxed. She addresses Walter as "Dear Wallie," "My dear old darling," "My old dearie dearie," and "Dearest darling old hus," and ends "Lovingly" or "Goodbye, dearest of husbands." In Florida, in March 1873, she writes of kissing the letters she has had from her older children and ends, "But I do want you here. I long for the children, but I long for you my own darling still more. . . . Oh for one goodnight kiss." Four days later she writes, "It is only half living without you."[85] But, however deep the affection, married life called for feats of organization and a capacity to endure misfortune.

Houses had to be chosen and managed. Servants were "a dreadful torment." In her parents' home, she had found them, all too often, "wasteful, disobliging, and conscienceless." In her own, they were seldom much better. Leaving aside the French governess, who had quite a different status, the Cabots' coachman, housekeeper, cook, nursemaid, laundress, and unspecified number of maids seldom gave satisfaction. Some of them were willing but ignorant. One could not endure country life. Some bargained about wages, left to better themselves, or absconded after borrowing money. One wetnurse simply abandoned the baby in the garden and made off. Scarcely a month passed without some defection. Probably she lacked skill at this kind of management, but a further comment is in order. At the same level of wealth in England, she would not have needed to maintain such detailed contact. Routine would have been laid down, and discipline enforced, by experienced butler and housekeeper, acting, as it were, as executive officers.[86]

Despite the presence of governess and nurse, she also had far closer contact with her children. The diary says little about their discipline or education but much about their health. Sometimes one child after another was ill. Sometimes several were ill together. Either way, she lost many nights of sleep.[87] All her babies experienced feeding difficulties while with wetnurses, but the pain of breast-feeding Harry in 1861 gave her no choice. Yet she was luckier than some of her friends.

All her children grew up, at a time when Walter's sister, Mrs. Henry Lee, lost three in Europe in the single year 1872, two in their twenties and one at eight.

Adults were of course in danger too. We have noted her brother Edward's death. Elizabeth expected William Powell to perish, amid the enormous casualties of the Civil War; he was, in fact, wounded and then invalided out.[88] Walter was often ill, and, when he traveled alone in Europe, Elizabeth insisted on his taking a stock of medicines. Private nurses could easily be found, but often she cared for him herself. She thought it her duty to spare him every possible disturbance. Once, in the early stages of labor, she let him sleep until daybreak; when he was unwell she gave up sleep to provide continuous help.[89]

As a young woman, Elizabeth herself was often ill, neuralgia an often recurring ordeal. Some ailments continued into her married life. Her pregnancies caused her discomfort. But it was childbirth that especially alarmed her. By the standards of her time, her family did not become very large, though four of her children were born when she was over thirty. Like most of her friends, she became pregnant almost immediately after marriage. But, unlike her friend Louise's nine children in seventeen years, she had no long series of closely spaced births. Just once the diary contains the thought that it was not God's will that a woman should have so many children as to endanger her health and deprive them of satisfactory upbringing, though she knew that some of her friends disagreed.[90] Her ordeals were eased by ether, and nothing suggests that she suffered much, certainly nothing like her daughter-in-law's second confinement as she describes it. But she feared not only suffering but death. She probably did not know the official statistics, which showed two or three hun-

dred women a year dying in childbirth in Massachusetts. She did not
need to. One after another of her own friends died that way; on the
last occasion she wrote, "It is too old a story for tears." Shortly before
her second confinement, she thought it appropriate to pen, for Walter,
her parents, and her friends, a formal farewell—though in fact she
lived for another fifty-five years.[91]

Less clear in its nature and origin is the depression so often mentioned between 1867 and 1873. She grieved that, despite resolutions
to the contrary, she was so often ill tempered with her family. After
several years, she confided to the diary that they might be better off
if she were dead. Then, from an entry in 1874 recording excellent
health, the subject is never again touched on. Was she one of those
nineteenth-century women for whom the end of child bearing and the
approach of middle age gave rise, not to despondency or regret, but
to feelings of happiness and well-being?[92]

In 1856, Elizabeth records a confidential conversation at Walpole
with Louise Slade, recently married to a most devoted husband. The
bride remarked that, if women could know all that lay before them, they
would not marry. No explanation follows, and the words may seem to
contradict all we know of the central position held by marriage in the
hopes and plans of young women. They must stand as a mysterious
reminder, perhaps, of how far the duties, responsibilities, and risks of
marriage contrasted with the freedom and opportunities of youth and
of how far, to young women, marriage was unknown country.[93]

IV

It must never be forgotten that my evidence comes chiefly from the
diary. No such document can be accepted as objective history or as a

transparent record of events. On the contrary, it is an expression of personality, a private discussion of strengths and weaknesses, hopes and fears, and yet also, in a sense, a work of art.

Elizabeth's self-portrait at fourteen was complacent, but far more common, in the diary as a whole, is self-criticism and self-doubt. She bewailed her lack of conversation, her inability to organize her time, her equivocal attitude toward her parents. Above all, she deplored her shrinking from expressing her feelings and the absence of the spontaneous emotions that she thought she detected in others.[94] Her claim to keenness of perception, used in this edition's title, was not a boast that stood alone. On the contrary, it was balanced by the depressing thought that "my affections, instead of being exercised to keep pace, have been neglected, and are withering away."[95] Knowing as we do her relations with her circle of friends and, later, her love for Walter Cabot, we may feel that she does herself an injustice, that she exaggerates, or even that, through repetition, she is writing herself into a pose.

What did the diary mean to Elizabeth? Certainly, she was often dissatisfied with it, thought of ceasing to keep it, even of destroying what she had already written.[96] More often, she found that it met one or another need. In her teens, visiting Niagara, she hoped to be able, in later years, to recall with its aid her feelings and the situations that had aroused them—to prevent time from slipping into oblivion.[97] There was another and perhaps deeper need. She viewed her diary as a companion, a friend, to whom she could talk even though a living confidant was lacking: "When my heart seems bursting from long suppressed yearning for sympathy, I take up this my ever-constant friend. It is a relief to talk even to the walls, stocks and stones."[98]

In Thomas Mallon's terms, the diary was largely chronicle, partly a record of travels, occasionally a pilgrimage in her desire to live by simple Christian principles, and sometimes confession—though by the standards of Pepys, Byrd, and Boswell she had little enough to confess.[99] She was confiding in a friend, but one who could not answer back, could not criticize, could not pass judgment. So it provided relief from the strains of daily life.

Even that is not quite all. The diary is a piece of writing, and Mallon's title, *A Book of One's Own,* deserves further thought. At one level, Elizabeth was writing exercises—describing nature, analyzing her friends' characters, reflecting on religion, summarizing sermons or her suitors' speeches—much as Mrs. Lowell had trained her to do. She enjoyed the act of writing, for she could practice it without the labor of publication or exposure to reviews. She was defining thought, shaping experience, imposing a pattern on the confusions and contradictions of the real world. Even frustrations and sorrows became more bearable if expressed in deliberate prose.

Walter died in 1904 after years as an invalid. The lack of information about Elizabeth's last fourteen years would be frustrating, crippling in a biography. But this is an edition; so to end when Elizabeth gave up writing has a certain logic. When they have reached this abrupt and inconclusive ending, many readers will wish to dispute my generalizations. But they will do so because they share my fascination with the record of this woman, intelligent and attractive in her day but now long dead, as they find her "writing down in as much order as possible the most striking events of the lost time."[100]

THE CAST OF CHARACTERS

In a diary covering so many years, hundreds of characters appear. But few of them have anything like central importance, and there is no need to strain after total identification. An effort must be made, however, for a central group of relations and friends, and any failures must be not only deplored but explained. That my rate of success has proved so high, I owe thanks, above all, to two sources of information. One is a set of notes compiled by Ruth Cabot Paine and included in box I, folder 1, of the family papers. Their emphasis is on the Masons and connected families. The other, with its focus on Walter's relations, is Lloyd V. Briggs's *History and Genealogy of the Cabot Family,* privately printed more than sixty years ago. From these and lesser sources, I present a very simplified picture of what is immensely complicated. I accept that a family tree in diagram form would be either absurdly unwieldy or quite illegible. So, in plain prose, I treat first the Masons and their connections through three generations, as far as an understanding of the diary makes it necessary, and then the Cabots in similar fashion. Finally, I introduce a circle of friends, with special emphasis on difficulties of identification, leaving many details to the notes on the diary text.

Masons

There is no need to start before Elizabeth's grandparents, and even they do not appear in her diary in person. Jonathan Mason (1756–1831) was one of the Mount Vernon proprietors and, from that and other enterprises, a principal source of the family's wealth. From his marriage to Susanna Powell, there were seven surviving children. The oldest, Susanna, married Dr. John Collins Warren, generations of whose descendants were also medical men, so he was our Elizabeth's "Uncle Warren." Elizabeth married Samuel D. Parker. Anna married Patrick Grant, so she becomes "Aunt Grant." Miriam married the wealthy merchant David Sears. Mary married Samuel Parkman, who deserted her, and as "Aunt Parkman" she becomes a central character in the diary. Jonathan married Isabella Weyman. William Powell (1791–1867), older than the two last named, became a lawyer, for some years reporter of the U.S. District Court, secretary of the Social Law Library, Fourth of July orator in 1827, and a member of the General Court 1828–31. He married a second cousin, Hannah Rogers (1806–72); Elizabeth was their oldest surviving child. Few of Mrs. Mason's Rogers, Bromfield, or Clarke ancestors concern us, though some of them were distinguished people. Two of her brothers, however, are often mentioned: John Rogers, who married Ellen Derby, and Henry Bromfield Rogers, who married Anna D. Perkins.

Elizabeth's brothers deserve a mention. William Powell Mason, Jr. (1835–1901), I have already treated, in connection with Mr. Mason's will and the life-style that was based on his fortune. I need add only that he married Fanny Peabody and that their children were William and "little Fanny." The other was Edward Bromfield Mason, Harvard

M.D., briefly an army surgeon, who transferred into the cavalry and, shortly thereafter, died from the effects of a riding accident in 1863. In her diary, Elizabeth calls them "Willy" or "Powell" and "Eddy." Before her marriage, Mrs. Mason had cared for the three children of a sister, whose husband had lost his money. There is no trace of their living with the Masons, but a quite close contact was maintained. They were Daniel, Ellen, and Elise Slade, the married name of the last being Schmidt.

Since some of the families were large, characters of Elizabeth's own generation are numerous. It would be rash to claim to have pinpointed all her cousins, but I can go through most of them family by family, as I have listed the older generation. John Collins Warren's son was Jonathan Mason Warren (1811–67), who in turn had a son called John Collins Warren. Of the Parker children, only Annie (who married Samuel L. Hinckley) and Isabella (who married John Codman) are at all prominent in the diary. Aunt Grant's children are not conspicuous, though Patrick, Charlotte, and Elizabeth are mentioned, and it is worth noting that a grandson, Robert, was a judge and novelist. Several of the Sears children appear: Frederick especially, who married first Marianne Shaw and then Albertina Shelton; and occasionally Ellen, who married P. d'Hauteville and was soon divorced; Anne, who married William Amory; Harriet, who married George C. Crowninshield; Grace, who married William C. Rives; and Knyvet, who married Mary C. Peabody. Aunt Parkman's three children were Henry (wholly in the background); Samuel, who married Mary Dwight (who became one of Elizabeth's friends) and died young; and Powell, "Cousin Powell." Jonathan Mason's children included the Rev. Arthur and Isabella. Of John Rogers's eight children, only Ellen and Laura appear prominently. Finally, Henry B. Rogers had one daughter, Annette, who never married; and his sister, who married a Loring, had a daughter Anna ("Annie"), also close to Elizabeth's age and unmarried.

Cabots

It was Godrey Lowell Cabot, one of Walter's nephews, who, in *his* huge diary, recorded at Thanksgiving 1881 a song that began, "We are the Cabot clan, just count us if you can. . . ." Marriage to Walter provided Elizabeth with another crowd of relations. We need note only one member of the grandparent generation, the famous merchant Thomas Handasyd Perkins (1764–1854). One of his daughters married Thomas Cary, and their children included Caroline (who became "Carrie Curtis"), Emma, and Sally. Another married William F. Cary and had a daughter Fanny. Another, Eliza, married a Perkins business associate, Samuel Cabot. He lived until 1863, she until 1885, often referred to as "old Mrs. Cabot." Of his siblings, one need only mention that a sister married Professor Charles Follen. Of Samuel's large family, three died young. Dr. Samuel Cabot married Hannah Lowell, and he was family physician to Elizabeth as well as friend. Edward Clarke Cabot, an architect who designed the Boston Athenaeum, married first Martha Robinson and then Louisa Sewall. James Elliot Cabot was trained in law, studied philosophy in German universities, acted as Edward's colleague, was a keen ornithologist, and helped the aged Emerson arrange his papers. He married Elizabeth Dwight, who became one of Elizabeth's closest friends. Elizabeth Perkins Cabot married Colonel Henry Lee of the Lee, Higginson firm. Stephen and Louis (who married Amy Hemenway) scarcely appear in the diary. Walter Channing Cabot married Elizabeth. Sarah (Sadie) married, when she was thirty-one, Andrew C. Wheelwright.

Apart from Elizabeth's own children, already mentioned in the introduction, exceedingly few of the next generation are even mentioned. Two of them were children of Dr. Sam: Dr. Arthur and Godfrey. The other, occasionally mentioned late in the century, was Elliot's eldest child, Francis.

Friends

I turn, now, to the circle of friends. When information can be had, it will usually be placed in notes to the diary text. But, as it happens, several of the key figures pose serious problems of identification. These must be explained to readers at once, not least because some of them may be qualified to offer suggestions and corrections. Three of the girls can be placed beyond question. Mary Quincy was the daughter of one Josiah Quincy (mayor of Boston in the late 1840s), granddaughter of another (mayor in the 1820s, then president of Harvard), and sister of a third, who courted Elizabeth. The families occupied two houses on Park Street and two at Quincy. Lizzie Ticknor, who married William Dexter, was the second daughter of George Ticknor, pioneer American specialist in Spanish literature, who lived at the corner of Park Street and Beacon. Jenny Revere (who married Dr. John Reynolds) was the sister of Edward, Paul, and Josephine; her two brothers were killed in the Civil War. But Susie Welles could have been a member of any of at least four families, whose homes were on Pemberton Square, Chestnut and Walnut streets, and Summer Street. Nellie Hooper also remains uncertain. Several juxtapositions in the diary make it rather likely that she was Ellen, the daughter of Dr. Robert Hooper and the sister of Marian ("Clover"), who married Henry Adams. She was four years younger than Elizabeth, but at eighteen was not too unlikely a choice as a reading partner.

Even more difficult is the problem of "Loulie" Gard{i]ner, a close friend, and "Joe," a suitor. Elizabeth states no relationship between the two, nor does she place them in any connection with parent, sibling, or any other third party. Loulie is often at Brookline. Joe's appearances suggest a Beacon Hill neighbor. The neatest solution would be to identify them as Julia and Joseph Peabody Gardner, whose brother John L. married Isabella Stewart. Joe would be about six years older than Elizabeth. Family homes would then be at 7 Beacon Street and at Brookline. Joe gets invited to a very small dinner party with Thomas Jefferson Coolidge, his business partner. He marries Harriet Sears Amory, whom Elizabeth is found visiting in the 1860s, and Julia marries Joseph Randolph Coolidge. The fact that neither the marriages nor Joseph's sudden death in 1875 are recorded could be explained by long gaps in the diary. Everything seems to fit, yet nothing is conclusive. John L. is never mentioned, nor are any engagements. But, although Elizabeth uses the spelling "Gardiner" more often than "Gardner," one piece of evidence points to the latter as correct. On 6 May 1856, Elizabeth hears, at second hand, opinions about Joe expressed by Georgina Lowell, described as his cousin. "Gardner" was her mother's maiden name and the middle name given to her elder brother George.

Two more doubts are worth recording. Another suitor was John Higginson, and his frequent calls, and his taking part in walks on the Common, suggest a near neighbor. So does a remark by Elizabeth about his disappointment at seeing their house shut for the summer, with months to pass before their next meeting. This could point to his being John A. Higginson, merchant, whose address was 2 Louisburg Square, born in or about 1824, but here too I have to admit a total lack of supporting evidence. Finally, there are early diary references to a Miss Nancy Perkins, already of mature years. Then a "Cousin Nancy" joins them for part of the 1867–70 European tour. It is never positively stated that this was the same woman. No other relationships are defined. The nearest to a strong candidate seems to be a granddaughter of Thomas Handasyd Perkins, vaguely mentioned in papers of his that have been printed.

Such remaining doubts are annoying. But one generalization is clear. The people in Elizabeth's circle were rich, of families that would have been thought old, who lived on Beacon Hill or at Brookline, and, to make a further point, who had names that often appear among the pew owners at Federal Street (Unitarian) Church.

The Diary

CHAPTER ONE

1844–1847

When her diary begins, Elizabeth is not quite ten years old. At the end of 1847, she is thirteen and a half. The very earliest entries are brief and plain, with uncertain spelling. But very soon she is writing full accounts of events and fluent descriptions of New Hampshire scenery. Although she does not yet write about the position of women or analyze her own character, she undertakes, in her page on the influence of the seasons, what can be called an exercise in formal reasoning.

Places begin to take shape: the more favored districts of Boston, Brookline, the North Shore, Newport, Rhode Island, and Walpole, New Hampshire. The cast of characters begins to appear: her parents and brothers, Aunt Parkman and less prominent relatives, Annie Webber, and her friend Mary Quincy. In the person of a young cousin, she encounters death.

1844

Boston   30 April

Father has decided to let me go to New York tomorrow. I am so delighted.[1]

21 June

It is not so warm as it was yesterday. You know I told you yesterday that I was going to take a ride. We did. First we went out to Mrs. William Amory's and there we got some beautiful cherries. You know she lives in Brookline. Then we went to Uncle Warren's and there we got some strawberries as big as a horse chestnut and I got a large bouquet. Then we went to look at Mr. Tom Parker's new house and then we went to Mrs. Guild's and then we came home. Mrs. Gavern my teacher has begun to come in the morning from 11 to 2. Before, she came in the afternoon from 3 to 6. My hair all cut short.

4 July

It is a very pleasant day though it is quite cool. I got up this morning at halfpast five o'clock. We ate breakfast at seven o'clock and at half past Mother, the boys and myself went down to Mrs. [Hayden's?] to see the floral procession.[2] It passed the house at eight o'clock. It was prettier than the year before, I think. They had a platform with poles at each corner and it was carried by four men. It was covered with moss and then strewed with flowers. On it was fixed an anchor covered with moss. On the platform stood a little girl dressed in white with a cap of moss, and round the edge of that was a wreath of flowers. She held the anchor in one hand and a bunch of flowers in her other one. She looked very prettily. Another of the things was a sort of summer house made of moss. At the bottom it was a yard square and about a yard and a half high; it sloped up to a point. In the middle was a little pond, and in the middle of that was the smallest little flower-pot covered with silver leaf and turned upside down. Out of the hole in the pot was a little spirt of water that went about two feet high and then fell down into the pond again. It was sweet pretty. Then there was a boat on wheels and covered with moss. Two little girls sat in it and every now and then they threw a pond lily to the people. I shall have so much to say about the fireworks that I shall not say anything more about the procession.

Oh I have had a most splendid time. I will tell you what they were. They had signal rockets from sunset to nine o'clock. Then they had Greek Bengola [Bengal?] Lights, rockets with red and green stars; but it would take a long time for me to tell you all of them, so here is a piece of paper I cut out of the newspaper that has them all printed on it. [Missing.]

28 October

It is a rainy day. I have just been to school to Mary Quincy's.[3] Miss Watson is teaching us.

31 October

It is not any pleasanter today than yesterday. Mary Quincy's furniture to her new room has come home. It is painted a fawn coloured ground with purple figures on it. She has got a beautiful white marble slab to her bureau and washstand.

16 December

It is a beautiful day though quite cold. Miss Blood is here. I am just going to school. I have been to Mr. Papanti's with Aunt Parkman and

Miss Elisa Boott, to see some young ladies dance. I danced twice in a cotillion.[4] I had a very nice time. I came away at half past eight.

1845

Boston   *14 January*

It is a rather pleasant day. I have been to school. When I got there I found that Mary had such a sick headache so she did not go to school. So I had to study all alone, which I did not like much. Yesterday evening I went to a child's party at Mary Quincy's where I had a delightful time. We went as soon as we could after seven. They danced all the evening and had Mr. Fergus to play on the piano. They had supper at about nine o'clock, they had it in the library. There were about sixty children, a few grown people. As I said before I had a delightful time.

25 February

It is a most lovely day. I have been to school but it does not keep today because Mary has gone to Dedham with her mother.

I have just been to Aunt Anna's to see how Ellen was and they said she was gone.[5] I turned away and went home. Mother sent over for me and Father to come over and see her. She died very quietly. Aunt Anna Rogers, Cousin Daniel and Mother were on one side of the bed and Uncle Rogers on the other. She raised herself up on her elbow and struggled for breath for two or three minutes, then she laid down on her side for about ten minutes, then she turned over on her back and stopped breathing. She looked beautifully. She has a smile upon her face and looks as happy as possible. She was a dear girl when she lived.

26 February

It is a most lovely day. I have been in to see dear Ellen. She looks more beautiful than she did yesterday. She looks as calm, happy and sweet. She has been examined today. Her heart was three times as large as it naturally is. The liquid in which it floats is all dried up and the outer skin is attached to the heart. Her lungs were perfectly good but the left one was pushed out of its place.

27 February

It is a beautiful day. Ellen does not look as well as she did yesterday. Cousin Eliza does not know that Ellen is dead.[6] She has just been confined and they do not think it safe to let her know. Ellen has had a cast taken of her. The funeral is to be this afternoon at four o'clock.

I have been to the funeral this afternoon. Dear Ellen was laid on a couch of white strewed with flowers. She looked perfectly heavenly. Dr. Gannett performed the services.[7] He made a very beautiful prayer. Ellen had a great many *old* friends as well as young. A good many girls that she knew came to the funeral.

4 April

It is very windy today. Mary, Emmy Edwards and myself have been driving our hoops, sending them in front of us, then the wind would carry them along and we run after them. I have taken my French lesson this afternoon. He is a very pleasant man.

6 May

I have been very kindly invited by Mrs. President Quincy to spend the day at their house at Cambridge with Mary, and go with them to the exhibition. I have spent a delightful day in going to the exhibition, going to the Library, and also going to see the Panorama of Athens given to the College by Mr. Theodore Lyman.[8] It is very beautifully painted.

25 May

It is my *Birthday* today and I am eleven years old. I had a beautiful present from dear Mother. It was a bracelet made of *Ellen's hair,* with a gold clasp. On the inside of the clasp is written Ellen and the year. I value it very much. I also had a present of a bag from Mary. It is made of ribbon and is worked over with narrow straw braid. Father forgot it was my birthday.[9]

Newport   1 September

It is a most lovely morning about the same as it was yesterday. We are going to bathe. I wet for the first time my new bathing dress, it does very well. I did not go with Mother to ride this afternoon but waited till half past five o'clock. Then I went for Anna Thorndike but she was out. I walked down to Aunt Isabella's where I met Isabella Mason and Harriet Amory.[10] We played with the swing and in the orchard, and at half past six o'clock walked home. When I got home I found Mr. Tom Appleton who has just returned from Europe.[11] He stayed and drank tea, and told us all about the Turks and Greeks and a great many other people and things.

13 September

It is a magnificent morning and the thermometer is sixty. I have not been anywhere this morning before breakfast though I was up at six. We are not going to bathe. We have been over to Fort Adams which is the largest and most complete fort in the United States. [12] It is not quite finished. Aunt Parkman, Cousin Annie Parker, Father, Mother, the boys, and myself got into a sailboat and sailed over. We entered a large passage and went up a pair of steps guarded on both sides by large cannons. First we came to a powder house built entirely of stone and immensely thick, with two iron doors. Then we went along a road paved with stone and went through a gateway on which in time of war would be placed two iron gates. As far as I could tell the walls extend about three-quarters of a mile round. The wall toward the land was composed of stone houses for the officers and rooms for the soldiers. That part toward the sea was composed of powder houses, places for shot and cannons, etc., etc. It was all of it solidly embanked with earth outside.

We went up a pair of steps which led to the top of the houses and rooms and there were cannons about 14 feet apart with cannon balls between piled up as nicely as possible. Father could but just lift one of them. When we came down we asked one of the men how many guns there were or rather cannon and he said 500 cannon and 3,000 men would be the full complement in time of war. How horrible it seems to make all this preparation to kill our fellow men. There were two subterranean passages, one leads to a small fort at a distance and the other round the fort, both of which are now filled with water from the sea but can be drained off. Mother or myself had never been in a fort before.

Boston   13 October

It is a delightful morning. Willy, Eddy and myself went out round the Common at half past six this morning. I have been this morning to school for the first time in my life. Mrs. Lowell keeps a school in Winter Place, a small court out of Winter Street.[13] She has an Assistant whose name is Lizzy Sullivan. I like the school very much. Isabella Mason goes there. There are six windows in it and it is heated with hot water and has four [word missing]. Miss Peabody is another assistant but for the older girls. Some of the girls are nineteen years of age and some not more than ten. We study French, Latin, E. Grammar, Mental and Oral Arithmetic, Physiology, Spelling, etc., etc.[14] Mother has been to dine at Mr. and Mrs. Lyman's.

14 October

It is a very pleasant day. The more I go to school the better I like it. At first I felt rather awkwardly among so many girls but I have got over that a good deal now. Father, Mother, the boys, and myself have been to see the Chinese Museum. It is very handsome. There are wax figures as large as life put inside glass cases. There was the Emperor with eight or nine figures standing round him. Then there was the Empress with her ladies, and the court of justice with a man in a tub and another kneeling down and some men sawing wood and making shoes and a boat with a family in it and a great many other things, too many to tell. They were all as large as life.

Then to crown the whole a Chinese man sang and played on instruments. If a cat had got up and sung I should not have known which to call the best. Certainly I never heard such a squeaking in my life.

25 October

It is very pleasant today. Mother got home from New York last night at about half past ten o'clock. She is very well and has enjoyed herself very much.

I went down to Aunt Parkman's this morning. She gave me a most beautiful little silver dove with a silver heart in his mouth. His eyes are red and there is a blue stone in the heart. It is for a breastpin. Father, the boys and myself have been to see the mastodon this afternoon.[15] It is most immense, 11 feet high and 22 long. The knees bend towards each other. It has two tusks and is supposed to have had a trunk. It is nothing but the bones of the animal put together. It far exceeded my expectations. Cousin Daniel Slade dined with us today. Mother brought us some candy from New York.

1846

Boston   1 January

It is very pleasant today. After getting up this morning and wishing everybody a happy New Year I proceeded to look at my presents. I had Bryant's *Poems* from Aunt Parkman, Thomson's *Seasons, The Castle of Indolence,* and his memoirs all contained in one book, from Father, and a large handsome book called *The Gift,* also from Father, and a beautiful gold pencil from Mother. I have since had Longfellow's *Poems* from Cousin Daniel.

I gave Mrs. Quincy a pair of slippers which I have been working ever since the middle of last summer. The boys had some very handsome presents as well as myself. Willy had a case with twenty beautiful books in it, from Father, a book from Aunt Parkman and the promise of a pair of skates from Mother. Eddy had a violin from Mother, a game from Aunt Parkman, and the four volumes of *The Arabian Nights* from Father.[16] I have been to dancing this afternoon. Last Monday evening I went to a party at Mrs. Mills'. I had a very pleasant time. I came away at 11 o'clock.

23 February

It is very pleasant today. I have been this afternoon to a dancing class. We have Mr. Fergus to play for us and we do not have any master but dance by ourselves, which is very pleasant. We meet at each other's houses at six o'clock on Mondays once a week. There are about 20 girls and ten or eleven boys.

5 March

It is *very very* warm today. I have been to Aunt Parkman's to dine with Father and Mother and Dr. Pierce and Miss Lydia Green. We had a very nice dinner. I tasted a banana. I did not like them, but I suppose the reason was that you cannot get any good ones here, they are generally decayed. I came home in the afternoon to play on the piano, and went to Aunt Parkman's again to tea where I met Isabella Mason (little Isabella). After tea we went with Aunt P. to Colonel Perkins's where we had a dance.[17] His children and grandchildren always come there every Thursday. I went upstairs into the room or rather study that is used by Mr. Perkins. He has got a beautiful collection of shells and busts. We had a delightful time.

13 March

It is very pleasant today. I have been this morning to riding school. I was never on a horse before except once or twice at Mrs. Guild's where I stayed a short time last spring when I rode on a little pony. I rode Millie.

17 March

It is very pleasant today. I have been to ride in the circus this morning. I rode Eclipse which I like very much. Mother and I dined at Aunt Parkman's with cousin Anna Parker. We have had a dinner party at 4 o'clock, Father's club. I have been this afternoon to play on the State House steps.[18] Mother has got a little headache but I hope it will go off.

30 June

It is a lovely day. We have all been to see Van Amburgh's collection of animals. It is very good indeed. Then there is a monkey rides round the tent on a horse; and then one of the elephants comes out into the middle of the tent and walks over a man who lies on the ground, it is wonderful to see with how much caution he steps over the man, come within an inch of the man's head, then he lifts the man on his back and the man puts his head into his mouth, and performs many more antics which it would take too long to describe. Then Van Amburgh went into the tigers' and lions' den and put his head into their mouths. The whole was very wonderful.

Walpole   25 September

It is rainy today or what most people would call so, sometimes raining, sometimes shining. We have finished reading the *Life of Sir Walter*

Scott. [19] It is very interesting. He was both a great and a good man. What a sudden change of life from opulence to poverty, from a married man with his wife and children about him to a widower and his children abroad; and yet how patiently did he bear it. I never read a more interesting *Life*.

27 September

It was pleasant this morning but is disagreeable and rainy this afternoon. The carriage and horses are both put away for the season, so we cannot go to church.

I feel *very very* sorry at going to Boston as we intend to do next Tuesday. How different are brick walls from hills, meadows and rivers. I was never anywhere where I liked the view so much as that out of my window, that I should like to see all the time, that is. [20] Down under and about my window, I can see green meadows and fields of corn and grain. A little further is the road, with every now and then a vehicle or a foot passenger, and beyond that is the river, the trees that surround and hide it in other places separating there and showing a sheet of clear smooth water with a boat now and then gliding along its surface and disappearing from view behind the trees. Look still further and you will see a range of hills covered with woods, in a nook of which is a meeting-house with its gilded vane and few houses scattered round it. Over the whole, scattered in different places, are vast woods. What is the view from my window in Boston: around it bright red walls, and beyond it as far as you can see in a level the same. One may now judge which is the pleasantest to live in. But enough of this.

Last evening I received a letter from Sarah Barrett containing a piece of "Mica" which she promised to send me as I could get none here, and informing me her "neck was not yet broken." This morning I received one from Aunt Parkman, which says she has not been well since she has been at Newport, for which I am very sorry. What a cold word "sorry" is! I wish there was some other that would express you really felt so. "Sorry" is so common. Everybody says it as a matter of course whether they feel it or not, and you do not know if another person feels sorry for you or not.

1847

Boston   30 January

It is raw and disagreeable this morning and snows a little. I went before dinner to Fanny Cary's to paint. Mother went to the Philharmonic but I could not go because I had a cold.[21] Eddy is much better.

16 May

The weather has been rather disagreeable this last week, even if it were not for the northeast winds which are enough to stamp a day cold in most people's minds. Today is delightful, however, to my feelings, and I am again seated at the open window in the same place as I was last year. The week has glided away very rapidly and nothing has occurred worth noting. I have been to school and come home, got up and gone to bed, just as usual; and with the exception of last evening, when Aunt Parkman and Cousin Powell came in the evening, nobody has been in the house but to make a call.

In six weeks I hope to [be seen?] climbing over the rocks of Nahant.

I anticipate the greatest pleasure this summer and build many castles in the air. How far my hopes will be realized remains to be proved. Many persons think that fall or rather autumn is the saddest season in the year. The leaves are all falling off, and although there are many beautiful days the weather is sometimes cold and dismal. But I do not think so. It is true that there is some gloomy weather which sometimes brings gloomy thoughts; but the cool weather and the bright sun, the colored leaves and the peculiar clearness belonging to autumn invigorate and strengthen you; and when one feels well they are generally in good spirits. But the warm days coming so suddenly after the cold of winter weaken and debilitate you which causes a sort of dreamy sad feeling which I think is very beautiful. It is not exactly sadness but a sort of calm peaceful feeling, which is most lovely. A year or two ago I used to think fall and winter the two best seasons of the year, you feel so well, there is so much frolicking and running. But I am now decided summer and spring (the former of which is the pleasantest on account of the debility felt on the sudden change of weather) with its more quiet enjoyments is preferable. The cold weather must be much better, however, to develop our intellectual powers and make us smart and active.

18 June

Mother went out to walk for the first time today and we all went to see Tom Thumb, as he is called, a dwarf of twenty-eight inches high and weighing only fifteen pounds! His real name is Charles Stratton. He weighed nine pounds at birth, which is considered a very large baby. He is said not to have grown since he was seven months old. He is certainly very remarkable. He could not put his cap on the head of an infant of five months old. He is fifteen years old and I have heard is very intelligent for a boy of that age. He has been in Europe four years, and during that time has gathered a large fortune. He has got a little equipage, an English carriage, a remarkably small pair of Shetland ponies, footman and driver all complete, just large enough for himself.[22]

23 September

I have been pressing some very pretty mosses that I brought from Nahant with me. I like pressing them very much. They are very easy to do. You take a small tub or anything of the kind, fill it with water, and float a flat piece of wood (the best thing a shingle) on it. Lay on that your piece of paper and then press it under water. After you have thoroughly cleaned your mosses, arrange them under water on the paper, the water spreading each little fibre out beautifully. Then lift your paper with the moss placed on it out of the water, fix it according to your taste and put it between a piece of cotton and under a heavy weight. The more each little fibre is picked out and separated from the others the handsomer it looks.

This afternoon I rode with Mother to Aunt Perkins's and Mrs. Snow's. Mrs. Webber and her daughter Lizzy are staying there. She says Annie is very well and is coming to Boston some time this winter.[23]

CHAPTER TWO

1848–1852

Just once, in her early teens, Elizabeth witnesses an historic event. In October 1848, after strenuous efforts by the first two mayors Quincy and Theodore Lyman, a modern water supply is brought into Boston by aqueduct from Lake Cochituate. Most of the diary, however, is occupied with the process of growing up. Elizabeth is being educated. She leads an active social life. She moves within a social circle of relatives and friends. She continues to visit Walpole and to love it "as a near, dear, friend."

On all this, she writes more and more fluently. Even at this early age, she devotes pages, not only to description, but to analysis of her personality and her problems. She feels responsible for an ailing mother and two brothers, for she is the oldest child and only daughter. She begins to discuss the situation of women. Inevitably, therefore, the selection presented must be much fuller, to reflect the shape of the diary itself.

One episode, in her private life, is mentioned without emphasis. On 16 February 1850, she dances with Walter Cabot, five years older than she. He makes no particular impression on the girl of less than sixteen. She continues visiting Cabot homes, for parties and amateur theatricals, while Walter, after Harvard, spends years in Europe training as an engineer. But, after his return, it will not be long before she singles him out as closest to her ideal of a man.

1848

Boston   9 July

Very pleasant this morning. Went to church with Mother, and have been writing, and reading, the remainder of the day. Began the *Life of Dr. Channing,* by his nephew.[1] It is a very beautiful book, being composed almost wholly of his own writings, which I think is the most satisfactory way. Mother has been reading it, or I should have begun it before. There is a great deal of reading in the book, and there are three volumes. Been talking with Mother this afternoon a little, which is very pleasant. I am now fourteen years old, and have a long vacation before me in which I shall, of course, have much leisure time. Many things, which I should otherwise do, are omitted in the winter, on account of my school, and other studies, which necessarily take so much of my time, but I have no such excuse in the summer, and I am about to try to make time if possible. I never, in the first place, have time in the winter to read the Testament, and not much for reflection and meditation of any kind. Reading the Testament every morning, or evening, or at both times, is an excellent habit, and one that it is important to form. In winter, in the mornings there is no time before my studies, and in the evening I often go to bed half asleep. I intend also to write a set of rules, or precepts, to act by during the day. These I can follow in winter as well as summer. I never thought of it before; but Mother was speaking of a person that did so, the other day, and it struck me as a good plan. These you can read at the same time as you do the Testament, and if you endeavored to remember them, and to follow them, through the day, they might be of much use. I mean also to read some, if not all, of Sparks's biographies.[2] This will not only be very useful, as well as interesting, but it will be of great use to me next winter, when we are to study American history at school. In the winter, after studying hard the greater part of the day, if I read at *all* I read lighter books; but in the summer there is no need of such a recreation, and I shall follow these, as a sort of study.

I mean also to sew a little, for in the winter I never take a needle into my fingers; and I think it very necessary that a woman should be able to sew nicely and quickly, so as to render her independent of others; although I would never spend as much time on it, or make it so much a matter of business, as to take some of your most precious time, as some people think it necessary to do; as it is a thing, if you are not absolutely awkward, you can learn at most any period of life, whereas some things if not learned in youth are lost forever.

The weather has become damp, and disagreeable, and it has rained several times today. I am sorry, for Willie has gone with Daniel Slade to spend the day at Nahant, and Father, and Eddy, walked out to Brookline, to spend the day at Mr. Crowninshield's or Mr. Amory's. They have neither of them got home, although it is half past six p.m.

Walpole   27 August

The scenery at Walpole is very fine, the Connecticut river runs through it, at a short distance from the village. Across the river is the little town of Westmoreland which appears very prettily from Walpole, its spires rising through the trees. The drives around Walpole are very beautiful, hills rising up all around and in one part one may catch a glimpse of the Askutney mountain in Vermont, quite blue on account of its distance. Through the months of July and August there is generally a dense fog lasting till nine or ten o'clock in the morning; but often it clears away when the sun rises, the tops of the mountains gradually appear wreathed about with the snow-like fog, rendering the effect peculiar and beautiful. Unfortunately for lovers of the country the railroad is making great havoc here, passing through green fields and hills and leaving only sand banks on each side. However, for the public good one *ought* to be willing to give up one's own pleasures; but it is hard to think that the railroad is of so much good, and to look upon it with any degree of Christian feelings, when we see dozens of men employed in digging away those places which we have looked upon with so much pleasure.

21 September

[The traveler will] pass at two and a half miles distance from the village Bog Meadow farm. To me, the scenery here is very beautiful, the house situated on the point of a high hill about a quarter of a mile from the river, white and perfectly plain and simple, surrounded by a piazza supported by large pillars. The interior of the house is very plain. The lower floor consists of a large drawing room with eight windows, opening on the piazza, a parlor, library, dining room, and kitchen. Two large chambers and four smaller but good sized ones, besides four in the back entry, finish the house, which is only two stories high. The farm is between seven and eight hundred acres in extent, nearly eight hundred. It is cultivated by two farmers, who with their families and workmen live each in farm houses on the place. Seven or eight hundred sheep, and twenty or thirty oxen, are kept here, and the former during the winter are put in a large sheep barn, which to me is a very picturesque object. The house is surrounded by no large trees, and although many small trees have been planted, it is very difficult, especially as the house is so often unoccupied for several years, and never [occupied] for more than four months in the year.

Boston   26 October

Yesterday there was a grand celebration on the entrance of the Cochituate water into Boston. The procession which they always have on such occasions was very handsome. It was said to be more splendid than any other that was ever seen in Boston. All the military not only of Boston but of many of the surrounding towns turned out and marched through the streets; also all the firemen of Boston and the surrounding towns; all the Odd Fellows and Free Masons of which there is an immense number, with their different banners and badges; all the public schools male and female. Different tradesmen followed with carts carrying different things belonging to their trades. There were a great number of market men following a very large cart filled with provisions of different kinds ornamented with flowers and evergreens, which looked very well. There was a printing press and all its accoutrements, and men with it who printed little billets and threw them among the crowd. There were two cabs belonging to "Oak Halls." A large ship was carried round, filled with sailors and followed by a great many sailors; a long procession of captains and commanders of ships followed. An elephant as large as life (of wood) was dragged around with a seat on its back, and several boys dressed as [words missing].[3]

1849

Boston   21 January

Life, how it runs away. I have been very much struck with this lately. One day a child is born, the next it is married, and on the third dies, and there is his end. On the fourth he is uncared for and forgotten.

Annie Parker, my cousin, was married last Wednesday to a Mr. Hinckley, to whom she had been engaged for some time. By most persons this is thought a very excellent match. I do not attempt to judge. I am not sufficiently acquainted with Mr. Hinckley. She seems to be very happy. Her presents have been splendid. She has a great many friends, besides a large number of relations, and all of them have sent her some gift, most of them very handsome ones. Silver seems to be the common present, of which I should think she had fifteen or twenty pieces, besides many other things. She was married at church, which seems to me the most disagreeable performance possible. The church is generally filled with people drawn merely from curiosity, and in whom you have no interest. It must be very trying to the immediate friends.

Saturday, I went to a funeral. What a change! One all joy and gladness, the other all sorrow, mourning and grief. It was the funeral of a girl of sixteen, young, beautiful and good, Fanny Lamb, with whom I have spent many pleasant hours. How little did I then think that in a short time I should go to her funeral! She was an orphan, and lived with a grandmother and three aunts. I walked with her quite often, in the early part of the fall. Soon after, she was taken sick with the typhus fever. New Year's Day I went to see her, and found her sitting up but very weak, and not able to walk at all. She was however in very good spirits and seemed very much pleased at seeing me, and was anticipating with much pleasure the next day, when she expected to go downstairs for the first time. I have been intending for some days to go and see her again, but was detained by different things; and Thursday morning I was told that she was dead. She had had a relapse of the fever, and died of utter weakness, perfectly quietly without a long breath. Such is life: one day he lives, the next he is among the dead. "As for man, his days are as grass; as the flower of the field, so he flourisheth. For the wind passeth over it, and it is gone, and the place thereof shall know it no more."

And yet, how little we realize, that this may be our lot, before another year, nay, before another month. We can say to ourselves, I am not made differently from others, I am subject to the same regulations and laws, there is no reason for my being more favored than others; and yet we do not really bring the idea to our minds, of our death, of leaving our friends and this world, and going to another. I think if we could really bring this to our minds, realize it, as we realize that we shall go to bed tonight, rise tomorrow, and go through the duties and pleasures of the day, that we should be better and holier creatures, that we should keep the great interests of eternity more steadily in view, and that we should follow them with more energy and zeal, and think less of the things of this world, since they are really to pass away so soon. Let me try to keep my own death and the death of my friends more constantly and vividly in sight; and this will teach me to think less of, and look above, mortal things, and see those belonging to immortality in a clearer light.

23 February

A schoolgirl's life, although a happy one as a general rule, and full of interest, is nevertheless often a *very* weary one. To rise in the morning and hurry down and breakfast and hasten to school at nine o'clock; to study from that time till two, recess and all; and never be allowed to open your lips or move from your seat unless in a recitation; to come home, swallow down a dinner, and seat yourself at the piano for an hour and a half; and then if the weather be too unpleasant to walk, to sit down to write a composition or learn some lesson that must be done during the week; and then to spend the whole evening in studying for the next day: to do this, I say, is enough to weary most anyone. And yet often and often do schoolgirls have to do so; and I sometimes feel, as I do tonight, as if I shall drop down dead with the fatigue of sitting still.

17 May

I have been walking a little way with Willy, and as I was coming home he asked me if I knew three young men that he mentioned, two of them brothers of girls I knew very well indeed. All three are gentlemen's sons of the first class in Boston—not that I think much of that except that it makes their actions all the more disgraceful. I know them by sight but have never been introduced to any of them and know nothing of them. He told me that himself and another boy met them in the street, very much *intoxicated,* so that they tumbled round, lost their hats, and so on, and he traced them down to a *billiard* room. I know that young men are sometimes very wild and even bad, especially at college, but I did not think that they would be in such a state during the day time (for Willy is never out in the evening) and when they could be seen. How dreadful it seems that immortal spirits, made in the likeness of God, should so debase themselves. It is not thought of as much as it should be, it seems to me. It is so common a thing it is looked upon as almost inevitable; but it does not seem as if this ought to be so. What temptations are boys exposed to, necessarily exposed to! How I should feel if I knew one of my brothers did so! If this is not so very bad, it would surely lead to worse. They are both now pure and undefiled, they are young, and also I think *very good* boys, better than the generality. They *must* be kept so. I have often heard how much sisters, and particularly older sisters, can influence their brothers. If in any way I can do I surely will. One of the first things is to win their confidence. I try to do this, try to make them love me, and I think they do. But I am not a person with much conversation, especially lively, and I am afraid that they find it dull to be with me. There is so little in common between a girl and a boy to talk about, when they each go to different schools, have different amusements, different companions; and a girl is always older for her years than a boy, and a year or two makes an immense difference in their minds. If you can get brothers to like your company, to be much with you, to give you their confidence, and to love and respect you, it seems to me that a great step has been taken in taking them from vice. Let me begin to try, and may God help me; for I should never forgive myself if I thought that two souls were led astray, who might have been kept in the path of duty by a little effort, or a great deal of effort, on my part.

Walpole   15 July

The sermon this morning from Mr. Tilden was on the sacredness of marriage.[4] I mean upon its influence on the happiness of mankind and the importance that the love that is felt at first should be kept up through life. I can imagine few things worse to bear than for husband and wife not to love each other, not to be willing to give up to each other, and yet linked together for life. How many persons marry merely for the sake of marrying or for money or some such low object, and sacrifice their comfort and happiness for life! A person of true feeling must suffer to be tied in this way and not to love or be beloved by the person they are tied to. It has the greatest effect on their own characters, and certainly on that of their children. How often might the irritability, peevishness and ill temper of a person be traced to their having been brought up when young in a continual scene of contention and debate, often reprimanded by one parent and praised by the other, or punished unjustly.

It is pure enjoyment to me to see a husband and wife who not only really love each other—for there are many persons who disagree in slight everyday things who would be willing to lay down their lives for each other if put to the test—but who have a constant and living love that is constantly springing up in actions of kindness and thoughtfulness for each other, and who respect each other, in fact who are all in all to each other in everyday life as well as in extraordinary events. Some persons, most persons, think that the husband ought to govern and the wife obey. It does not seem to me that this is right, at least as much as I know. Women are generally considered as inferior to men; but here again I disagree with the opinion commonly entertained. In some and many respects, women are inferior to men, and in many respects also they are superior. The reason, or one reason it seems to me, why women are thought inferior is that the qualities in which man excels over the other sex are the most showy qualities, and therefore are the most observed; whereas all the qualities found in the greatest perfection in women are the passive qualities, and these excite much less attention. The active virtues have also a preference in the public opinion over the more retiring ones; but I doubt very much whether the latter are not often the most difficult to acquire, or do not deserve the greatest admiration. For instance, it is thought a much greater proof of strength of character to defy a command and await the consequences than to submit to it; but I doubt whether it could not be often much more difficult to obey than to disobey. In the one we follow the natural bent of our inclinations, and the excitement takes away all fear of the effects. In the other, we not only force ourselves to undergo the pain of the obeying the command, but we have also to subdue our own temper and inclination. The preference given to the manly virtues was greater formerly than it is now, when physical force was esteemed more than any effort of the mind; and it is in a great measure on account of the gradual change in opinion that women are valued and respected more than they used to be. Education has also been extended to women as well as men, and has put them more nearly on their level. It seems to me in the case of husband and wife that there ought to be an equality. In some respects the man has the most experience and is most fitted by nature, here he should take the lead. But also in some respects the woman would be the best guide. Persons say that in this way there would be no order in a family, that there would be continual contention, and that two persons necessarily with different opinions and ideas on many subjects cannot govern at the same time. Even if this were true (which I deny) is this any reason why a woman should give up her liberty to a man who, her equal as to the whole character, is superior to her in force? I do not think that woman ought to govern: it is not in accordance with her character. Neither do I think she ought to be governed, and become a mere instrument in the hands of another. Woman has desires and opinions as well as a man: why should not hers be consulted as well as his? She has powers of thought, will and action: why should not they be exercised? A man has the power to give up his own ideas to those of another: why should woman be the only one required to use it? If we examine the nature of man and woman, we see that they are made and beautifully adapted for each other. If man has strength and courage, woman has patience and fortitude. If man has force, woman has delicacy. In one way man can be best, in the other woman.

One can support the other. Man is more fitted for public life and
bustling scenes, woman for private life and quiet scenes. But because
the man's part is public and makes much more noise, do not give him
all the praise. The woman, although she is neither seen nor heard,
may have as much pain and as many hard battles as the man. If then
this is true, give her the respect and station she is entitled to. Then
they are equal. The woman, feeling that she is appreciated by those
around her, and has some responsibility, will rise higher and higher;
while the man, seeing her real worth and respecting her, will not only
be forced but pleased to give her her full half of influence and consideration. Their mutual love must increase; for we can never love to
the full extent those whom we look down upon, nor those looked
upon as above us, and themselves deeming themselves superior.
Besides, although a man may love a wife inferior to him, as a sort of
plaything, if she is never permitted to be interested in his affairs, and
to think and talk about things in which he is interested, she can be no
companion, and to find one he must leave home and go elsewhere. If
also a woman is not allowed to exercise her higher faculties they must
fall into decay; and therefore she can no longer enjoy the company of
one who is unwilling to lower himself to her level. We see in all
countries where women are entirely passive, and are not allowed to
use or improve their minds, they become an inferior class of beings to
those women who enjoy the privileges of society in an equal degree
with men. If men in such countries should say that women are inferior and are unable to govern themselves, the answer would be that
it is their own fault, that they themselves have rendered the women
inferior, and that they are doing a great wrong to half the human race
by so doing. They also lose a great deal themselves by this deteriora-
tion. Education is as important to women as to men. It cannot be

expected that a mind that has been left to itself should be equal to one that has been highly cultivated. I am glad that they do such things now as found public schools for girls. There is no reason why the minds of girls should not be cultivated as well as a boy's. It may want a different kind of *practical* knowledge on account of the different path in life; but it needs and should have the same purifying, the same enlargement and cultivation. Many persons cry out that *girls* should learn at school Latin and different languages, and in fact anything that is not needful to pass through life with, but think that the time would be much better spent in learning to sew and keep house.[5] Those people do not seem to consider that school is a place to improve and enlarge the mind, but think of it as a place necessary to attend in order to acquire a certain amount of practical knowledge. Some practical learning is certainly necessary, as we all live in a material world and shall therefore need it. But the chief object is the cultivation of the mind, and this is alike necessary both for men and women, the rich and the poor. If once the mind is put in the right direction and ennobled, the practical knowledge is easily acquired; for it will be seen then how necessary it is, and what is wished by the person is easily obtained. Fortunately, practical knowledge improves the mind, and therefore two ends are gained; but we cannot by any means confine ourselves to this alone.

19 August

How strange is the heart! It seems to go by contraries. This afternoon, when I was thinking about religion particularly, Mother came in and made a few observations upon the same subject, spoke about my reading the Bible and Dr. Channing's *Life;* and it, instead of giving me a desire to do as she wished, and to become more religious in my employments, had a directly contrary effect. I always feel uneasy when anyone, and especially Mother, speaks to me on the subject. I feel as if I do not wish them to know anything of what was passing in my mind. I think I am very reserved on such subjects, and as much if not more with Mother than anyone else. Several times I have tried to open my heart and feelings to her, but have always had a feeling of regret for doing so, afterwards. I dislike very much to have a person tell me what to do. I am willing to take advice, but when I am reproved in that way for anything it is often undeserved by me, as the person does not know my real thoughts, that it makes me more reserved and seems to turn me the other way. I often feel that it is wrong, and try to correct it; but although you may compel yourself to *do* a thing, you cannot easily alter your feelings.

28 September

It is evening. The round, pale, peaceful moon is resting in the sky looking down on man, and trying to purify his thoughts. It sheds its mild light on hill and valley, wood and plain and water, on all the beautiful scene before my window, that I love, oh! so well. I have been walking alone on the piazza. Father is asleep, Mother has a bad cold and is half asleep, the boys are in bed. I walked alone on the piazza, and felt lonely, a loneliness that nothing can take away; for is not the spirit always alone, and yet if we could believe it, there is a being that is with you always, with you more than any human being can be. Why cannot we bring it to our minds that God is with us always, that He is thinking of and loving us wherever we are? If a person could believe this they could hardly ever be unhappy, never unhappy.

I love Walpole as a near, dear, friend. Every nook, wood and hill is

familiar to my eye. If I feel sad, I look out of my window on the still
[?] blue scene, on the hills covered with bright sunlight, on the val-
leys in shade, on the woods clothed in a thousand different greens. I
hear the wind in the trees, it seems like a sweet song, low and plain-
tive, sighing and singing with me. Everything is quiet but the birds
who sing happily, and the crickets buzzing always. I look out at
night, the moon is bright and lights everything, not a sound is heard
except the ever-sounding insect and the owl. Everything is the same
as in the afternoon, but it is quieter and sadder. The two views are
like the different views we take in early life and when we are fast
going to the grave. But is the moonlight less lovely? If Tuesday I
leave Walpole; perhaps never, never shall I pass such pleasant hours,
never shall I find a place more beautiful in my eyes. I feel like leaving
something very dear to me, and I long to return to it. It has never
been so beautiful in my eyes as now; all that I have comes before me,
as I gaze and think it may be one of my last looks, that I may never
see it again. If I never do, if circumstances prevent me from ever
looking on these hills again, I shall always look back and remember
it as an almost sacred place where I had all my happiest and holiest
feelings, and where the happiest hours of my life were passed. In
many, many years, when I am old, when parents and perhaps brothers
have gone, I may come to this little room, and look out of this window at the same scene I look at now. What will then be my circumstances, thoughts and character? What will be my thoughts on looking back on my own life? What shall I have passed through, and how
passed through? It is vain to imagine. We must go quietly on, doing
faithfully what we think right and just, and have trust to one who
never forgets us, and loves us.

My writing in my journal, although I try to make it otherwise, is
very irregular. In the hurry of life there is very little time to devote
to meditation and employments in one's own room. All the times
for reflection one can get must be at odd times, when there is no
opportunity for writing.

I feel a continual desire to seize on time and make a part of it at
least my own. It seems to be flowing away so fast without profit,
without great pleasure, without anything of importance.

I feel very undecided about my schooling, for the future I mean.
There are so many conflicting duties, or what seem conflicting. School
is very important; a fine education is in my opinion as important for a
woman as for a man, in private life. I do not mean the knowledge of
so much Latin, Greek, or anything of the kind, but an education to
strengthen and improve the mind. I also think that in many respects
school is better for gaining that education than home; and I think,
although I am not perfectly decided, that it would be better for me
and that I should prefer to go another winter, till I am seventeen,
and then study the two following years at home. But there seem to be
a great many reasons why it would be best for me to leave school
after this winter; and it is very difficult to decide to which reasons to
give the most weight. In the first place, *and as the very first motive for
studying at home,* is Mother. She is all alone; I am her only daughter;
and as I now live, see her only at my several meals and a few minutes
in the afternoon. Every year she is growing older and needs more and
more a companion. She seems to be particularly tried, for she is often
unwell, so as to prevent her going out; and yet her eyes are not strong
enough to enable her to use them constantly at home. Then she is
naturally of a melancholy and desponding temperament, and I think

that every year her cares of various kinds connected with her house, her own health, etc., bear more heavily upon her. It seems under such circumstances I ought to be at home and with her as much as possible, at any rate if I can do so without seriously injuring myself in any way. Sometimes I feel very well content and think that I shall do nicely; but at other times I feel rather sorry to leave school so soon. One very important motive for going to school is that it brings you into connection with other girls; whereas I think that if I left school I should be very apt to lose all connection with them in the familiar way one must see a companion at school. Another thing is that I am much afraid that as I am the only daughter and necessarily of more importance in the home than if there were more girls, it will be very difficult to continue my studies as regularly and thoroughly as I should do at school. Then I think that there are many studies for which I could have no special teacher, and yet which I should learn with much less advantage alone than if I had some one more advanced to go on with me. Besides all this there is something very healthy for the mind in the very air of school. It teaches greater industry, regularity, promptness, rigidness of attention, and system than anything else; and girls especially need this drilling in early life as they have much less of it in after life than a man. I think that school teaches one to overcome difficulties, accustoms one to continual and unremitting effort, makes them think less of any difficulties, taking them as a matter of course, to be overcome continually. It gives also chances of thought, and as I said before, promptness. It also exhilarates a person and is a continual incentive to effort often severe, without which one would be apt to become lazy and slow. I often wonder what married ladies and girls out of school do with the time in which I accomplish so much and they so little; but I think it must be that they have no decided occupations, nothing fixed to be done, and that they become, not idle, but waste their time in things that if they had anything urgent to do they would not *think* of doing. I began to write this morning, but was obliged to leave off and have finished since I came to my room for the night. I should like to write much longer but have no time.

1850

Boston   9 February

I have been dining and passing the afternoon at Aunt Parkman's. Just before that, I went up into Annie Hinckley's chamber to see herself and the baby. It is about three weeks or a month old and is a nice fat looking little thing with the smallest imaginable hands, beautifully formed. Annie has very pretty hands, he no doubt takes them from her. She looks very thin, and *dreadfully* pale, perfectly worn out. She is still very weak, and suffers a good deal of neuralgic pain, which keeps her down. She is now accountable for the education of an immortal soul. How little we know of that child's future destiny who is now lying in the nurse's arms apparently without any sort of mind. He merely lies and stays perfectly helpless, cries when wanting anything or feeling sick, otherwise sleeping or else in a kind of dormant state. May not we be children on this earth, helpless, and knowing little, in comparison with a future life in which we may live?

I admire young Mrs. Parkman's character in some respects (Sam's

wife). She certainly has managed in relation to Sam, with the greatest
wisdom and tact. Many wives, nay most, give up entirely and foolishly to their husbands when they are first married and then when it
is too late feel sorry for it. Mrs. Mary Parkman married under a good
many disadvantages. In the first place he had been used to have his
own way entirely in his mother's house and had become on that account
rather selfish, wayward and thought everyone wrong but himself; and
was very much in the habit of picking at and worrying his mother
about every little thing. It therefore must have required some tact
and wisdom to have been able to have changed these feelings. But
now his wife has her own will just as much as he. There is no quarrel-
ing and disputing, and no arrogance on her part; but he believes her
capable of taking care of herself and her affairs as well as she did
before her marriage, and also allows her judgment to be as capable as
his, only hers more in one way, his in another. He allows that she can
do things right as well as himself; and he is willing to give up to her
in some things as well as she to him. He is also much pleasanter
towards others, than before he married. Men have a curious idea, or at
least their conduct would seem to show, that it is their feeling, that
their wives do not know how to do anything half as well as they do,
even as to taking care of their own health, conduct, etc., even if they
are equally old and have been used to taking the charge of themselves
all their lives. I think a great deal of after comfort and happiness may
depend on the first few married years. Then habits are formed that
can never or at least without great difficulty be removed.

16 February

I went last evening to a party at Mary Quincy's. There were about
seventy persons, most all of them girls of sixteen and seventeen and

college boys.[6] I very seldom, never go to parties; but Mary was very desirous that I should go, and I went. Today I feel tired and low-spirited, as one always does after a party. Low-spirited in the common acceptance of the term seems rather high-sounding to apply to the feelings one has when you are tired and a little dissatisfied with many things; but still, it is the only word there is, and it is a very expressive one. I enjoyed myself very much, at least for a party. I was dressed in a simple white "taillon" muslin with two skirts and capes trimmed with a sort of quilted silk lace. The dress was simple and quite pretty. My hair looked very well I suppose, although not as well as sometimes. When I arrived, I thought I should not dance at all; but in the end I believe I danced four times, once with Arthur Dexter whom I like, once with Walter Cabot, son of Sam Cabot of Temple Place.[7] It would be a great comfort to me if I could learn to talk. I cannot imagine how it is, but some people have the happy faculty of having everything to say upon nothing, and to a person perhaps they never saw or heard of before and know nothing of. I cannot do it at present and I always feel after I have been to a party, or anywhere where there are persons to talk to, that they must think me the most heavy stupid person they ever knew, and that I have not two ideas in my head. If I went anywhere I doubt not I should improve, but I am afraid, as it is, that I shall grow worse and worse every day.

Walpole   7 *September*

What is life? a conflict of emotions. How falsely are our actions and outward circumstances considered as making up our lives. Often when outwardly we seem most quiet, does the true current of life run most swiftly, and the most roughly. And often when our outward being is the most busy, our true inward life is the most quiet, being kept smooth by its attraction to a regular round of objects. We should be careful that when we are much occupied, our moral life do[es] not fall asleep being forgotten amid the whirl of other things.

I have been reading this morning a letter of Mother's from Uncle John, in which he raises my esteem for him, much higher than it had ever been before. Among other things he says that, in his walks from Roxbury to his business in Boston, it was his habit to think over (or try to do so) what he *ought* to do, what were his duties, how he could best fulfill them, etc. What an excellent plan it would be, if one could devote some time to this occupation, every day of their lives. There are so many different currents in life setting against each other, and often making us entirely forgetful of what we would wish most to remember, that it is almost necessary to have some time, in which we can free ourselves to think over what we are doing, and what we ought to do, what our situation is, what the duties belonging to it, how we have executed them, and how we can best execute them in future.

We are very apt, not so much to neglect duties, when they are positively before us, as to allow ourselves to forget them, allow other things to veil them from our sight. This is almost as great a fault as to neglect them when they are plainly before us, and brings the same results. I have often tried to think over the occurrences and thoughts of the day, at night after coming to my room; but one cannot do two things at once and do them both faithfully, beside which I am often very tired and sleepy, and am forced to give it up; and such a thing as that should never be neglected for a day, if once begun.

It is more difficult to find time in winter than in summer, but find time I must and will. If I could only succeed in getting up early in the morning, I should be able to do a great deal more; but whether it is really want of energy on my part, or whether it is natural to one, I very seldom succeed in having more time, than just to hurry to school, and do not get there at the proper time either. I often feel disheartened about this coming winter, for there is so much that I want to do and feel as if I ought to do, and I am always able, or at least succeed *in accomplishing, so much less than I intend.* There are several things that I *must* do. First and principal is attending to Mother. Her eyes are yet weak, the slightest thing hurts them; and I am afraid when cold weather comes, and she is shut in the house, they will be worse rather than better. Her health is poor, miserable, and I almost totally despair of its ever being better. She gets low-spirited, and depressed, from sitting by herself and having few enjoyments; this of course is bad for her body; and mind and body are *continually reacting on one another.* My next duty is my education. I have a mind and soul to be formed and now is the time to shape them. They demand all my time. Now often I do not succeed in executing and carrying out both of these duties, and am perpetually harassed, as to which ought to be sacrificed to the other. I more often feel, and feel now, that Mother has a right to the first attention, but I so often feel the opposite, and seem to do her so very little good even when I sacrifice my studies to her, that I feel discouraged and uncertain. My great object now is to do as much as I possibly can, but so arrange it that my different duties shall not clash; and my great difficulty is that, to do this, I *am obliged to give up so many things that I long to do.* There is another set of duties that I must not lose sight of, and those are the duties I owe the whole family. I feel that, situated as I am, an only daughter, with a mother often sick and depressed, never gay, it rests upon one, to make our home bright, cheerful and attractive to the boys, and comfortable to Father. When I think how much boys are exposed to, how much a happy home may keep them from, and how much depends on me for making it happy,

I feel almost discouraged by my own responsibility. I am very conscious, that I am very apt to be easily bruised and discouraged by difficulties, and it often makes me much less cheerful at home than I ought, or will, to be. In reading a new novel of Dickens' this summer, *David Copperfield,* I have felt very much impressed by the character of *Agnes.* [8] It is the kind of character I would most aim at imitating. The calm, quiet and cheerful goodness that seems to form an atmosphere around her, and affect all who come within its influence. She has great dignity, is able to advise, and commands everyone's esteem and confidence by her good sense, judgment, firmness, truth, and love; and yet she makes herself beloved by everyone, for her gentleness, sympathy, love, and sweetness. There is nothing the least weak or silly about her, you feel that she is able to take care of herself and others; and yet she is the personification of modesty, humbleness, and all womanly and lovable traits. There is an atmosphere of quiet goodness around her, which is more lovely to me in a woman than any other characteristic. I do not know what the feeling is exactly, but I always feel as if she had a certain line of conduct that she always pursued, and which made every outward difficulty appear nothing. She has no doubts or anxieties: all is smooth and quiet. I long so much to make myself like this, to go through life always quiet and cheerful, doing good in an invisible sort of way, to everyone, and doing all my duties without a murmur or without a doubt. I have constantly floating in my mind the idea of such a person, she seems like a kind of little angel. I have expressed my ideas in the most clumsy and hidden manner, but it is because it is an idea difficult to be made understood. To go back to myself: if I devote as much time as I want to my own school and music, where is the time to give to Mother? Besides, Mother is unwilling I should give up anything for her. And yet when

I come home from school, as I often do, and find her sick, unable to use her eyes, and feeling so depressed and lonely and nervous that she can scarcely keep from bursting into tears, I feel as if, come what would, I would put everything aside and devote myself to her, doing what I could afterwards. But I cannot do this, because one cannot go to school and be constantly unfaithful to it; therefore I must leave off some of my studies. But when I do I am dissatisfied; Mrs. Lowell is unwilling I fall behind; and I do not find after all that I do much good to Mother.

What can I do? There is such a state of things when I get behind-hand with my lessons, and behindhand with my music, when Mrs. Lowell [is] complaining, and my music is neglected, and then Mother is weak and sick and miserable, I feel as if I should give up every-thing, and lose all gaiety, get irritable and cross and worried. One of my greatest troubles is, that I am surrounded with two or three people, who all pull different ways. Mrs. Lowell of course expects me to have all my lessons, and does not understand that a person is very often interrupted; therefore I always feel very unwilling to go to school without all my lessons learned; therefore if anything prevents my learning them at the proper time, I am often tempted to take the time from my music, and finish my lessons. Now Mother thinks that I study a great deal too much; she has nothing to do with my lessons and does not know all the circumstances, and thinks that I ought to give those up to my music, rather than my music to them. Father thinks that I have a great deal too much to do in every way, wants me to be more with Mother, and have my evenings to myself. And finally I feel as if I must give up some of my time to Mother. Therefore, if I get behind in my lessons, and have laid out a [long?] plan, by which if I give up music, walking and everything for that day, and get all even, Mother will often insist on my doing my music; or Father will want me to walk; or I will see Mother sitting in her room alone and unoccupied, and wondering why I should do nothing but study; and I get so worried and have all my plans so overturned and everything goes so wrong that I cannot do anything, and am irritable and dull for the rest of the day. It is all the result of having too much to do, and too little time to do it in. It is not I alone, but many girls whom I know, who have the same difficulties. As Mrs. Lowell always says, American girls have a whole lifetime crowded into the first eighteen years of their lives. In England, girls until they have finished their education live in their own rooms, see no company, have comparatively little to do with their own families, and have no cares but their own education. Formerly in America the women had comparatively little education and devoted themselves to housekeeping, sewing and so forth; but now girls study as much as boys, especially if music be included, besides being expected to see to things at home; and many go into company. Of course when all these things come in a bunch they cannot be done well, and are more than half the time the causes of women's being sick and anxious in after life. There are two things I mean to keep if possible, and to which everything else shall yield, and these are good health and cheerfulness. They have a vast effect on a person's character, and shall never be sacrificed, as they so often are, especially in women, by want of proper attention.

5 October

I have just read a letter from Mrs. Wm. Amory to Harriet, and it gave rise to feelings which often trouble me, and which I cannot pass over. Harriet and her mother are dear and confidential friends: why am not I, an *only* daughter, open and easy with my mother, and why

cannot I feel towards her as a friend and companion? I hardly dare
write it or think it, yet I cannot help feeling and believing it, that I
seldom speak to Mother except as to an everyday friend, who had no
particular interest in me, or I in them. What is the reason? When I
daily pant for a dear friend in whom I can confide, and who can advise
and comfort and aid me, why is it that I have never found such a
person in my own mother. It is entirely or principally my own fault?
Am I blinded and unjust when I say that it is her fault? It is all my
fault that we so often speak quickly, unkindly and complainingly,
and that we so seldom speak tenderly, confidentially? If I could only
solve those questions, it would still many unhappy feelings.

1851

Walpole   *11 July*

[Looking back to Niagara . . .] The roar of the water is a very beautiful part, and when you think that ages ago the Indian heard the roar
and saw the waters rushing by, and that ever since they have rushed
on unceasingly by night and day—always—you feel awed at a thing
so vast and eternal. There is something to me very beautiful in the
feeling that there are some things that do not change, that last for
ages the same, unmindful of the changes of men and the lapse of
time. This same great river has been rushing away for centuries the
same; but if a record could be written of all the human beings who
have looked on these waters, of all the feelings of the thousands of

souls who have stood on its edge, what a record would it be! The
Indian warrior looking upon it with awe and mysterious dread, as if
in the presence of some mighty power, the Indian girls wondering
where it is going always, always, and singing a song of love, or a wild
lament. The adventurer, thinking of the home he had left, of the different scene he had been brought up in, but taking heart, as if the
great spirit who seems to sweep over it would protect him. Then
the settler with his family, who have left their native land to dwell in
these wilds. The party of travelers, young girls and their lovers, who
breathe over these waters their vows, and dream of perfect happiness;
and these same young girls grown to gray hairs, with the husbands
they pledged themselves to love years before, looking back upon years
of sorrow and joy, pleasure and disappointments, thinking of friends
gone then standing beside them, hopes, castles in the air, then bright,
now fallen to the ground and forgotten, perhaps feeling calm and
happy, grateful for the pleasures of the past and trustful for the
future, or embittered by life and despairing. Oh, the prayers, the
hopes, the griefs, the joys, the innocent thoughts, and high aspirations, borne down to eternity with that rushing water! If twenty years
before, when Mother was there a young beautiful girl, with Father at
her side, she could have thought of herself, twenty years passed by,
again looking over that current, married, and a daughter of seventeen,
worn out by sickness, and the wear and tear of life, would she have
wanted to have lived on? . . .

[Looking back to West Point . . .] The life must be tedious in the
last degree. They were all in tents pitched out in an open barren
plain. Sentinels were walking to and fro guarding space, for that was
all. The parade which is every day at sunrise and sunset is merely to
collect all the students and see that they are on duty. I did not see the

rules, but they are extremely strict. While we were there, there was a
long list of punishments read. One who had smoked was confined to
his tent, except when on duty, for ten days. Another, who went beyond
the limits, was to keep to his tent for a fortnight, etc., etc. They cannot go beyond certain limits, which are very circumscribed, except
with an express permit. They only are allowed to wear so many clean
clothes a week, and if these are soiled they are punished. The rules
extend to the smallest trifles and the punishments are very severe.
Sunday we went to church at the government chapel, and heard what
I consider a most miserable sermon, dogmatical, stupid, and without
sense or talent. The cadets were perfectly quiet, not a sound to be
heard, but some read, some drew, and they did everything but attend.
Can you wonder that men are what they are, when you see them
brought up in such a way? Taken from home at the most critical time
of life, when their characters and minds are entirely unformed, and
yet when their bodily activity and spirits lead them into temptation
and disincline them from reflexion, they are put into a school like
this, with two or three hundred boys most of them older than themselves, surrounded by nothing but men, separated from home, older
friends, women, all softening and elevating influences, and taught by
[force?]. Force and hard law are the only barriers placed against all the
evil around them, and this forces them to outward obedience but dis-
gusts them with everything good, and teaches them hypocrisy and
deceit. Indeed I cannot understand how men come out from such
training for five years as good as they are. By this process they are
thought prepared for life. Then what is their life after they graduate?
Three years spent either in war, where if they live they are likely to
lose health, or in some fort placed in the wilds. After this it is rather

late to begin another mode of life, even if they are not destroyed for it. And what is it to be in the army? A soldier is no longer considered one of the first rank in the kingdom, and he must pass his life in hardship and poverty, without the power of improving his condition by marriage or wealth. For who would marry a man to go with him to the world's end, or else be always separated from him; and I should not think a man would want to ask any woman he loved, to do it.[9]

3 August

I went last evening to Mrs. Grant's or rather Mrs. Bellows' to tea. They begged me to be there very early and so I was there by five.

Young Mrs. Grant was taken sick while I was there, with a sort of choke, sickness and great pain. They had all been that day to Bellows Falls to see the place, and dined on lobster and champagne. They attributed her illness to the former. Before tea, however, she was relieved, and soon was quite restored. In the evening we had quite a large collection of the villagers, and, to show how the place is emptied of young men, the only two men of any kind were Mr. Abel Bellows and old Mr. Willis. I don't know what will become of the farms. There seemed no one to carry them on, all the young men going to the cities to enter into business; and I am not surprised, for the life of a farmer, although it has its pleasures, is one of constant toil, and no advancement, for they succeed in comfortably supporting their families, and that is all. On the other hand, an intelligent man goes into business and makes money in a short time, sufficient to live comfortably and well, and then has the chance of continual improvement. I believe it is true, that there is but one young man from among the aristocracy of the village who remains here, John W. Howard;

and he is forced to it by his health.[10] Villages have as decided an aristocracy as cities, strange as it may seem; and it is often impossible to see a difference between those of the upper *ton,* and those excluded.

The case is almost the same with regard to the women as the young men. All the girls go away in winter to some of the cities, some for less time than others, but go there to have some gaiety.

12 August

I finished yesterday *The Disowned* by Bulwer, and like it extremely.[11] I feel this with a great many books, but it is not from want of discrimination. I do not mean that I like the whole of the book; but either as a whole, or else parts of it, have given me much pleasure and go to the right place. Bulwer's novels are not generally considered very moral, and perhaps in a certain sense they are not. They are not books one would want to read aloud, to everyone at least. But I do not think this is always a proof of a book unworthy to be read. He writes like one brought up amidst the follies and vices of fashionable life, and although now fully sensible to its defects, remains partly guided by habit. His books have to me a great deal of true sentiment and right feeling. I prefer the style of novel very much to that of Walter Scott's. I finished a few days before *Old Mortality,* and was struck by the contrast. The Waverley novels are justly celebrated and praised.[12] They show great talent, but in a way that, although it pleases you for the time, does not last. He gives an account of the outward life of his heroes and heroines, but nothing beyond; and one never feels that they could have lived in the same world as oneself. This arises partly from the difference of manners and the times, but more I think from the superficial view given of their lives. The great want to me in all histories and most biographies is the want of a clear view of the inward man. Everyone has two lives, his deeds and his thoughts; and I think the latter make up the true man. If he is bad, his bad thoughts are worse than his deeds. If he is good, they are better, in as much as the soul is purer than the body. Many persons say that deeds are the true test, and they are to a certain degree; but the spirit is often willing when the flesh is weak, and when we are freed from the last, the spirit will rise triumphant. Though this must be said, that a man who unites goodness in both is more perfect than one who fails in half. I do not take much interest in adventures or in the outward *mechanism* of the world. History, I will say unreservedly, I find very wearying, except when taken as a study. A book of history to *read* is the dullest book in the world, and the same with a biography; but when you study either of these for a course of reading, and can compare them with other histories and biographies, in their connection with civilization, progress, etc., etc., in fine, when one can read them not for themselves but as helping to throw light on a great subject, they are very interesting. This is the course of study I intend to pursue next winter (as far as one can intend anything for the future), and think I shall enjoy it very much. History, to include the lives of great men of each age, and their works, the improvements made in all branches of civilization, and in fact a history of man, as shown on a certain spot of earth, and through a series of ages. I am lamentably ignorant at present of all history and geography, even that of my own country; but I had always much rather work out a mathematical problem, or study an abstruse philosophy, than read a common history or biography. In the latter, however, are many lives that I enjoy above most books, when the writings, public but more especially *private,* of the individual constitute the life, and not an account of certain events, strung together without sense or interest. I am reading now a life of the Rev. James Perkins, lately dead in Cincinnati, and the brother of Miss Nancy Perkins before mentioned.[13] It is little more than extracts from his journal and private letters, with his other writings, and interspersed with an account of his movements when it is necessary to keep up the connection. This to me is delightful, it goes to the bottom and gives the true account without any flattery or misrepresentation. Most biographies are a collection of the pleasant parts of the character, the faults being omitted. Can one feel interest in such a life? Much as I enjoy myself here, I long sometimes to be in Boston, in order to get the books I want. I dislike very much this kind of desultory reading, when you seem to know no more at the end than at the commencement.

1852

Boston   22 *February*

The winter was begun with high hopes, brilliant plans, good intentions; and it is ending with plans unperformed, and but little accomplished. One of my plans was to keep a regular diary this winter, and write every day, in which I certainly have most signally failed. I feel sorry for this, as it has always been a very pleasant idea with me, to be able in future years to recall my old self. People seem to forget their younger selves so much, and almost feel as if their earlier life no longer belonged to them, that I have always felt it would be very pleasant as well as useful to have a written account to refer to, which should recall as letters do all your old feelings. I shall try this morning to write down a short picture of the winter, as I do not wish it to be lost. It has been very quiet, that is, void of excitement, and has been very busy. My studies, which I limited in the autumn to the morning, have increased very much; and I have been much more busy if possible than usual. There is so much to be done that I do not in one sense regret having filled my time with lessons, although I shall try another winter not to do the same again. My plan of proceeding, which is very regular, is as follows: Mondays and Thursdays at half past nine in the morning I go to Mrs. Hodges' room in West Street for a little more than an hour, when I read the lesson I have completed, and take those for the next time.[14] The studies and their plan I think very excellent and they are as follows: Mondays are devoted to English history, Biography, and a Question. For the history Mrs. H. gives us the notes one Monday for the next, of a reign, that is to say the heads of the chief events of a reign, and during the week we read that portion of history in two or three different books, she herself does not care whose or what, and then write an abstract of it making one reign about 3 pages of a common blank book. This when carried to her the next Monday is read aloud, and the composition and facts revised and corrected. Besides this book we keep what is called a book of key words, that is a set of words each of which is the most prominent word in one event and therefore recalls it to the mind. Once in four weeks the study is reviewed, and we relate from memory the date of the commencement of the reign (which is the only date we commit to memory) and all the events in it repeated in chronological order. We also keep another book called a chart, where in eight divisions, one by the side of the other, we put down the name of the king, his death, etc., his family, wars, battles, and events, great men of the time, any odd things such as the foundation of buildings, etc., contemporary history of the surrounding countries, such as crusades, wars of the popes and emperors, etc., and then all the contemporary kings of the time.

For Biography, we select a particular man, and write from any good authority we can obtain an abstract of his life. These abstracts are all to be written as clearly as possible, with nothing omitted and everything superfluous cut away. Her third lesson is a question she gives us to look out, on any subject, such as the house of Condé, a list of minerals, a list of important treaties, etc., upon any subject with which we wish to be acquainted. For this we look at encyclopedias, large maps, histories, geographies, etc., etc., and write a short account. Everything at stated intervals is reviewed. On Thursdays we learn French history in the same way as English, except that instead of learning the dates of the kings we learn in the reign of what *English* kings they flourished. For the second lesson, instead of Biography we have Geography, when instead of learning any geography we take the map, say of Europe, and first draw in our blank books its countries and its lakes, seas, gulfs etc., then take its separate countries and divide these into counties, towns, etc., etc., giving the rivers, etc., in this way making a geography for yourself you have it impressed upon your mind. For a third lesson we have another question. Besides all these, on Mondays, we have, at stated times, to learn all the German contemporary emperors, to write a description of certain places in the form of a letter, called a Tour, and to read any piece of prose or poetry we particularly like. Also to read at home the works and life of any author and give our opinion upon his character and works, and lastly to write a theme on any subject appointed. I have written this long account because I think it so good that I wish to have it written down. Besides these studies, I take a lesson in French twice a week with Mary Quincy of Dr. Arnett, for which I have to write exercises, and alternatively write a note or relate an anecdote—the last two are horrid. [15] My singing, which I enjoyed so much last winter and meant to continue so religiously this, has failed most signally. Signor Corelli, of whom I took lessons last winter and whose teaching I liked extremely, was taken sick this autumn after I had taken one lesson, and went to the South, as his physicians said never to return; but I have heard of him since in Charleston, S. Carolina, giving lessons, and he thinks of returning here this spring. [16] In the meantime, having so much to occupy me otherwise, I have neglected my practicing very much. I have just begun to take lessons of a Miss Baumann, a Frenchwoman who has lately come here; but her style does not please me very well, and if Corelli returns I shall certainly take of him. She seems pleased with my voice; but it is much more than I am myself, for no one else seems to enjoy my singing at all. Friday evenings I go to the Ticknors' to sing, which I find extremely pleasant. [17] Our music is entirely *masses* of Mozart's and Haydn's, which are extremely beautiful. Anna Ticknor plays on the piano, Lizzie T. and myself sing the soprano part, Sallie Cary and Miss Ware sing the contralto, Mr. Charles [?] and Mr. Tom Frothingham sing the tenor, and Mr. C. G. Curtis Jr. and Dr. [Oliver?] the bass. We have very nice times. I think it teaches you a good deal, as we have to read a great deal at first sight. Lately we have engaged August Fries, one of the Music Fund Society, but a German, and who knows a good deal about music, to beat time, etc., etc. [18] Twice a week, in the afternoon from half past three until 5, I go to the rehearsals of the Music Fund Society, and of the Germania Band. [19] These are, or rather were, very pleasant on several accounts. You can go by yourself and you can hear the same music played at the concerts without the trouble of dressing and going to them. But they are sold so cheap, the Musical Fund 16 tickets for a dollar and the other 8, that there is a great crowd and you have to go early to get a tolerable seat. These various pursuits and occupations have filled up my winter. There have been very few public amusements, and I have not been to these. People have been very much fascinated by a Madame Thillon, a French actress who has been playing here in little French vaudevilles and who was certainly very pretty and graceful, but who did not carry me away with delight.

The great event of the winter, to our quiet household, was a ball Mother gave on 10 February, this month.[20] She has been intending to give it for many years; but in the old house it was always put off to this, and since we have been here there have been various objections. Now that we have at last furnished, we decided to give one. We sent out [blank] cards, that is invitations, and invited about [blank] people, but only [blank] accepted and on the night of the party so many dropped off that we did not have more than [blank]. The house looked very well. The flower room was filled with plants and looked beautifully. We had dancing in the dining room and center room where the floor is made for dancing—in the dining room a cloth was put over the carpet. The musicians were six of the Germania Band, and the music was very fine. The supper was down in the library where everything was moved away and a table laid the whole length of the room. The ornament in the center was a gold basket, with exquisite artificial flowers, and two bunches of real flowers at the ends. My chamber with everything moved out and other things moved in was the dressing room for the gentlemen. Mother's room was for the ladies, and the best chamber a card room. My dress was very simple and pretty I think, white tarlton [tarlatan?] muslin, two skirts with plain hems, a silk waist with Grecian folds, satin bows on the shoulders and some very beautiful natural flowers in the front. My hair was very handsomely dressed behind in a sort of medley of puffs and braids, and puffed in front, otherwise plain. Mrs. Upham lent me a very pretty bunch of flowers and I looked very spruce. Mother's dress was one she has worn before, a light green watered silk, an application lace mantle, and artificial flowers in her hair. About an hour before the party the lamps were lighted, when to our great dismay they refused to burn; and although the gas man was sent for, and worked hard for half an hour, the company began to assemble and the entry was almost dark, while the lamps in the parlor flickered and burned very faintly. At about ten o'clock, when nearly all the people had arrived, Father announced that all the lights must be extinguished, and accordingly every gas light in the house was entirely put out. The only light downstairs was an oil lamp in the vestibule, a small chandelier of candles in the flower room, and our candelabras on the pier table in the very end of the dining room. We remained in this way for between ten and fifteen minutes, when they were re-lighted; but they did not burn brightly all the evening in either the front parlor or the entry. When the lamps were put out, it was so dark that people in entering the room did not recognize Mother. The ball as everyone has said went off very well, and I think it did. The people did not go until quite late, and when they did a few remained to the German cotillion, which they danced steadily until a quarter past one. They had a very nice chance here, as they waltzed into the center room. I danced several times; but I did not begin until the middle of the evening, and then only dancing the cotillions did not have much time. As I, however, did not receive with Mother, very few people knew me at all. A short time before our party Miss Sarah [Inches?] died, which took away some of our friends; and the very day before came the news of the death of Edward Otis, Mrs. Harry's son, which kept away Mrs. Bates who was extremely anxious to come, as she had never seen the house, and the two Misses Otis, Emily and May, who are great belles and beauties and whom I was anxious to see in a party. The girls of the present day are all pretty, there was hardly a plain or ugly girl here; but there are very few or no handsome ones. Ellen d'Hauteville was the only really beautiful woman in the room, and all the handsomest ones were either married women or an older set. Those who had come out this year or last are all very small and all pretty, but nothing more. It is the same with the men, the present set are mostly dwarfs in size and appear to be dwarfs in understanding; but there are of course some exceptions. The most fashionable are those who dance the polka and are not the most desirable by any means. The manners too of the rising generation strike me as anything but elegant; and it arises in a great measure from the parties being composed entirely of almost children, instead of a mixture of older people. We are now quite restored to order since the party, but it was a long business.

20 May

It is all over. What I have feared, and yet hoped was not true, at the same time. All, all, all is confirmed. How can I think of it? I took this morning a singing lesson of Corelli, and he told me exactly what he thought of my voice. I don't know whether, knowing I was going away, he thought it better to tell me, or whether he had hitherto been hoping it would improve. But that matters not. The cold dreary fact is the only important thing. My voice is *poor*. What misery, what disappointment that sinks down to my very heart, that I must always feel, that I can never cure! I never fully realized, until now, how much music was to me. How great a loss the want of it. My sole comfort now is that I know the truth: that there is nothing now to hope or fear. All is decided. *There is no hope now. Why was it?* Why has nature denied me this great blessing? There is some good reason, and I must make the best of it. I am vain, too fond of applause, of the approbation of the world rather than of God, am too prosperous, and am worldly, when I should be pure and high-minded. And yet why this, why touch me in this tender spot? A child of heaven, but nevertheless mortal and earthly, how little thou knowest thy true good! Submit patiently, yes, and thankfully, to God. Have you not a Father watching over you for your true good, and do you not believe in the depths of your soul, that you will one day rejoice at this seemingly great misfortune? I feel that I could have given up Europe if I could have a truly beautiful voice. And yet poor weak child, am I to say what is best and what is not?

I can yet hear music, and it will be doubly pure enjoyment if self-denial is added and joined with it. You have had power hitherto to wander in any direction you liked. You needed only to stretch forth your hand and you could have. This is your first repulse, made for your good, to try your strength. Do not be found weak. There is a high calling for you. Be ready for it. Life is a school in which we must all be trained. Not enjoyment, and not sorrow, are our destinies' end or way. But to act that each tomorrow find us further than today. God Almighty, my Father in Heaven, I solemnly and earnestly pray to Thee for strength; and let this disappointment, heavy to me though it may seem small, lead me and help me on my heavenward path. Thou wilt not scorn as trivial any earnest prayer of Thy creatures.

CHAPTER THREE

1852 – 1853

After envying friends who have enjoyed the experience, Elizabeth at last sets off with her parents on a European tour that is to last sixteen months.

Much of what they do repeats the experience of innumerable American tourists. They disembark at Liverpool, from their tiny Cunard paddle wheeler, go at once to London by train, then move back through the Midlands, Derbyshire, and York, on their way to Melrose and Sir Walter Scott's Abbotsford. They penetrate Scotland as far as the edge of the Highlands, then, via the Lake District, return to London. Crossing to Europe, they travel through the Low Countries and the Rhineland to Switzerland and as far into Italy as Milan, still, like Florence and Rome, with its fortifications. Soon, they settle in Paris for three months. Early in 1853, they go to Lyons, down the Rhone valley, along the Riviera to Genoa, and take a steamboat to Leghorn, Civita Vecchia, and Naples. Soon they are in Rome, where they spend nearly seven weeks. From Rome, they make the accustomed progress up the Tiber valley and through Tuscany to Florence, where they spend a month.

Their next stage is rather more original. They go to Venice, then by steamboat to Trieste, then to Vienna for a week, then by Danube steamboat to Linz. They continue through Salzburg, Munich, Nürnberg, Leipzig, Dresden, and Berlin. They return through Magdeburg, Cologne, and Brussels to Paris, for a stay of five more weeks. They go through the Low Countries again, before reaching London, Liverpool, and their ship.

Much of Elizabeth's account is plain description, of historic buildings, art galleries, artists' studios, and shops. She has read much English history and literature and some French, so at Versailles she can relate the palace and its pictures to the panorama of French development.

On three occasions, her life is touched by history, though I print only the first of these entries. In October, half understanding its meaning, she watches a procession for Louis Napoleon, somewhat before he became emperor. In November, she learns of the death of Daniel Webster. From the newspapers, she reports deathbed scenes and assessments of his public life. Then she ventures opinions of her own. She thinks that he greatly decayed in his last year. Acknowledging that she has never heard one of his speeches, yet she knows that he has been a great man and is glad that, quite recently, she has met him. For, on 30 May 1852, at tea at Thomas Handasyd Perkins's Brookline home, she saw him and admired his magnificent head and his deep-set dark eyes. Then, early in December, she watches another parade for Louis Napoleon, when the Empire has just been proclaimed.

1852

Paris   14 October

Arrived at the Place de la Bastille, the weather was so clear that we
were tempted to ascend the Column of July. This is built of cast iron,
unsupported by masonry, and standing on a pedestal of stone or
marble.[1] It was consecrated to the memory of the victims of the 27th,
28th and 29th of July 1830, who are buried in vaults constructed
beneath its base. Some of the insurgents of 1848 were also buried
here. The exterior is surrounded by belts, and the interior engraved
with the name of the sufferers. The column is surmounted by a gilt
figure of the "Genius of liberty" holding a broken chain, and as it
were just taking flight. The figure is very finely executed, but I do
not like exactly the contrast of the gold and black iron. The stairs
inside are much more spacious than in the pillar of the Place Vendôme, but they are very dark and seem anything but solid. The view
of Paris is superb; and certainly no city could present a more magnificent panorama. Unlike London, which seems an impenetrable maze
of human habitations, Paris seems to be clearly divided into portions
easily recognized, by certain grand objects. In the furthest distance
looms up the noble Arc de l'Étoile, making a most impressive feature
in the landscape.[2] It looks fit for an Emperor to pass under and is to
me one of the finest monuments in the city. This side of the arch, the
Champs Elysées, Place de la Concorde, and gardens of the Tuileries
form a large open space covered with trees, in the midst of which rises
the point of the obelisk. Nearer, the Hotel des Invalides with its
magnificent dome, the Palace of the Tuileries forming an enormous
square, the Madeleine hardly discernible, the Pantheon, Notre
Dame, and a hundred domes and spires, palaces, gardens, and

squares give a grand and brilliant aspect to the city. Near the Place de la Bastille took place some of the most violent fighting in the late revolution; and the "quartier" immediately around it, I was told, is one of the lowest in Paris, but I was surprised to find that it looked clean and respectable.

We have been astonished to find the degree of motion given to the column by the wind, and motions of the carriages in the street, and ourselves, we could actually see it sway beneath us, and it seemed incredible that it should withstand the wind. After gazing for a long time over Paris with our opera glasses, trying to pick out and make clear to ourselves the various objects and situations, and amusing ourselves by watching the numerous jugglers in the Square sur-rounded by their crowds, we descended to relieve poor Mother, who, too tired to mount so many stairs, remained seated waiting for us below. Father and Eddie walked home. We rode. As the Boulevards are filled with preparations for arches, etc. in honor of Louis Napoleon's approaching entrance, we were obliged to turn aside and pass through some of the smaller streets; but nowhere have I seen the miserable habitations, dirt, and squalid misery that I often saw in riding through London. The people seemed respectable, and here and there a well-dressed man or woman walked composedly along; and decent shops one finds everywhere.

Fred and Marianne Sears spent the evening with us. She is a great favorite of mine, and is certainly very handsome. I am very sorry to hear that they have decided to go on next week to Italy.

15 October

As we had intended to go to Versailles today, I sent word last evening to tell Mme. Montfort that I should not take my lesson. So after

getting rid of my coiffeur, of a woman with some cloak patterns, and
various delays of a like nature, I prepared myself to shop. We all
walked with Father to see a very pretty pond and fountain surrounded
by people basking in the sun, in the Tuileries garden, and then
proceeded on our winding way. We did not get far, for the weather
was so very clear and lovely that we determined to enjoy it by visiting
Père Lachaise. Riding up the Boulevards, it is just within the *barrières,* not far from the Place de la Bastille.[3] A quarter of a mile from
its entrance, the road is lined with shops for the sale of tombstones
and monuments, and of candles, flowers, immortelles, and everything needed in a graveyard. The entrance to Père Lachaise is singularly unfortunate. A broad straight avenue, paved with stone, and
lined on each side with offices and square stone tombs, or rather
temples, leads from the gate. When we were there, too, the road was
repairing, and was filled with dirt carts and stones. Following as far
as we could the plan laid down in Galignani's guide, we turned into
another straight avenue leading to the right. This was also bordered
by tombs, as thick as they could be placed, some very plain, some in
the form of chapels, with an altar, candles, flowers, crucifixes, and
other emblems of devotion and affection inside. They were alike in
one point, that of having suspended upon them wreaths of what we
call everlasting flowers. The wreath is called an immortelle, and is
not only hung upon graves by friends, in expression of their love and
remembrance, but is often placed on monuments, as round the pillar
of Napoleon. They are not always made of these everlasting flowers,
but are composed of a kind of white chip, sometimes black, and
marked with letters either in the name of the person, or as *souvenir,
amour,* etc., etc. One often sees on a tomb a dozen or 20 of these,
some brown and dead, some quite fresh; and though at first sight it

gives to the tomb a finical and odd appearance, yet it is pleasant to think that the surviving friends visit here, if only to place a wreath. Many of the tombs were planted with flowers; and several very beautiful rose-bushes, covered with flowers, hung over the mortal remains of one who had lived and felt and walked on this earth. After a little time, we found our way to the tomb of Héloise and Abélard, one of the most beautiful. The monument is a kind of temple, supported by pillars, and very graceful in its proportions and ornaments. Beneath its roof repose their two figures in marble, side by side; around stand young trees, bushes and roses; the withered leaves of autumn were strewn around, and the wind played in the trees, and whirled the leaves over the ground, the warm autumn sun streamed through the arches, and threw delicate shadows on the stone; and it seemed to me pleasant to lie quiet and still.

While there, a large funeral approached, and one of the tombs very near was opened; but I did not wish to look at it, but preferred to wander abroad and sit in the sun. I picked some leaves from a young oak tree which threw its shadows over the figure of Héloise, and then we pursued our road. At the end we came to the monument of Casimir Périer, supporting a large handsome figure.[4] From here, wandering down to the right, we passed the tombs of many of Napoleon's generals, and read names very familiar to everyone. Some of the monuments were very magnificent, some simple, some very clumsy, some very beautiful; but their beauty, and the solemnity of the place, is very much hurt by the immense numbers; and so crowded are they, that often it would be most difficult to carry a coffin behind the piles of building that surround a tomb. In returning to the monument of Périer again, we passed an enormous pillar which stands far above all the others, but which we found to be a private

tomb. The chapel is in another part of the cemetery, and is very plain
and simple. In front of it the view of Paris is superb, and every
building stands out clear before you. Just below is the part of the
ground reserved for paupers, and absolutely crowded. Some of the
avenues we walked through afterwards are arched over with trees, and
form very beautiful walks; but Père Lachaise is not the lovely spot
that it has often been represented. The situation is fine, and in former
days it must have been retired and beautiful; but now the number of
tombs and publicity of the place destroy its quietude and appropriate
solemnity.

On our return we dropped Father at Galignani's, rue Vivienne,
and stopped again to see about my cloak. I find the same trouble as
in Boston. After dinner, Aunt P. and Father went to call on Mrs.
Brooks, and I wrote to Annie Webber.

16 October

The sun rose this morning with unusual splendor—as the novels have
it—and soon after breakfast we walked to the Place de la Concorde to
see the arch and various preparations for the reception of the president.[5] Everything is very handsome, and the Place was filled with
admiring crowds. The arch itself is in imitation of stone, and surmounted by an eagle. Various inscriptions cover the face and the
whole effect is in very good taste. Pillars surmounted with a kind of
vase, and tall staffs bearing flags, are placed on each side. In the
bright sun the whole appeared very pretty. The pavement of the Place
had been covered with sand to prevent the slipping of the horsemen
in their maneuvers here. The speed with which all these arches had
arisen is truly wonderful, for last evening a few rough beams and
boards was all that could be seen.

At half past one o'clock we walked to Mrs. Edward Brooks', whose rooms form the corner of the rue de la Paix and the Boulevards, commanding a view of the latter a long distance up and down. The room was filled with Bostonians—Mr. and Mrs. Franklin Dexter, and their son Mr. Arthur D., Mr. and Mrs. Goodrich the consul, and their two daughters, Mr. and Mrs. Rotch, Mr. and Mrs. Weiss and child (Miss Everett that was), Fred and Marianne Sears, Mr. and Mrs. Boppinger, Mary Coolidge and her husband, and several more whom I did not know.[6] The street was filled with people, and soldiers hurrying to their respective places, and *vivandières* belonging to the different regiments were running here and there with their wine for the soldiers. The dress of these women was very pretty—a short cloth skirt trimmed with velvet ribbon, red pantaloons, an open corsage, epaulettes, a canteen on their backs, and a hat on one side—they were however very ugly and coarse, and destroyed all my romantic ideas at once.[7] They seemed however to be very good natured, and did a great deal of coquetting. From the confusion that had reigned through the morning, perfect order was brought about as it were by magic. The National Guards, arriving almost without being observed, took their posts, forming a double line along each side of the street; the people fell back; the road was cleared; and punctual to a moment the procession started, of course arriving later at our situation. At about 3 the old soldiers of the Empire appeared in sight, many in their peculiar uniform, but many only designated by a number in their hats, showing the regiment in which they had served. Some of the dresses were very superb. These old men were the most enthusiastic of the procession, and stalked on, some without arms, some with wooden legs, old, gray, and weatherbeaten, with joy and triumph on their faces. It was touching to look at them, and recall the scenes they had been through. I cannot pretend to give the order of the procession, but the number of troops seemed endless. Some of the dresses were very superb, and I was especially taken with the hussar jackets—the cavalry was very superb—and one could hardly believe that so many men and horses were constantly supported. Opposite our windows there was a pathway over the street of asphaltum; and no less than 5 horses fell flat on the ground, the men rolling off to some little distance. I thought once or twice they must be hurt, but they all mounted immediately. At last came Napoleon himself, and though I fixed my glass on him, I can hardly describe his appearance. As for his dress, I did not observe it, but his horse was superb, and his riding still more so, he seemed a part of the saddle and bowed to each side slowly as he passed. He seemed to me an older man than I had supposed, and I thought his hair was gray, though I am told that this is not the case. His head is very large and finely formed, and I should say his features were good; but the expression of his face is, not heavy, but stolid, wanting in expression, or the face of one who does not choose to show his thoughts. His eyes have the same fault, and want brilliancy, still I should say, from the impressions I now have of him, that he was a handsome man, and *anything* but insignificant. The acclamations were not as enthusiastic as I expected. There were shouts as he passed, and cries of "Vive l'Empereur," but not the thundering and continuous applause I anticipated from the French people. I have since heard, however, that they are generally quiet. As the president passed down between the files of the National Guard they fell in behind him, and thus made a very long train. I believe about 60,000 soldiers were under duty during the day. The houses on each side the Boulevards were filled with people, who paid (according to the newspaper) an average of 4 dollars a place. They were not very enthusiastic; and our rooms, filled with Americans, attracted the notice of the president so much by their hurrahs that he gave "two decided bows" which were claimed by each of the ladies in the room, especially those whom he had spoken to. A little question may be entertained, as to whether it were possible for him to see them; but this was not thought of at the time. After passing a pleasant hour in chatting, etc., we left, and arrived "chez nous" at half past 4.

In the evening we walked to the Place de la Concorde, to see the illuminations, which we found so pretty as to tempt us to go further. The ministerial palaces in the rue de Rivoli were lighted by a long line straight round of gas, forming a very pretty effect. On each side the arch in front of the gardens were groups of figures of different colored lights; and two or three brilliant pillars stood in front of the gates. Opposite, on the other side of the river, the House of Deputies was ornamented by a line of gas lights along its wings, and rising to a point in the center. As we passed along the rue de Rivoli, we saw all the hotels lighted, some with colored lanterns, some in figures, some in gas. The Palais Royal was ornamented on one side by a line of gas lights, and was very brilliant. Many of the shops hung out colored lamps. When we arrived at rue St. Honoré, Mother went home with Father, and we walked on by the passage and rue Choiseul to the Boulevards. Here the illumination was more general and brilliant; in two or three places we saw lights in the shape of eagles, very perfect, and very brilliant. Nearly all were put up by public companies, theaters, etc. The initials "L. N." were seen everywhere, and colored lamps were hung from nearly all the stores. We walked to see one of the arches, and then turned homewards. The crowds of people surpassed anything I have ever seen. In looking at the arch I mentioned, we became so wedged in by the people, that when an omnibus turned down very near us, we were almost afraid of being crushed, and run over. The whole length of the Boulevards was crowded as far as we could see in the same way, also all the side streets, and the middle of the way with carriages. Yet notwithstanding all this, there was no uproar, no dirt, but little pushing, no rudeness, and all seemed to be quiet and orderly. We, after a fatiguing walk of pushing and sidling through the people, arrived at our own door. The Place Vendôme was in several places quite brilliant, and the pillars standing against the dark sky looked nobly. I suppose, because everyone else does, that Louis Napoleon will very soon become Emperor, and perhaps he will be crowned while we are here. I hope so, for the fêtes would I presume be very magnificent, and it would be a most favorable time for seeing Paris and the Parisians.

1853

Rome   18 March

I was disappointed in my first impressions of this famed basilica, but not as I expected to be. The exterior, the grand court and surrounding colonnades, are magnificent and fulfilled all my expectations by their immensity, their beauty and grandeur. Indeed the pictures give you so good an idea of all but the size that I had formed a very correct opinion of it. But the one great defect, and which is not given in the engravings, is the facade which, standing out a square and heavy front, quite hides all but the very summit of the dome, making it appear as if far back, and indeed belonging to another building. This defect is most striking and painful, and not to be overcome. For instead of seeing, as in St. Paul's, the whole of the graceful building surmounted by the dome in all its proportions (which in St. Peter's are fine seen from the hills, etc.), you see merely the front which looks heavy, out of place and awkward. The effect of the long line of steps is fine, from which you enter the long and superb vestibule and thence the church itself. This arrangement I do not particularly like, as I prefer entering at once from the outward world. You enter the church, the church of St. Peter's, the church famed for its overpowering splendor and beauty. These thoughts fill the mind of everyone I suppose. I was disappointed, not in the size (for though unappreciable at first, I felt it to be enormous) but disappointed in the effect. I was prepared for the solemn stilling feelings caused by such grandeur and immensity, but I failed to feel them. In vain I tried to lose myself in the contemplation of its splendor. It was like gazing on a magnificent and brilliant theater or ballroom. All was light and bright, and "unchurchlike." People were lounging about, gay in handsome dresses, talking, admiring and laughing. I did the same, everyone did, for there was no influence to check you. I do not pretend to criticize St. Peter's, for I know nothing about it. I cannot pretend to call it anything but magnificent. I do not even pretend to speak of its defects in my opinion. I merely give my feelings when comparing it with what I had imagined it to be, and in seeing it the first day; for doubtless it will be more appreciated by me every day I see it. I compare it too with Milan cathedral, which embodies all my ideas of beauty in a church, without a defect.[8] There, as you enter the door, from the glare and bustle of the world, you felt yourself entering a sacred place, breathing a holy atmosphere, and almost held your breath in dread of breaking the profound stillness and profaning its sanctity. The church before you was a perfect and beautiful picture; the light was mellowed and made solemn by the richly colored windows and their exquisite colors glancing on the floor; the white marble pillars, the beautiful arches added an almost unearthly beauty; you could not stop to admire the size or beauty of any particular portion, but lost yourself in admiration of the whole. St. Peter's is quite different. The whole effect is glorious, as anything must be made of so many superb parts combined with such size; but you admire the parts, the whole fails to strike you with its perfection. The walls, or rather enormous half pillars (for there are no aisles) which almost compose the walls, are of white, with colossal statues in marble. The ceiling, which is arched, of white and gold, I do not like. The intermediate portions of the walls are covered with a variety of beautiful marbles. The dome, which surpasses all description by its size and magnificence—for *this is perfect*—is inlaid with . . . [the entry breaks off here].

CHAPTER FOUR

1854–1857

As a diarist, Elizabeth Rogers Mason has now entered her prime. She has had experience of European travel. She is continuing her education, though in no regular institution. She has a circle of friends, young men and women, though her closest ties are for some time still with girls. Then courtships begin, though for several years she finds them unwelcome, confusing, painful in having to inflict disappointment on others. In addition to those prominent in these pages, the years 1855–59 see the rather shadowy suitors Phillip, Hubbard, Kerl, Delano, and Van Schaick. Josiah Quincy troubles her most, partly because his intellectual qualities appeal to her, partly because her impression of his coldness forces her to reflect on what may be her own, partly because his sister is one of her closest friends and she often has to meet members of his family.

She may complain about her confusions, worry about her temperament, fear to remain single but expect it; but she can continue commenting on many matters with some degree of detachment. She criticizes others: she criticizes, even condemns, herself.

The process of selection becomes increasingly difficult, if only because so many entries are very long. A few passages have had one large section cut. Her Washington trip of early 1857 has been wholly omitted. So has the entry in February 1856, describing the only episode in Boston streets that she ever found alarming. A man accosted her, quite near her own home, annoying rather than dangerous it would seem, but causing her to take refuge in a friend's house, whose door was fortunately unlocked.

At the very end of this period, she meets Walter Cabot once more. She has had social contacts with his family. She has heard much about him. Never, since 1850, has there been any communication or sign of interest. Now she is at once impressed. Chapter 5 will show how soon that impression becomes overwhelming.

1854

Boston   25 May

My birthday, and my twentieth too, old age and decrepitude are approaching, if they have not arrived. Mother sent me, before I rose this morning, an exquisite bunch of lilies of the valley, white and sweet, the prettiest birthday gift possible.

My foot is better, and I was very busy until eleven sewing, putting away summer garments, etc., then had a short snatch of *The Heir of Redclyffe,* and at half-past Susie Welles appeared.[1] We are reading the *Modern Painters* by Ruskin, very interesting and particularly pleasant for me, as I have seen much that he mentions.[2]

Fanny Cary dropped in for a few minutes, but would not interrupt us. Susie Welles and I had a long discussion on the duty of a woman to *obey* her husband. I cannot feel it to be just, and though I think one ought to yield, and sacrifice oneself entirely and freely, it seems to me obedience to a fellow human being is a step too far. She quoted a passage from one of the gospels, teaching subjection. I had nothing to say, but that I was still uncertain. After reading I had intended to go to see Amelie Rives that was, now Mrs. Henry Sigourney, but it rained hard, and I found I could not get on a shoe.

Isabella Parker and Elizabeth Grant came in to tea, and Charles Parker, Father and I joined them in going to the Howard, to hear Anna Mowatt perform *Ion* by Talfourd.[3] The play, which I never read before, is beautiful; but I never like the kind of piece on the stage, the dress is to modern eyes, and on degenerate modern figures, so trying, and the whole character so unnatural, that when brought to the reality of imitation, it is difficult to enjoy it. Mrs. Mowatt performed, I should think, well. It is a difficult part, and requires not only appreciation of the character by the performer, but also by the spectator. She looks like the engraving of her, and in the last act, when she wore a scarlet mantle, was pretty and brilliant, her hands are remarkably handsome, and she is graceful in figure and motions. I wished I could have seen her in a different play; for although I enjoyed this better perhaps, I felt that I could not judge fairly of her. Mr. Marshall took the part of Arastus—and did it well—the others were hardly bearable, Clemanthe the very ugliest female I ever saw, and Phoeion a great ugly man, in a woollen undervest and skirt.

I felt almost sorry to sit in a box in the Howard, and, not seeing a single person in the house I ever saw before except the Lowells and Mr. Lamb, destroy the thousand pleasant associations I have with it, when sitting in a box. I listened in ecstasy to Stiffannia and Salvi— Bosio and Bettini, or further back Truffi and Benedetti and Tedesco; and between scenes saw hardly a person in the house that I did not know personally, or by sight and name.[4] Oh what visions of happiness have I enjoyed in that little theater, and what intense present delight have I reveled in! I was then at school: I am now twenty, and yet I can hardly feel that a year has passed. Oh if one's faith were not firm, of a world beyond this, life would be passed in regrets that it was passing.

11 June

A beautiful gray day. Dr. Gannett preached a sermon on the slavery question, which exactly met my feelings and views.[5] It was extremely moderate, and he evidently was most anxious to do justice to all parties. He said what I never realized before, that many southern planters conscientiously sustained slavery, on passages from the

Bible, on the inability of the black race to take care of themselves, on the advantage to them of living in intimacy with white people of intelligence, and other arguments.

He said too, that as we were enjoying the many privileges arising from the compact made by our ancestors, it was a sacred duty to keep the promises they made, in the spirit and in the letter, and that violence should never be resorted to, to sustain our principles; but for this reason we should be careful not to allow ourselves to become indifferent, and should firmly oppose all propositions tending to any extension of slavery. He thought, too, that though the fugitive slave law was a law, and therefore must be obeyed, that we ought to remonstrate against having the Northern States made the scene of such tragedies, as we had been undergoing the last week; that until the last year or two, few slaves had been reclaimed, but that now it was a constant occurrence, and subjected us to the most injurious consequences. Finally he said that if we could not agree with the South, without consenting to the increase of slavery, he thought we were forced on disunion. He said he had always been so strongly for the maintenance of the Union, that he had been severely blamed; and he still thought the evils immense, incident to a separation; but we could not, feeling the wrong of slavery as we do, we could not give our countenance to its boundless extension, without dishonor, even for the sake of the maintenance of peace and prosperity. It seems to me so too, but Father and Mr. Ticknor both blame Dr. Gannett much, for inculcating and suggesting this doctrine, to the minds of his hearers. If we were to separate from the South it would be impossible to do so in a peaceable manner, and it would be as impossible to defend ourselves, without a more despotic and energetic form of government—here would be the fall of liberty. I sometimes think, is it possible that I may one day see in this happy land, bloodshed and the destruction of liberty? I cannot believe it.

In the afternoon Mother and I went to the King's Chapel, where we heard Dr. Lathrop.[6] I walked with Mary Q. after church, and had a very nice "talk."

23 June

Class day at Cambridge, and also, rainy and damp. Up very late, and never dreamed of going out, until first I received Laura's bundle of dress, then a note from Jenny, and then Willy *in propria persona*. Therefore, in defiance of the fears and doubts of the family, arrayed myself, sent word to Jenny, and *ran* with Laura and Willy to the depot, somewhere at the end of the world, that is to say behind our house, beyond the Jail, (upon the whole I will spell that another way, Gaol).[7] When we arrived, exhausted with our speed, we were early. Jenny and her sister Josephine soon appeared. We met also Richard Fay, with his sweet smile, and Rose Lee, the betrothed of Leverett Saltonstall. Augustus Greenwood joined us. In time we started in the cars, in time we stopped, landed, walked to the chapel, were refused entrance, as our ticket was not a senior's, were carried in by Charles Lowell, and found excellent seats, downstairs though afar off.[8] My comfort, I will confess, was somewhat diminished by my costume, which was a simple silk, a straw bonnet, a black and not new cloak, a pair of thick boots, an umbrella, and a pair of dark and dingy gloves, seized by mistake in my haste of departure, while the rest of the world were in gala array,—white muslin, crape and flowers and yellow kids. I could not but feel that theirs was hardly fit for fog and rain; but when it continued fair, though clouded, and the dampness diminished, I desired ardently to fly home, and seize the nice silk, white lace bonnet and crape shawl, that were laid on my table, and above all, to search for fresh gloves. I have confessed my weakness; now I will add, that having once regretted them, and felt it impossible to do anything, I became calm, resigned, and even forgetful. Robert Winthrop delivered the oration. As the first I ever heard, I cannot say if it was good or bad; but it struck me that he might have felt more at leaving Cambridge and youth behind, more romance if not love for the faculty (at least in parting) and more good resolution and hope for the future. He made some rather poor jokes about women, and said several quite good things, was very pale, but not in the least excited, or apparently interested. The Poem was so full of allusions that none but collegians could understand, that I could not enjoy it. The Ode, sung by the whole class, was fine. I only knew several members of this class and so was less interested, but Oh, why do they not feel more: youth gliding away, never to return; then those four years truly spent, might have been so delightful, perfect freedom, choice of friends, pleasures of intercourse, opportunities of study, the pleasure of a regular employment, the time for all kinds of reading, and the pleasures of skating, walking, etc., with whom, when and where you liked. They are not certainly appreciated. I really believe girls would do better. After the exercises, beginning at 12 and lasting about 2 hours, we walked to Mrs. Lowell's house, where was a collation and various people, among whom I saw chiefly Mr. Henry Higginson.[9] He is not elegant in appearance, but is truly sensible, and well informed. He is a friend too of Mrs. Lowell's, an excellent reason for liking him. I left the Reveres, and with Laura and Willy went to Holworthy to a collation given by the orator, Mr. Winthrop, having been invited several days. I found the Sears, Amorys, Cora Shaw, Marianne Sears, Mrs. George Gar-

diner, all the fashionables; talked with Mr. Joe Gardner, who has just
returned from New-Orleans, and whom I have not seen therefore,
since he left Paris. He desires to go back, and thinks America
generally, and Boston more particularly, a very stupid place of
residence. He is very agreeable and *manly*, but I cannot agree with his
feelings on this subject at least.[10]

Newport   22 August

Soon after breakfast, at ten or a little after, rode with Mrs. Lyman to
the beach, where she and Florence take their daily bathe. I should
like to have joined them, and when I saw them floating on the water,
and dashing under the waves, I almost repented my decision. Almost
I say, for there are two powerful objections for me: one that I do not
think it agrees with me very well, for so short a time, and destroys
besides all my garments; and second and still more weighty is the
crowd of people, men, women and children, both bathers and spectators, who always attend. Strangers always consider the morning
bathe one of the lions to be visited, and young men drive up and
down to have a little fun. By what argument or means, mammas,
who faint at the very idea of their daughters polking, overcome their
scruples here, I cannot imagine.[11] Each one for themselves. Happily I
am not compelled to go and do likewise. On our return, in about three-
quarters of an hour (for your habitual bather is very expeditious), we
stopped at Aunt Grant's. Speaking of hasty toilets, it struck me that
by some it was carried to rather an unnecessary extent, as I saw several
dames or demoiselles enter their open carriages, without stockings,
collars, or muslin sleeves, a degree of negligence that was not becoming. Salt water for the time being, at least, seems to sour the temper

too, and I never heard such sharp voices, angry speeches, or impatient demands, as I did in the ten minutes on the shore. In fact all the world seem to feel that they can cast off externals of all kinds with impunity; and sweet young ladies in dainty dresses, too languishing and delicate to live, do not hesitate here to appear as ugly, undressed, cross, and coarse women. But a truce to bathes and bathers.

Aunt Grant and Elizabeth are well, their cottage as cozy and pretty as ever, and their place much improved by the astonishing growth of the trees. They have been much worried all summer about Pat, who until with[in] a few weeks, has not at all improved in health, and his misfortune in business has weighed, I am afraid, on their minds. Isabella Parker is staying here, and has been nearly 3 weeks.

On my return home, I found Mary Quincy, who is with Mrs. Greene her Aunt. She was dressed in a straw bonnet, trimmed with purple velvet, black lace and dark flowers (dark bonnets are the fashion) and looked remarkably well. She alarmed as well as pleased me considerably, by the mention of a musical party, to which I am to be invited.

Dined at 2 ½, and after dinner, at about six, rode with Mr. Lyman, in a little trotting wagon, to Bateman's Point, which extends into the ocean beyond the fort, and is a favorite drive, when the beaches are impassable. The fort is now garrisoned by an old man with but one leg, the soldiers having been moved this year.

The weather was warm, and the roads so excessively dusty, from constant traveling and long continued drought, that when we did not suffer actual pain from the state of the eyes, the mental agony gave one no peace, at the thought of the sad fate of the new bonnet and fresh dress. The dampness of the sea air, combined with the red dust, form a paste which, even if one is happy enough to remove it, leaves its tinted traces on lace, silk and muslin. For this same reason, as they say, the drive was less crowded than usual, but we found some 15 or 20 carriages standing together at the point, enjoying the breezes.

Walpole   17 September

Mr. Henry Bellows today preached a very splendid sermon on the Last Judgment, showing that the manner or date or circumstances, were nowhere given in the New Testament, as in some places the Father was called Judge, in another the Son, and the descriptions contradicted each other, proving that they were metaphorical, and meant to impress on our minds and imaginations the great fact, without the details, which were unimportant.[12] He could find no reason in the Bible, to believe in the popular doctrines, and thought that each day's experience, and each new acquisition in science and knowledge, went to show that sin was contrary to the laws of our being, and that each man was therefore his own judge, inevitably suffering, from the construction of his own nature, exactly in proportion as he disobeyed her laws. I must say I have never been able to feel any other but this belief to be true. He spoke in a hopeful way of the great and general progress of mankind in all ways, Slavery, War, and among other things, the unjust oppression of Woman. All now had their opponents, every day gaining more and more ground. I confess I was glad to hear him speak in the pulpit in this calm way, of The Wrongs of Woman, as among the evils, yet to be effaced, classing it with widespread and acknowledged evils. It is useless for people to laugh, and men to reason; the time will come when a woman has a higher place in the world, not as statesman, or public officer or character of any kind perhaps, but as a thinking, reasoning, feeling, human being. Father and all admired that sermon very much, though

Aunt P. said many times that it was "very bold" and many more, I
dare say, disapproved of it.

Boston   29 October

A half rain, warm and muggy. Only three of my pupils at Sunday
School, but I had two little boys, Frank and Willie Brewer, added,
as they were too young for any gentleman's class.[13] The former was a
fine, bright and well-mannered boy of nine, his brother a little fellow
of only six and a half. Mr. Gannett, in addition to other exercises,
gave a kind of lecture on St. Paul, very good for the older scholars,
but too difficult for the younger ones and to my mind not as useful as
a lesson from the teacher, who, being nearer, can interest the pupils
in one subject, and command their attention. It left us very little
time, too little to combine interest with instruction; but Mr. Gannett is very set in his ideas, and I think he is too anxious to have it
a lesson, and too little solicitous to please and interest the children.

1 November

The last three days have been oppressively warm, and yesterday was a
rain during the morning. I have occupied them chiefly in shopping,
and I am happy to say have purchased two dresses, and have only two
more simple ones to find, for the winter.

Monday I took my first singing this season of Corelli, and Wednesday, this morning, began the Bible class at Dr. Gannett's. I feel rather
encouraged than otherwise about my voice, and mean to study very
hard. I have kept to my resolution firmly, by not opening the piano
today, but necessity will excuse today I hope. This afternoon I went to
the Quincys' for a few minutes; the success of *Lyteria* has been very
great, all the papers have highly approving critiques on it, and an

extract from the paper edited by the poet Bryant, in New York, was very flattering in its commendations. [14] For myself, I liked it the first time I read it, before speaking to anyone of it, or seeing any notice, and each perusal has pleased me more. The originality of the plot is very refreshing, and it is remarkable for simplicity, ease of diction and a wholeness and oneness of impression, which is very effective. Besides, taken in detail, there are many fine and elevated sentiments, and finely and aptly expressed, and the management of the plot is very skillful. I admire much the want of bombast, for which it is remarkable, and the little effort and struggle for effect. The first dawning of the true interpretation of the oracle in the mind of Lyteria, her struggle, and her half repentance and weakness after all was confessed, are very fine passages; also the passage in which she replies to the greeting of Aulus in the Temple. In fact there is a great deal that one must admire extremely, and one is surprised that it should have come from the pen of one so young, and inexperienced in writing. if he continues as he has begun, great things are in store.

I must not close the day's journal, without mentioning the engagement of Julia, the youngest of the two Wainwrights, to a gentleman, Mr. Robbins in New York. She is only seventeen, I believe, but they say it is a very good match.

19 November

All my scholars, but one, were assembled today, and but that the time was very short, had a very pleasant lesson. I am going straight through the gospels, that is, teaching them the life of Christ in as clear and connected a way as possible, so that they may be thoroughly acquainted with every part. I do it in my own words, reading from the Bible, however, whenever it is in simple language. I have been much assisted by Palfrey's *Harmony*, a most invaluable book, now out of print, but lent me by Mr. Ticknor. [15] I spend a great deal of time in reviewing, so that they may all know the whole thoroughly, and in a connected story. I learn more than the children, for in preparing and teaching and review, I learn all the details with a minuteness that I shall never lose, I think.

27 November

Have been busier than any bee all the morning, taking a singing lesson, reading, etc. After dinner 28 girls arrived to sew. This is the first meeting of the sewing circle for the winter. We have invited many more, nearly sixty, including all the young girls of our acquaintance, and the young married ladies. Of course not all can join, and I imagine that there will be seldom more than one-half collected. We are to assemble every Monday, as soon after three as possible, and remain until tea time, having no gentlemen, and no fuss. I hope it will be successful: it is certainly very pleasant. We accomplished a great deal of work, too, and may do a great deal of good, I think. As for the cutting out, we have divided it into four or five departments, which will be attended to by the Carys, Jenny Revere, Susie Welles and myself separately, each having certain materials, and certain articles to arrange for each time, so that each will be responsible for their own things. This will save me much trouble and be more sure and regular.

This evening I have passed at Sally Cary's, who invited me to join a club, got up and arranged by Mr. Dresel to sing German music, quartettes, choruses, etc. We sang a beautiful quartette and chorus from *Midsummer night's Dream*, and several more fine pieces. [16] Unfortunately, there has been some mistake, however, and instead of my voice, soprano or mezzo-soprano, they need one to sing the second soprano with Sally Cary, or a kind of contralto, so that I shall not continue. I regret it, as the music is very beautiful, and I long for something regular in the musical line.

1855

Boston   10 January

This morning had two pieces of news, one painful and the other joyful. The first, the death of Mr. Arthur Payson, who, while talking with his father in his office, said he felt a sharp pain in his head, fell back in his chair, and expired in about 20 minutes, a kind of apoplexy. He has not been perfectly well for several weeks, and had overworked himself and taxed his strength too far. Side by side with misery stands happiness, and this I found in a note from Lizzie Ticknor, announcing her engagement to Mr. Wm. Dexter, no surprise to me, though I had been rather uncertain for some weeks of the probable result. She seems very happy, naturally, for what can be greater bliss, than to feel certain that the right person for life, is found and secured—no doubt, nothing more to desire.

This evening rode out with the Reveres and Isabella Mason to Cambridge, to a theatrical representation. The plays were two from the French, translated by Mrs. Lowell, I believe. The first, *The Short Road to Fortune*, represents a young man, a lawyer who, notwithstanding his talents, fails from his integrity and disdain of intrigue, in making his way in the world, until becoming the friend of Zoë, the wife of a French officer, he is made deputy, by her deception towards her friend Mme. de Montancourt, who, all-powerful by *her* intriguing talents, succeeds in securing to him this office, quite unknown to himself. It is very good indeed, and admirably fitted for private theatricals. Ida Agassiz, in powdered hair and an old-fashioned dress, with her pretty foreign accent, made an enchanting Zoë; Miss Whitney filled with much success the part of Madame M., and Mr. Emerson, Mr. Alex Agassiz, Mr. Erving, Mr. Gambrill, and Mr. Colburn, law students, or Cambridge young men, took the other parts. [17] Hattie Lowell was Agatha, the daughter-in-law of Madame de M.

The second play was *The Bear and the Pasha*, a very excellent farce, which several of the spectators had seen on the French stage. The audience was not large, but very agreeable, and I had a very pleasant talk with Mr. Charles Follen. His mother was there, and also Miss Catharine Sedgwick the authoress, both of whom I was glad to see. [18] We rode in at about half after ten.

17 January

Have passed the whole morning out, from ten until half past two, notwithstanding the bad weather, for it snowed nearly all the time. My occupation, was enquiring chambermaids' characters for Aunt Parkman.

This evening passed again at that enchanting and enchanted spot, the Opera. [19] *Lucrezia Borgia*,—Isabella M. went with us. Grisi looked most charming in a black lace dress, and then in a yellow with blue tunic. The scenery was in Venice and *very* beautiful. Mario's dress, red cloak and small clothes and dark jerkin, with the peculiar Venice cut, was most becoming—but—the whole opera, until the last act, was cold, cold, cold. "Com'è bello" was sung, to my ears, without soul, or expression, and "Di pescatori" less well than I have heard it, but the last act was fine, and Mario, who always reserves his powers, died most splendidly and awfully, not continuing to sing to the last gasp, but writhing, struggling and falling like a man in his last agony. I did not expect it, because he is not, in the general opera, a good or enthusiastic actor. The house was crowded—full to the very last seat.

Have not been out yesterday or today, for one day it rained hard, and the next snowed. Today the snow is really quite deep.

The opera was *Favorita* this evening, my favorite. Mother, unfortunately, had so bad a cold, that she was afraid to go, and so Willy took her ticket. Mr. and Mrs. James Parker, being disappointed by their own coachman, rode down with us. The house was not as full as on Wednesday, though very brilliant, and the opera pleased me much more than any I have heard.

The orchestra is decidedly poor, but I enjoyed every moment. Grisi was superb in looks, her dress was the most splendid I have ever seen, with the exception of some of Rachel's. A white brocaded dress, *en disposition,* of the most brilliant colors, and a pink satin tunic also brocaded in white in a regular pattern, and covered with the most brilliant diamonds, imitation of course, but most splendid. In the last scene too, as nun, she looked, acted and sang well, and Mario most delightfully. His dress, a dark velvet jerkin, embroidered in gold, with a gold jeweled girdle, and gray small clothes, was very elegant. He certainly is a very handsome man, and looks 30; they say he is 45, and Grisi at least 47. She must have been magnificent in her prime,—now she is very stout, and has lost her voice to a certain degree—her hands are very beautiful still, and her hair. The opera seems to me more perfect, every time I hear it.

22 January

Rain this morning, but cleared beautifully, after dinner. Sewing circle at Mary Cooke's, very small, only six members.

This evening the opera was *Norma*,—Mother went for the first time. It was well sung, though "Casta Diva" was to me very disappointing. Grisi has not sufficient power for it now. She went through it like a difficult lesson, learned by rote. Mario was fine in the little he has to sing. Mlle. Donnovani (Miss Donovan, an Irish girl, in other words), has a fine voice, but is wretchedly thin, ugly and awkward, and did not sing well with Grisi. The dresses were not in as good taste as I have seen them for the women, but Mario's was very successful, in a blue tight frock and red cloak, instead of white, the usual dress, or rather undress.

1 February

Went down this morning to Dr. Warren's to ask him about my health, which certainly has been less good than usual all winter, and is growing worse, instead of better. Shortness of breath seems my great trouble, walking up hill ever so slowly, exhausting me so, that I lose all color, and almost all strength to stand. So with the least exertion, dancing, going upstairs, walking against the wind, or very quickly, etc. He says it is weakness, arising from no one knows what, I am sure I don't. However, weak I seem to be, reason or none. I am to take a mixture of iron, three times a day, to eat well, and to exercise, fatigue or no fatigue. So on the strength of that, I ran down to the apothecary's, returned to my dinner, and notwithstanding the snow, which fell fast, called for the Hoopers, and with them proceeded to the omnibus for Jamaica Pond. Mrs. H., Annie, Susie Welles, Charlotte Gray, Lizzie Winthrop and myself, with Mr. Higginson, Mr. Gardner and Willy, formed our party. We thought ourselves very energetic, and were mutually surprised to find each other. Lucy Sturgis rode out with Mr. John Reed. Arrived at the pond and we found Mr. Otis, (Willy), Mr. Peabody, Mr. Palfrey, and all the world—Sheltons, Mary Coolidge, Mr. Dixon, Mr. Brimmer, an assembly in fact.[20] Mr. Otis was in great distress, because having promised to carry Mattie Parker out in his wagon, he had thought her in joke, and had driven out without even calling for her, while Charlotte Gray left her at half after ten, waiting with all her things on! I enjoyed the afternoon more than ever before. The sun had checked the wind, it was very mild; good skating, and I felt remarkably well. I crossed the pond with Lucy Howard, who does not skate better than myself, several times,—we found long lines of a dozen all taking hold of hands, we were pushed in a sleigh belonging to the Bacons, and in a kind of high chair on runners, which Mr. Joe Gardner had made expressly for the purpose; and altogether it was splendid. I never felt a sensation of cold, even in my feet, which generally suffer horribly, and was in high spirits,—a little as other people. In crossing the pond on our return I had my first real fall, for being behind the others, and dragged very rapidly by a long stick, I came suddenly to very rough ice without perceiving it, and measured my length, without injury, however, except to my bonnet, and in getting very wet from the snow.

We rode in sitting in each other's laps, the omnibus being perfectly crowded, and at home I found Aunt Ellen and Uncle John to tea, with Laura.

7 March

Went to meeting at Dr. Gannett's, then read with Lizzie Ticknor, and then dined with Aunt Parkman. Heard that Marianne Sears, who was confined last week on Thursday, is not so well, and they feel anxious.

In the evening went to a teachers' meeting at Dr. Gannett's, where three females, unknown to each other, sat on one side of the room, and four males, likewise strangers, stared at them from the other. A few questions were asked, a weak attempt at conversation was made, and the meeting broke up, after an hour and a half of smiling misery.

9 March

Marianne no better,—rather more drowsy, and does not recognize even Fred. Willy came in to go to a party at the Ticknors'—but I gave up going.

10 March

Marianne died at 12 last night. Young, strong, handsome, beloved, rich, happy, she had nothing to wish for on earth, but wherever she is, we know that her enjoyments are still greater, if she can appreciate them. I cannot bear to hear people say, that it seemed a pity she should be cut off in the midst of so much happiness, as if heaven were no brighter, and fine clothes and gold were the greatest joys. I believe it was a week ago Monday, that I went down to see Marianne, walked all over her house, sat in her room some time, as she was dressing to go out, and then rode up the street to Mrs. Howland Shaw's. She talked of her plans for next winter,—their intention to go to Europe when Minnie was eight years, and all her arrangements for living in town. Ought not our plans be for heaven, when Sam Parkman, Arthur Payson, Marianne Sears can exchange life for eternity, with so short a warning? Another melancholy death is that of Annie Thayer, Mr. John E. Thayer's only daughter, and eldest child, who died of the measles in New York, where she was at boarding school.[21] The dispatch arrived Friday night that she was worse, and another came Saturday morning, soon after Mr. Thayer's departure, saying that she was dead. She was a bright, pretty, intelligent girl, and her father's pride.

23 March

The eventful day is come. Corelli called in the morning to beg me not to go out, as the weather was windy and dusty and horrid. I ventured, however, as far as Tremont St., to Mr. Greenough's studio, to see his *Franklin,* which will be cast next week.[22] It is eight feet high, in the old dress of shoes, small clothes, long waistcoat, and a coat trimmed with fur (as they say, the badge of a printer), he leans on his cane with one hand, and holds his three-cornered hat under his arm with the other, and has altogether the appearance of a portly benignant old gentleman. It is really splendid. We then went into Mr. Rogers' studio, to see his little model of Adams, to be placed at Mt. Auburn, in the Chapel.[23] He is in the act of speaking, one foot and one hand and arm thrown forward. I am not quite sure that I like it; but one cannot have all statues in repose, else, taking off the heads, one would be as good as another. Mary Q. went with us.

I took what rest I could after dinner, and then slowly dressed for the grand occasion. I wore a black skirt, high-necked velvet spencer, as the most appropriate.

After a small tea, and an egg, taken raw, we rode down, arriving at seven. The hall was crowded, so that Father, coming a few moments later, had much ado to find any place.

The singers, 54 in number, I believe, all sat round in the rows at one end of the hall, three pianos and two chandeliers of candles in front of them. Nearly all were dressed in high-necked silks, very simple and appropriate. Corelli was very quiet, and behaved extremely well; so did the girls, no whispering, giggling, or folly, and not the least affectation of manner. The music, all of it remarkably beautiful, and some difficult, was sung really *well*. The solos, many of which, if not all, were difficult, demanding strength, execution and expression, were extremely well sung, speaking as you would of artistes. The duets were fine, and all went off admirably. This I cannot help saying, because I think so, and I believe every one else, the most critical, felt so too! I feel it to be remarkable, and much to the credit of Boston, that there should be so many young ladies, with really well cultivated voices, and *it* says a great deal for Corelli. Between the two parts, the singers went out, and had ice and cake. All was done in a most perfect manner, no hurrying, and no failures of any kind, a decided improvement over last year.

As for one's own sensations, they are difficult to describe. It is not fear exactly one feels. The trembling in every limb, the beating and throbbing blood in one's head, the cold hands, and the awful faintness, seem to be not exactly fear—a part is excitement. While singing, especially in the duet, which is a very exciting piece, my lips trembled and quivered so, that I had to press them down with my shaking hands, or I believe I should have burst out crying; then, singing, you forget the audience, but stop for one minute, and raise your eyes, and the million eyes, and eager faces, seem as if they would pin you to the earth. After returning to one's seat, however, is the most severe, for then the tension is over, and for ten minutes you can hardly contain your sobs. At least these are my sensations, and yet, in singing, my voice trembles merely at the first note, if at all. Fanny Adams, who was to take a solo from *Elisir d'Amore*, sent word she was ill, rather a piece of good fortune, as hers was the only poor piece.[24] At half past eleven we left, it was over—Oh, what a relief!

3 June

I was confirmed, or admitted to the church today, a thing I have long thought about, and postponed for many reasons, but which I am very thankful to have done. The ceremony is very simple, and therefore less trying than I feared.[25]

The communion I do not regard in the light of a privilege (though a great one) only to be conferred on advanced Christians, else how little right have I to join it; but it seems to me a help, a kind of manifestation that you have joined Christ's great army of believers and workers, the earnest ones of the earth, the searchers for truth, the privileged beings of the universe.

One is often shocked to find themselves cold and untouched in moments when you would feel all, when it seems impossible that your heart should not overcome everything—and it was so today. I felt choked with tears, and repentance, but I at the same time could dry them soon, and even had some trouble to prevent my thoughts from wandering. But I try to believe this is not entirely sinful, that it arises in part at least from our human weakness, which is increased by the very causes, which we had hoped would cure it, and that as we grow generally purer and stronger, we shall become more able to control our spirits. Let me at least hope and endeavor.

It is a great thing to feel that you have chosen your life, and that now it is greater sin to fall away, than before. It is a great thing to feel that you have life still before you, and that with earnest purpose and endeavor, you can become like unto Christ, pure, strong, noble, free; and it is a fearful thing to feel that you may be tempted aside, you may descend instead of rise, you may become weak, sinful, despised of God, instead of His faithful servant, His beloved child, an angel in powers and purity. Yes, we can be one or the other, either as we give way to temptation, or follow what our souls tell us is true and good. Let us pray with all our hearts for strength and an humble faith, and a loving heart. Life is made up of efforts, either well or ill directed. Let each moment be one of earnest search and endeavor for the right and pursuance of it, regardless of all circumstances, which are made for us, not we for them.

Willie Amory and Daniel came in after tea this evening followed by Mr. Baldwin and the two Quincys, whom I was very glad to see, as I owe so much to Mrs. Q. that I am glad to be able to do anything for them.

Nahant   15 September

A beautiful autumn day. Passed several hours over my hair, which drops out slowly but surely, and is becoming very thin in front, owing to my health, without doubt. At noon Mother took a drive through the Lynnfield woods, and did not get home until four. I did not go out, but sat sewing at Aunt P's window, looking out on the blue ocean and brilliant sunlight, and fair skies, (she was out). There is more enjoyment in two or three hours of this sort, when you seem

to embrace and become a part of the beautiful universe, than in weeks
of every day life; they seem to be glimpses of the pleasures we may
enjoy more and more, as our being becomes purified, and more sensitive to the beauty and goodness of God and His works.

After dinner I walked to the William Carys' to see Miss Nannie
C.—she was at Gloucester; then went to the Tom Carys' where I
found Sally and Emma, and then Carrie Curtis and her baby, who
arrived from Winchester, to pass Sunday.

Sally told me of the engagement of Susie Welles to Russell Sturgis,
told her in the morning by Lucy.[26] It was a dreadful surprise, so star-
tling and unexpected. I felt as if Susie would be long disengaged, she
was so little in the world. I hope Russell is worthy of her. I have heard
of him as very amiable, and very handsome, but not as intelligent as
his brother or sister; however, this was as a collegian, and was only an
opinion from a mere acquaintance. I consider him one of the luckiest
of men, and he ought to be very good to deserve her. Emma walked
up and down the cliffs with me until dark, and then I returned by the
light of the new moon, and the glow yet left in the heavens. It was
very beautiful.

At home I found a small wood fire throwing its cheerful beams
through the room, and making the scene a perfect picture of domestic
peace. I could not help wondering a little whether the time would
ever come when I should sit at my own bright fireside, with those I
loved gathered about it. It seems to me we made too little of these
external influences, and that it would add much to one's quiet happiness, if every evening could renew the family gathering, each having
their own place and occupation, perfect freedom and the conviction
that this was the pleasantest corner and hour in the world.

Powell got home at nine, having walked across the beach, and

brought me a letter from Susie. I was sure it must come. I did not
read it until I went to bed, and was a little disappointed to find it
rather formal, but I can easily excuse the feeling, knowing that it
only arose from the novelty of the case, and too much feeling, rather
than too little. So she has gone. One by one we quit the raft of common interests and pursuits on which we have been floating, and embark in our own little boats. We may still keep side by side, but the
helmsman is no longer the same, and our paths may separate never to
meet again in this world. Never shall we forget, however, our old
ship-mates; nor will our hearts beat the less warmly in sympathy with
their joys and sorrows, though we may have our own separate ones to
fill our hearts. Oh how earnestly do I pray for her happiness, and that
the new joy which has now entered into her soul may be perfect and
lasting. Lucy, Mr. Codman, Susie and Mr. Sturgis must make a happy
quartette indeed. She gives me no particulars, but as Russell has been
here little more than a month, there must have been a strong feeling
before. Oh dear, it seems all very unreal—I can hardly feel sure of the
fact now.

Ned came down today, having walked all the way from Cambridge, a
distance of about 20 miles, in five hours. Willy did not come.

Boston   26 October

My room will never be in order, I verily believe. The bedstead is gone
to be mended, and to get it back again is past my power. My closet
has just been varnished and has to be avoided as a fly shuns molasses;
my sofa covering is not only unfinished, but has been cut so small
that I fear it is almost ruined; and in fine the whole apartment is
laden with Mother's things, which lie about in all directions.

At eleven went with Annie Loring in the omnibus to Brookline.

Read aloud before and after dinner in *Evelina*.[27] Mrs. Loring came out for us, and after a run round the place, and shelling some corn, returned to town.

Father and I went to the theater. Powell went with Charlotte Grant. The play was *Marie Stuart* by Lebrun. Rachel as Marie, her sister Sarah as Elizabeth, M. Randomy as Leicester.[28] Rachel's dress was a black brocade perfectly plain, with the full puff sleeves tight at the wrist and white cuffs, a rosary at the girdle, several strings of pearls around the neck, and on the head the close cap of open gold work, with points of pearls standing around the face, the hair being rolled back in a large puff above the temple. Behind, a white gauze veil fell to the hem of her dress, nothing could have been more perfect than this picture of the unfortunate and beautiful queen; and her face, her figure, her movements all told you of beauty, of grief, of wounded pride, or queenly dignity, of feminine weakness, and touching sadness, mixed with purity and faith.

The play they say is poor, and the scenes when she does not appear long and tedious; but I was so carried away in interest for her, that as they were connected with her fate, they interested me. She is much less passionate in this play than in any other. With the exception of her interview with Queen Elizabeth, where nothing could exceed the grandeur and vehemence of her indignation, she preserves a sad, sweet despair, that is infinitely more touching than the most vehement abandon of grief. I have often been surprised that I could not be moved by acting in the opera or theater, and sometimes felt that it must be from a want of sensibility; but tonight I cried as if my heart would break, and from no exaggeration of feeling, for I felt ashamed, and anxious to stop my emotion; but I felt as if I had seen Mary herself led to execution, after having vainly used every effort to save her. I could not believe that Elizabeth would really sign the death warrant, and hoped to the last, making the final blow the more terrible. That a woman with all that earth could give, beauty, a queen, the world bright and beautiful before her, should lay her head on the block, it must not be, something must save her. But no, she lingers, she bids adieu to each, she tears herself away, and then returns for one last look; but she must die, and nothing can save her. She does die, and it is too late for change; repentance and interference are vain; it is done. Oh, it seemed too terrible.

3 November

Raw November day; at ten minutes after ten went to Mrs. Jackson's, Hamilton Place, where Mrs. Lowell begins her readings.[29] Felt just like a guilty school girl a little late and without excuse. The room was filled. I should think fifty or more were assembled, chiefly, almost entirely, Mrs. L's old scholars. It would have been pleasant enough merely to have sat with them in her presence, so forcibly did it bring back old times. I wish I could give any account of the reading, but although I remember every word, the subjects are so abstract in character, that they hardly admit of description in few words.

She divided our nature into thought, feeling and action; our intellectual faculties into intuition and induction; showed the difference in development of these in man and woman, in races, in individuals; analyzed our perceptive faculties, the difference in our enjoyment of nature and art, the cause of melancholy connected with enjoyment of nature, the difference in different people, etc., etc., etc. Copious quotations from various authors were linked together by her own words, and then the whole discussed amongst us. There was not a great deal of conversation, but yet more than I expected, and as we feel more used to each other, I think there will be a great deal. There are some of the girls with very bright, enquiring minds, and if we can only become bold it will be delightful.

To me two hours of this kind have the effect of an exhilarating drink; all my powers seem to be sharpened, my eyes opened, and I am raised into a higher world, where freedom and joy and peace reign eternally, unchanged. I feel more able to do and be what I long for, my spirit spreads its wings, and if soon wearied, for the time I soar high above the mists and vapors of my everyday existence, and am able to keep in mind that there is a purer air and freer sky, if I cannot perceive it always.

Nellie Hooper and I, after twelve, walked over the Milldam to the Brighton branch, and when returning were caught in a heavy rain. However, it was a great satisfaction to have walked over three miles of earth.

The afternoons are dark as Egypt. Annie Loring came over and nearly finished *Evelina*. At six I went to take tea at the Amorys' with Nellie Hooper.

21 November

Snow falling all day. Uncle John to dine. Passed the evening with Isabella Codman and the Codman family. Held a very warm discussion with Dr. Derby on the proper discipline of women.[30] He thinks the effects of the present want of restraint disgraceful and dreadful. He thinks woman by nature, at least until she is quite matured, incapable of standing alone; she needs, and must always need not only parental advice, and social influences, but positive rules, restraints, and authority. I wonder if it is so. I sometimes have a strange glimmering of a theory in regard to women, though as a woman I dislike to feel that vanity may suggest it, or appear to. But is it possible that woman's true place is yet to be perceived, that she is by nature higher, purer, nearer the perfect image than man, and that as all delicate and high things are only appreciated as true civilization advances, so she has been neglected, but will be understood? Is man the pioneer, the first worker, the struggler, and she the more delicate and spiritual guide and teacher, taking her part in beautifying, purifying, spiritualizing what has been plowed and prepared? Can she be the finer instrument, cast aside as useless and worthless, only because applied to clearing the wilderness, previous to sowing the seed? Will she ever stand out perfect, sound, adapted unassisted to perform her proper work? Or will she always retain the air of an appendage, an ornament, beautiful, but for no end, too weak to have a place, and too frail to be serviceable or independent?

Are the faults we deplore radical defects, or unsoundness and feebleness resulting from cramped and artificial nurture? Is man our fellow worker, our stronger and coarser brother, or is he the guide, the object, the protector and master in whose service and under whose direction we dance and sing?

Heard strange news: by the evening paper, this day in the Liverpool packet, have sailed Mr. and Mrs. David Sears, Mme. Hauteville and Mr. Fred Hauteville! Father passed Monday evening with them and was invited to come again tonight; saw Uncle S. in the street yesterday, and heard not a word. All the family in surprise and wonder.[31]

30 November

Nellie Hooper and Ruskin. Went in the evening with Powell to the last of a series of lectures at the Lowell Institute by Mr. Dewey.[32] The subject was the three agencies in the education of man: Labor, The Church, and Character or Example. His treatment of the last was particularly fine and inspiring and eloquent. Is this eloquence a gift in itself, or the necessary result of a feeling, earnest soul?

Powell and I had quite a chat on love and marriage.[33] What an immense comfort it is to have him at home, and yet I must own to a painful feeling of effort, resulting from a fear that I may not do and be all I can to interest, sympathize with and please him. I am afraid to allay the feeling by remitting my exertion, and yet I feel suspicious that it gives a constrained and uneasy air to the result, exactly counteracting what I strive for, pleasant, intimate intercourse.

1856

Boston   14 January

The storm has lessened, though not quite ceased. At twelve went down to Susie Welles'; sat with her in her room two hours, talking and sewing on her wristers for the evening. She seems to me to realize her marriage as little as I could. I do not quite understand her feelings. Sitting in her little parlor for the last time, where she has passed so many hours, of joy, of sorrow, of devotion, of reflection, quitting it with her maidenhood, her comparative independence; quite shutting the gate, behind which she has been gazing at the world, to enter that world, still an unexplored country; at the very act of tying the knot, which is to mold to a great degree all the circumstances and influences of her journey on earth, parting with home and parents, never to return to them: all these would it seems to me form a tide which would rush over my soul, breaking down every prop and barrier that firmness, hope, and the pressure of the present cares had raised, and forcing me to cry aloud in an anguish of trembling hopes, fears, remembrances, sighs. But Susie was calm as if arranging for a ball, or a sister's wedding, rather than her own.

Before dinner I ran down to see Miss Prince for a minute; and at six in the evening was at Trinity Church with Powell.[34] The church was rather dimly lighted, which I liked, with no crowd, though some strangers in the gallery. Susie spoke calmly, and distinctly so that her firm tones could be heard all over the church. I sat quite far back, behind the Peabodys, and Carys and Laura Rogers, Mr. Sohier and Mr. Henry Saltonstall in the pew.

We walked quickly home, dressed, and were at the Welles' before eight: she received only her family and intimate friends. Her dress was a white silk and a tulle veil fastened with orange blossoms and other flowers. I have seen her look prettier, but she seemed to me the type of perfect, holy womanhood, her eyes full of love, cheerfulness and joy and kindness on her lips, calm, steadfast, devoted piety in her smooth broad brow. I could not leave her, and stood near, and parted, with a sprig from her flowers.

All left at nine. They go out of town. And then we rushed to Mrs. Mills', where was assembled a very gay and rather odd omnium gatherum, who diverted themselves with edifying discourse, dancing, games and supper. At steeple chase I won a cornelian ring, and a pair of small china boots! And Susie is married, and I am going to bed, and the scene is ended, the curtain dropped, and we prepare for a fresh act.

27 January

Beautiful at nine o'clock, but became raw and cloudy. The church was cold as a barn, the thermometer only 50°—Pretty tired and glad to get home. Mother not well enough to be at church, she does not sleep, has a constant headache, and seems miserable enough.

I begin this week with a new spirit, for the load of things to be done at a certain moment, bows, dresses, calls, and letters, and work of all kinds, seems mostly cleared away, and I breathe again with a little freedom. This pressure of petty necessities demanding time, thought and action, are very oppressive to me, and yet I seem unable to rise above them. I am constantly doubting whether my want of energy, activity and lightheartedness make them seem unduly onerous, or whether they really are too many, and ought to be straightened and lopped away. Reading and music become impossibilities, my temper becomes ruffled, my nerves uneasy, all is wrong; and yet I know not even whether I should increase my activity or lessen my cares, much more how I can achieve each of these objects. I wonder often and again, whether the tranquil faces, the light steps, the gay laughter I hear, belong to people whose whole being is in the constant state of restlessness mine is, eager, wishing, fearing, doubting, resolving, regretting, hoping, and often fainting, sometimes dancing; and yet when I see how little my life is open to others, why should I doubt it? Peace, rest, are they nowhere found; if we are freed from regrets and present vexations, we are striving to grasp that just beyond us, one as fatiguing as the other. Do all long for a loving heart to cheer, understand and help them? Do any get it, or is disappointment to meet all those who look for such an earthly staff? It seems to me if I could get rid of self, could get rid of this all-absorbing restless being, and become absorbed in something beyond, I might hope for more tranquility; but I still doubt, and hope, and despair, and so go on.

13 February

A dinner at Miss Emily Parker's for Lizzie Mifflin at half past five. Miss Parker sat at the head with Mr. Gardner Hammond on her right, then Isabella Mason, Charles Gibson, Mary Deconnick and Powell, Miss Palfrey and Daniel, Mrs. Parker and Mr. Nat Russell at the foot, Miss Mifflin and Mr. Palfrey, Miss Bowditch and Mr. Sam Hammond, myself and Charlie Appleton, Miss Russell and Mr. Wm. Rogers.

The dinner was very handsome, almost too long, a bouquet at each lady's plate, and one in the center, a great improvement, as you could see over the table to the other side. The service of china and glass was very magnificent. The house is also a remarkably nice one, and beautifully furnished, especially the chambers. Had a very good time, though I did not expect it.

At nine most of the company went to Mrs. Fay's where were to be seen some extremely good tableaux. I cannot remember with distinctness the details, as the room was filled to overflowing. I stood all the time, and did not arrive until several had been performed. Alice Mason and Tina Shelton seem to have carried off the laurels, especially the former. She was dressed as a Greek girl, her hair in hanging braids, a little scarlet cap on her head, black velvet jacket embroidered in gold, white satin skirt embroidered, and very dainty feet. The dress was in itself very perfect and rich, and on Alice was exquisite. Her dark eyes, beautiful hair, thinly cut features and slight figure made the wild, timid, beautiful Greek girl to perfection. The tableau was the letter-writer, Aug. Perkins on the ground with his writing materials, and Alice and Lilly Fay dictating and then reading the epistle. All the arrangements were excellent; the back room was hung with drapery, forming a large kind of tent, a black lace screen was stretched between the folding doors, which were also draped with damask curtains, and closed by a movable one. Gas reflectors arranged with gutta percha tubes threw a strong light on the actors, and a platform was raised on which to place them.

Tina Shelton took the part of Mary Queen of Scots; her dress black velvet, with pearls, made her complexion more dazzlingly white than usual, and the rather sad expression natural to her face, suited the part well. The other figures were John Adams as Roland Graeme, reading to her, Miss Bloodgood as Catharine Seaton, seated on a low cricket embroidering, and casting a sidelong glance at him, and Miss Fay as the other maid of honor, pointing at these two figures and addressing the Queen.[35] John A. made a very handsome, and with his curling red hair and light complexion, a most appropriate Scotsman, and Miss Bloodgood in a plaid scarf, and little cap, an equally pretty and appropriate Catharine. A third tableau was from the Rape of the Lock. Kitty Fay looked surprisingly handsome as Belinda, in her powdered hair, with flowers erect on the top of her head, and the old-fashioned dress. The other characters I have forgotten, though I believe Montgomery Ritchie and John Bates were two of them. Mrs. Jacob Rogers took the part of Lady Teazle, and suited her character admirably, with her fresh complexion, and little Frenchy air and toss of the head. I believe Frank Peabody and Mr. Joe Gardner were in the same tableau, but I forget how. The former looked eminently handsome, and gentlemanly. The last was the Seven Ages of Shakespeare.

Mrs. Fay holding the infant (Mrs. Ritchie's baby's doll!), Willy Fay as the school boy, John Adams with a guitar as the lover, Mr. Rogers as the soldier, Mr. Snell as the lawyer, Mr. Fay as the miserly old man, and as the dotard, John Bates recited the appropriate lines. I think there were seven tableaux in all. The Rivals in which Alice took a part and the statue where Kitty Fay and Montgomery Ritchie were the figures I did not see, and I have forgotten what I was told that the seventh was. Nothing could have been better I think for the beauty of the actors, the splendor of the dresses, the care of the arrangements, and I was surprised that so much could have been accomplished in Boston, where there is little use for articles of fancy costume.

A very pretty entertainment, and in one respect at least better than amateur theatricals, that they can be given in much greater perfection. I don't think, however, that I should ever be willing to take a part, such things should be done in the best manner, or not at all, and rather a marked figure and style are necessary.

28 February

Out until twelve; then received callers. In the evening Mother went with me to the dancing class, the 13th and last. The room was very crowded, many strangers, everyone in their best dresses too, and looking very well. I wore my new pink; carried a bouquet sent by Mr. Aa. Hubbard. Sat through the German with Mr. Gardner, and stayed until half past one, Mother having left at eleven. It was very brilliant, and I had a sufficiently good time; but though I feel very sorry to think that this is about the end of society for me as a young lady, and sigh that it should be past, I feel no desire to continue. When I say the end, I mean that in America, and Boston, a girl who has been in society three winters, has nearly climbed the hill, and must begin to give way to new aspirants, absurd as it sounds. The middle-age society, where those who have tried dancing, can turn to conversation and a pleasant intercourse, is wanting here, and the leap is immediate from girlhood, to old maidism or matronship; a leap often postponed, but to be made, no easy pleasant slide possible.

If I could see gentlemen and ladies of my own age, easily and often at home, I would never care to see a party again; but this seems impossible until one by marrying has the means and then becomes undesirable.

7 March

Have written a quantity of invitations to gentlemen. Am growing thin on the tea party. Nellie Hooper to read. Made a few calls, and looked for some trinket for Isabella. The weather cold and windy.

In the afternoon received through Mrs. Blanchard a gold locket from Mrs. Tracy of Newburyport, containing her hair. It is a very charming remembrance from an old lady of 78 years. I have never seen her, but she was a cousin and warm friend of my grandmother Rogers, and always expressed a very kind feeling for me.

Have been this evening to a musical party at Sally Cary's, the German singing club being the sole performers; several of them are artists, professional singers, and nothing can be better than the voices, the drilling, the taste, and the selection of music. A selection from *Orpheus* is splendid, Sally taking the solo; part of Weber's *Oberon*, where Ellen Ward shone conspicuously, as indeed she did all the evening so pure and sweet is her voice; many pieces of Mendelssohn, Bach, Frantz, etc. all beautiful.[36] It is like a glimpse of the bright skies, green woods and fresh airs of summer, as the imagination paints them in their perfection. In German music I can smell the violets, hear the

1

Elizabeth's parents, Hannah Rogers Mason (1806–1872)
and William Powell Mason (1791–1867)
Courtesy of the Massachusetts Historical Society

2

Elizabeth's brother, William Powell Mason, Jr.
(1835–1901)
Courtesy of The Bostonian Society/
Old State House

3

Elizabeth's brother, Edward Bromfield Mason (d. 1863)
Courtesy of the Massachusetts Historical Society

4

63 Mt. Vernon Street, the house where Elizabeth grew up
Courtesy of the Boston Athenaeum

5

*Boggy Meadow, the favorite Mason summer residence, in
Walpole, New Hampshire*
Courtesy of the Society for the Preservation of New
England Antiquities

6

Elizabeth's teacher, Anna Cabot Jackson Lowell
Courtesy of the Boston Athenaeum

7

Elizabeth's mother-in-law, Mrs. Samuel Cabot
(1791–1885), with Dr. Samuel Cabot (1815–1885), a
medical practitioner and Elizabeth's brother-in-law
Courtesy of the Boston Athenaeum

8

Elizabeth's good friend and sister-in-law, Sarah (Sadie)
Perkins Cabot (1835–1917)
Courtesy of the Boston Athenaeum

birds, feel the cool wind on my cheek, it is the singing of the green free earth, the music of healthy, happy souls, sweet and pure. Oh dreamland what art thou, shadows flying at the touch of human fingers, lovely, most lovely! In thy delicious fields existence seems priceless, everything good, no need of sympathy, here all the world creation is around us, is ours, our universal friend—but the void when its bright visions have faded!

29 March

Went to Mrs. Lowell's, the least interesting reading. On return found a note on my table—the blow has fallen unexpectedly indeed. From Mr. G. not an offer of hand and heart, but an approach to it; how ridiculously one feels! I trotted up and down my ten feet of spare chamber blushing and laughing to myself, and sighing too; for I am indeed very sorry, and yet I cannot think it is my fault. How can one know, how absurdly vain it seems to suspect, it makes one grind their teeth in shame to think of it, and yet if one does not, the trap springs as now. What can he know of me, excepting that I have pretty manners and brown hair and can smile—alas, alas, is this the way one is to stumble on their lot? I can't believe the thing to be true, and stare at the sheet of paper, as if I expected to see it fade away before my eyes; but there it is, and to be answered too. I then feel, I think really without laughing, I must cause him pain, more or less, but disagreeable at the time; and yet what can I do, what could I have done, and how absurd it is.

I finally went down to sing, stopping at each bar to decide whether I ought to tell Mother or not, finally called her and gave her the note, she of course if anything more surprised, though rather at the suddenness than at the fact.[37]

My Sunday School children came for the afternoon, and Arthur Mason dined with us, and I was obliged to keep my attention to them, and think over an answer at the same time. At last after tea I wrote it, and read it to Mother, and sent it, without betraying it to the family. It is very hard to be truthful and kind and prudent and negative all at once. Well, it is gone.

6 May

An east wind, but pleasant and mild. Went to Grace Rives' and, not finding her, to Mrs. Welles'—Susie sails on the 17th, the last letters were from Edinboro', she seems happy as any bird. May she ever be so. At half past ten read *Walden* with Nellie; it improves as it goes on, and is delightful, suggestive and rousing.[38]

Trimmed Annie Webber's bonnet partially, and at half past five, walked with Nellie on the Mill Dam, the weather delightful, a very cold spring, however, I think.

Mother went to bed early with one of her raging headaches; they are terrible, nothing to be done but live through them.

Nellie said this morning that Nina Lowell was speaking to her about Mr. Joe Gardner, of course neither of them knowing that he was in anyway connected with me; but she said (he is her cousin) that she thought all his faults were on the outside, and that he had very sensitive deep feelings, and a very warm heart, though so cold a manner.[39] I really hope not. It is very painful to think that you may have caused a person real suffering; the consciousness that it may really be so, sometimes rushes over me like a flood; for generally one connects these kind of feelings with novels, and plays and unrealities of all kinds, and feels as if it was a kind of pleasing fiction, not belonging to real life, not pleasing in this case, however. I suppose a lady of propriety would hold up her hands at my allowing my thoughts to recur to this subject so often, and yet I feel as if forgetfulness or indifference were an unkindness. Why should not one feel sorry for this pain, as well as any other? I do and I cannot help it.

Walpole   15 August

I have finished this morning Thoreau's *Concord and Merrimack Rivers*; it has given me a little tidbit of reading every day for a long time, and is far from exhausted yet, for I am eager to go back and examine some of the truths more thoroughly.[40] It is a life-giving book, and gives a picture of life from a point of view entirely unaffected by the artificial world created by man. He is a man without money, not poor, because able to get his daily bread with small toil, and desiring nothing more, untrammeled entirely (as no man with very warm affections I think could be) by the opinions or feelings of others, afraid of nothing, intimate with nature as with a bosom friend, learned in all the wisdom of the world handed down in books, ignoring ambition, position, aimless as far as concerns this world, and as unbiased as I can imagine possible. Added to these advantages are a pure large nature, vigorous intellect, and healthy life moral and physical. He is all-convincing at the time, and ought to be, for he is merely putting in practice, the principles which all daily preach, but none entirely make facts. Yet when we would follow him, our old habits of feeling rush back on us, making his purer practice a sort of dream, from which we awake, sorry that it is gone, and almost doubting still which is the unreality, the world we have left, or the world we awake to.

I believe solemnly and sincerely that the spiritual life should be first, material last, and needs a very small corner, and yet we place it practically first, because—other people do. I know no better reason.

After some little doubt, decided to accept Mrs. Bellows' invitation
for tonight. Father did not come in the noon train, but sent a note.
Louise also received a letter from Daniel, (he has written every day,)
saying that he would come up for her on Saturday, and pass Sunday.[41]
She has already arranged to go home Saturday morning, however, and
says Daniel is too fond of running about, therefore she will not allow
him to leave his business.

Mother left us at Mrs. Bellows', and we found a large party assembled come up from Keene, Miss Dinsmore, Miss Edwards, and
the Misses Jarvis. The theatricals were a repetition of the first performance, and were good, though several of the parts were changed,
Scraggs for the better, Mr. Ticknor for the worse. The two Misses
Wilson from Keene, were present; they are pretty girls.

Louise and I slept together, and had a pleasant talk. One learns
much more of another in passing a week with her, than in the common intercourse of months. I am very much pleased with Louise. She
is quite different from any one I ever knew, uniting the simplicity of
her youth, to the gay, impetuous lightheartedness, and quiet sensibilities of a foreigner. She is the most confiding, affectionate, lively,
simple little person I ever saw, and yet has much character, Yankee
capacity, and goodness. She is not foolishly talkative of herself, but so
frank and simple, that one knows much more of her whole soul than
is usual. She is certainly devoted to Daniel, and absorbed in him. It
is funny to see all the energy of impulse and feeling, which has before
led her in a gay dance, from flower to flower, now all settled on this
one object. Daniel is certainly wrapt up in her, as kind, thoughtful
and attentive as man can be; and yet she confessed, that she doubted
whether a girl would every marry, if she could see the future plainly

before her. It is hard to sustain a wife's part to any man, for whom you have given up all, and involves many bitter experiences, though more sweet ones. If one loses much one is saved much. Louise has not felt well here, but she bears suffering with womanly courage. I confess my reverence for woman as one often sees her increases: their quiet disinterestedness, their patient courage, their loving hearts. Their faults are first seen, their virtues last, because unobtrusive, deep hidden. I pray very earnestly that I may be able here to find much power of doing good. Louise is alone, no relations, no mother, sister, cousin even, and a woman needs a woman's affection, however much her husband's love may be to her. God grant that I may use this precious opportunity of love, with a faithful care.

19 September

I am particularly anxious to stay with Mary Quincy, because besides great pleasure to myself, I could do her some good. She has suffered with the same doubts and struggles that I have, only in more intense degree, and has never until lately looked upon me in any other way, than as an affectionate acquaintance. She has believed from my outward calm and propriety that I was incapable of understanding, far less aiding her, and has always maintained a reserve which I have felt in no light degree. Within a few weeks she has written me as she never has done before, frankly and confidingly as well as affectionately, and I long to secure the love I so much prize. For I consider her a person superior to most, with a character unsettled now, but capable I believe of the highest development, she has warm feelings, noble aspirations, and a grand intellect. For this last I especially prize her, because I miss it so much in others. I am grateful for the warm hearts that surround me, and the examples of lofty character; but I

long for a fine intellect, which can understand my doubts, is unsatisfied with voluntary blindness and servitude to forms and creeds, and
can struggle with me for purer stronger faith. Every friend has a
sphere. To Jenny I look for a warm sympathy that nothing can take
the place of, and which she possesses above all others. To Susie I
would go for a steadfast looking to God and duty, with cheerfulness
and affection. But Mary can aid me in overcoming the obstacles which
I alone can overcome, and must struggle with, for the others either
have risen above them and forgotten their size, or from difference of
nature and character do not see them.

I think a great difficulty in struggling in spiritual affairs, is their
want of tangibility. What at one moment seems all-important, in the
next has as it were lost its body and in contrast with the hard material
of everyday life, appears all a fog after all. But if you see another soul
in the same fight, your belief of its reality is kept alive.

Quincy   3 October

Mary followed the carriage on horseback this morning. The gentlemen, Mr. Q. and Joe, go to town. There is a delightful kind of ease,
and freedom from restraint in the movements here, which strikes me
very much. The horses are apparently expected to be used, the women
are given liberty of speech and action, rather uncommon, and their
plans go unmeddled with.

After dinner Mr. and Mrs. Henry Upham called, and Dr. Minot
and a Dr. Stone drank tea. Mary's voice is really very splendid, it has
improved, and some notes are perfect.

In the evening we called the spirits, and succeeded in obtaining
raps at a small table, but no very satisfactory communication. I think

Mrs. Quincy is almost a full believer. There have been great wonders in the village, hands of fire, etc.

7 October

Powell has postponed his departure a week, so that I shall not return today.

Had a very pleasant talk with Joe Quincy last evening. I have never known him so well before. He spoke of his stuttering as a great trial, and especially united with natural diffidence. I believe him to be a person of very pure character, and refined tastes, but he wants a something which I do not yet know how to name. He is to publish a new classical poem this winter. I imagine he has suffered a great deal during his life from sensitive feelings, and unfortunate externals. His face bears the marks of it, and is at times singularly pure and intellectual in expression, very handsome, if only on another figure.

Took a ride this morning with Miss Abby, Mary following on horseback. Powell walked over to see Stephen Perkins, and we followed him—the first time I was ever on Milton Hill though I know nearly all its inhabitants, at any rate by reputation.[42]

Mr. Thayer, editor of a New York paper, and Mr. Charles Hale of the *Daily*, came out with Joe to dinner.[43] I was most unwisely silent, but there seemed so many to talk.

After dinner all the young 'uns but Mr. Hale, went to walk to Mt. Wollaston, Powell, however, strolling off by himself. A beautiful evening. Returning, I can hardly say I was surprised by a declaration of love from Josiah; for it was preceded by that awful warning, when, separated from the other members of the party, a word, or motion tell you, with a conviction that makes a chill fall around you, and the blood rush to your heart, beating, that another soul has stepped from commonplaces to deep realities, and breaking over forms, speaks of interests belonging to the soul. He told me that for six years, ever since I stayed at Milton, he had loved me, why he knew not, for he hardly knew me, that he had tried to overcome it, that he had become intimate with many other women whom he admired, that he had tried in vain to break through my reserve, but though I was always silent, though he seldom saw me, his feelings only increased. Diffident of his own worthiness, and quite despairing from his outward deficiencies, he had kept away from me as much as possible, and last winter had gone abroad, only that he might not be obliged to meet me, and hopelessly keep silence. Now he could do it no longer, and begged me not to blame him, for seeking the relief, that pouring out his feelings to me, gave him. He said nothing of hope, asked nothing, and what could I say? What did I say? I seemed turned to stone; instead of trembling from excitement, as a moment before, it seemed to me I was as cool, as indifferent as if he had told a commonplace anecdote. I felt grieved, surprised, embarrassed, and could only mutter, that I could say nothing, that I was very much pained to give him suffering, that I could say nothing more—and hurry on to get home. How sorry one feels afterwards that they could not say something grateful, something kind, but one seems to become ice. I almost determined to return with Powell the next morning, but unfortunately I had promised to remain, and I was afraid of causing too much of a commotion by changing. I talked as well as I could on the piazza, then came down after dressing for tea, and then we rode to the town hall to hear a speech by Mr. Quincy for Fremont.[44]

In sober thought, one cannot but feel what a grand, holy, noble offering any man's sincere love is, cannot but believe in the great suffering which must attend, for a time at least, its rejection; and yet, in novels, poems, plays, in conversation, and in everyday action, it is so constantly treated in a light, silly, trifling incredulous manner, that one feels it almost vain and ridiculous, to believe in it as a true heart-felt sacred fact. One almost imagines it a farce, or a dream. Certainly we have little right to do so.

Boston   2 November

The weather as warm as September—very beautiful. I stayed to the Communion today, but I doubt if I shall again, and yet I dread to make a demonstration. I am afraid I joined it too thoughtlessly, and yet my motives were honest at the time. It has never given me real satisfaction, and is painful to me in its formality. I cannot believe that Christ ever instituted it as a lasting ceremony, and it does not serve to bring me any nearer to Him. The act of eating and drinking is disagreeable to me. It has not the solemnity belonging to it with the Catholic belief, and yet it is too formal to be grateful to the feelings. I suppose people will wonder if I do not continue, and yet I do not like to continue an empty ceremony.

I have been reading Theodore Parker's book on religion, and cannot but like it; it is not only that it convinces me, for it goes little further than I had gone alone, it merely makes clear and supports my own feelings.[45] Doubts which have always been clouds between me and faith, now vanish. I feel the presence of God, I aspire to worship, love and obey Him, I can rest on His power, wisdom and goodness; but Christ is a being we know only on testimony, and that of so imperfect a kind, that one cannot calmly repose on its statements.

How can God have favored only a portion of the world with revelation? If He meant we should regard the Bible as His word, Jesus as

His inspired son, why should He not have stated it so clearly that we could not doubt? I am but groping still, but I have a glimpse of daylight, and I will not believe that it is wrong to think to the uttermost. Falsehood falls before investigation, Truth must stand.

8 November

A summer's day, so warm and balmy, but although several wanted to ride with me, and I wanted to ride with several, the day passed without going. Gentlemen are abundant, but being of a ferocious nature, it does not do to trust so tender a creature as a damsel with them, even for two hours, in a thickly populated country, on a fleet horse, and women to ride are scarcer than flowers in winter,—poetical that last!

Met Mary and we went together to see two old ladies, the Misses Adams. I found she could have gone with James Savage this morning as well as not.[46]

After dinner went out to Rogers' and drank tea on my return with Aunt P. Glad to have a chance to cheer her up a little.

12 November

A mild still day, but no escort, and therefore no ride. I regret fine weather at this season, lost.

Mary brought me Joe's new poem *Charicles*. It is the same style as *Lyteria*, but more elaborate, and the Quincys think much better. I cannot as yet decide. The plot has less beauty, and the female character less development. But it seems to me a work of much talent, and showing great elevation of thought, and exquisite delicacy of feeling. Reading over the passages containing expressions of love in this and *Lyteria*, which are some of them very beautiful, I was very much impressed, almost awestricken at the idea they give of the author's conception of it. Am I then the object around which he groups these yearnings, these aspirations, hopes, dreams of his holiest, highest life? Can I, the vain, sinful, earthborn creature, be to him the image of all that is holy, pure, beautiful, good? Is it reality, or a dream of novelist and poet? How I long to be the being I seem! And I say these things in all purity and simplicity. I do not merit such love, and I must force myself, in order to believe it. How ill can I reward it too, by indifference stern and unyielding. What is the right course? Oh that I knew and could follow it.

13 November

A very beautiful day—mild, and the air entirely at rest. Rode out with Mary, Josiah and Mr. Savage. Took a road leading on beyond Theodore Lyman's into a thin wood, where by taking a road hardly formed, we crossed to Brookline again. Very wild and pretty, and the horses went delightfully. I went rather unwillingly with Mr. Joe Quincy, but it has turned out rightly. How or why I cannot say, but in some way I told him that it was vain for him to hope, that I was no divinity, that he was not doing right to keep up this dream. Oh I don't know what I said or did! All I know is that I felt like a stone, things seemed as in a dream, and that I said what I did not believe, spoke of what I did not intend, and far from showing human kindness, sympathy, pity, spoke like an icicle. Oh if we could only speak to people as we feel in our own chambers, instead of becoming machines! Thank heaven, however, it is done, and I no longer feel responsible for every word. It *is* a fearful thing to overturn a man's whole dream of happiness, whether that dream is founded on shadows or realities, and one's own unsatisfied desires seem almost merited. Self will come in too. Oh God, am I too to be alone in this great universe, am I to spend a life time rendered somber at least by hopes disappointed, yearnings unanswered, a flood of love and devotion pressed back on my own soul? Oh my Father, let me rest in Thy arms, Thou art all good, all wise, I will look up to Thee and trust Thy will like a little child; and when the flood is too bitter in its overwhelming strength, I will cling the closer.

23 November

Another glorious day. Tried this morning to talk more with my Sunday School children. I find they are all twelve but Julie Robbins, I have not got at their hearts yet, but I will not despair. It would be a great pleasure to me to be a friend to them, a true friend whom they could turn to for advice and sympathy. I think girls always need some such friend, even if surrounded by parents and relations.

Laura is in town for the day. Henry has most suddenly gone to New York, probably to remain permanently, some new business arrangement of the house he is in—it is a terrible loss to the family. I am very sorry for them. It is trying to have their only two brothers away so far.

Have been walking with Mary. Joe has told her all, though I think not all the details. She is very good and kind about it, and feels as much affection for me as ever. I appear to her and everyone, however, so cold, that I begin to think I am cold—perhaps reserve has nothing to do with it, and I have no heart, no sensibilities, no cravings for human affection. Oh my Father in Heaven, my prayers are then make-believe. When will this struggle cease? I feel as if I were willfully throwing away a priceless treasure. I believe Joe Quincy's love is pure and deep, why should I not accept it? I may never get such another gift. I sometimes feel as if it was some hidden pride that made me so indifferent to such devotion, but I dare not, dare not, run the risk. Is that the feeling I should have for my husband, the first being to me after God in the universe? Oh that I could know what warm love is! I could almost say even, hopeless. Is it possible that a heart that so longs for it should never get it, and yet how many women are apparently without it. God give me faith and strength. I will lean on Thee, and try with all my heart and soul to bend to Thy will.

Evening. I cannot help writing, for I have no one to speak to on the one topic of my thoughts. Oh if I only could have a calm bright faith! If I could only so realize spiritual things, that this life should shrink to its proper proportion! But no, a solitary unloved life will seem long and dreary, dreary, dreary, and the life beyond very far off and dreamy. If I could live for others, for their good and happiness! I humbly pray the Father to help me; and will He give stones for bread? Sufficient for the day is the evil thereof. I will not look forward, so help me God. But alas, I resolve one thing and do another.

13 December

A perfect day—mild as September. Received a letter from Powell dated Paris Nov. 26. It almost reconciles one for the moment to having him away.

Dined at six at Mrs. Jefferson Coolidge's—a party for Mr. and Mrs. Lincoln Baylies.[47] Guests Mrs. B., Mr. Martin Brimmer, myself, Mr. George Lowell, Charlotte Gray, Charlie Appleton, Mrs. Richard Parker, Mr. Baylies, Mrs. Coolidge, Mr. Parker, Lizzie Gray, Mr. Dabney, Miss Newton, Mr. Joe Gardner, Mrs. Lowell, and Mr. Coolidge. Mr. Brimmer agreeable, though he does not exert himself much. Had an hour's most lively discussion with Mr. Gardner, and I am afraid rather shocked him with my opinions, which I could not help expressing rather warmly.

He is all conservative, approves an aristocracy, thinks the common people may be taught too much, is accustomed to value liberal living, wealth, position, appearances very much. Has a horror of freethinking, spiritualism, and the host of isms, is inclined to think as his great-grandfather did, etc., etc., etc. This is hardly my plan and I suppose he is now very much surprised and sorry, and will soon consider himself to have escaped very luckily. Such is a man's love, to resist life and death, stand against time and circumstances, be all in all!! Ah me, is my dream all mist to dry up with the noonday sun?

18 December

Susie Sturgis has a son, born on Tuesday at five o'clock P.M.—how very funny! I am thankful, for I could not but feel a little anxious, and now she is nicely.

Tonight the dancing class—Mother not well and did not go. Had a very nice set of partners, and much complimented on my dress, buff, with branches of imitation coral in my hair and corsage. Was too worried, however, to enjoy much—Joe Quincy, Joe Gardner, and Richard Fay, seemed omnipresent, and I never could raise my eyes in any part of the room, that one of them were not looking at me. Joe Quincy looked so very pale, that it almost frightened me. What can it all mean, some rose-colored glass must be over their eyes, through which they see me?

It vexes me to do it, and yet I cannot help thinking of them all the time, and I am humbled to find how hard it is to put aside vanity, and act as a pure-minded generous, loving woman. It is difficult to realize that one is no nearer an angel, for other mortals believing so, or that one's sins are just as great, although others are blind to them. I wish so much that I could use some of this influence for good, but it seems impossible to effect anything; but let me not lower to them the ideal of womanhood, purity, love, holiness. If I cannot benefit them, I will not pull down one of the bulwarks of their goodness. God, help me to be pure and good that my light may shine to their blessing and good. Oh that a ballroom were not the scene of these experiences of the soul, it is so hard to preserve them untainted by the glitter and frivolity around!

1857

Boston   26 February

The last dancing class—Had the longest conversation with Joe Quincy that I have had this winter, and now I am afraid that he was driven away by some one, and felt hurt; for he is so delicate and gentlemanly, that as he imagines I prefer to talk to anyone rather than himself, he moves away as soon as any gentleman approaches me. He looked very handsomely tonight; but it is distressingly painful and awkward to dance and have every motion watched, as I was all the evening by Mr. Gardner and J.Q. If they thought I knew it I am sure they would be careful, but I cannot help seeing it whenever I raise my eyes, and I feel it when I do not. It seems like a spell over me. The last of the evening was made very uncomfortable by Mr. G.'s attentions, which I have resolved shall cease. He sent me tonight a bouquet which I should have been glad to leave at home, but Mother thought it would be rude. He is so reserved and quiet and gentlemanly, that though I have taken great pains never to be more than politely indifferent and coolly civil, still I felt that it was too little marked to have any effect; and I have determined that as a duty I would be decidedly ungracious even if I must be rude. It is dreadful, I shrink from it as from having a tooth out; but I know I am wrong in delaying, so when the German cotillion began which Clara wanted to see, he came to sit by me, and I was as still as I could be. But of what avail, I must say yes and no, must grimly smile occasionally, and must make a remark after staring ten minutes at space, instead of sending him off. Alas he stayed and stayed till I became almost frantic, there was nowhere to move to, no one to speak to and I got so hot and embarrassed that I could hardly think what I was about. At length Randolph Coolidge passed for the third time, and I could but just restrain myself from asking him to have mercy on me, and stop. Seeing I suppose that I was not all engrossed he did stop and sit down behind me, and I turned round and talked a half hour, hardly noticing Mr. G. It was dreadful for him and for me, but what could I do? At last, oh happiness, Clara was ready and we went; but Mr. G. looked red and wretched and did not even offer to escort us to the door, so we went alone. What is the reason that a gentleman's attentions are pleasing as long as they are meaningless, and if they become marked are so dreadful?

8 March

The last words I wrote in this were at Washington, and in despair of making up this long interim, I sit down to begin again. Laura and

Clara are both staying with me. Jenny whom I have not seen before for an age, has passed the evening with us, and also Willy Amory. Laura has been playing on my grand piano.

Have heard that Mr. Gardner is going to Europe. I was a little startled, as it is quite sudden I am sure, and must be the result of my manner very lately. It seems to me very strange that he can leave without saying anything to me, if he has really any feeling, but men are in such cases often enigmatical to me. I don't know that it is not best, but I should have a much pleasanter feeling towards him, if he said one single word from his heart to me. I cannot doubt that he has one, perhaps as warm and tender as a woman's, but certainly it expresses itself little through his tongue. Can a man really and truly love, and yet talk of nothing but his travels, his business, his little everyday adventures? I find it very hard to be sorry for him, because in appearance he needs it so little; and yet I may have overturned all his day-dreams, a sharper grief than many a greater one—for I suppose even he has them.[48]

How I long to be able to say to him, be nobler, rise higher, look deeper! How hard it seems that this great influence, by chance given into my hands, should be entirely lost; yet it is impossible to achieve anything, to move, as to stop the earth or the planets.

I can pray for him as a human soul with hopes, fears, aspirations, however few, a future, and a sphere on the earth. May God help him —I have been only a misfortune to him and a cause of suffering.

I long to know if he blames my conduct. I cannot say now even, how I could have acted differently. His manner is so cold, so commonplace, that it was impossible to be very marked in manner oneself. But probably he gave much more importance to slight actions, than I did—I should be sorry to shake his trust in women, in goodness.

31 March

Mary came up this morning to ask me if I would see Joe in any way; he wanted to speak to me once, and then if I did not wish it he would never trouble me again. I agreed of course. It is very painful, but anything I can do for him I ought to do and long to do, and especially as he is so reluctant to annoy me, so delicate and considerate.

Passed the rest of the morning with Mother in making calls. At Mrs. George Lyman's Mrs. L. was rude enough to say that a friend of mine was going abroad, laughing when I did not understand, and saying that he was driven abroad she presumed—he always had urgent business under such circumstances, meaning Mr. Gardner. I could have cried with vexation and indignation. So all the world know it.

Mary came for me after dinner, Joe joined us in Chestnut St., and she left. We walked into the Common and paced up and down Charles St. and Boylston St. malls. He said he wished to speak this last time, he was unhappy, wasting life and energies and health. He must end it, he did not think it right to make an appeal to my feelings, and therefore he should coldly state facts. He had loved me since I was at Milton six years ago, he had never loved anyone else, or thought of anyone but me for a moment. He had tried to put aside his feelings, despairing of their success, had been to Europe, made other friends, but last autumn they became stronger than ever—I had given him no encouragement to hope, and he had tried energetically this winter to forget me, to interest himself in society; but it was no use, he was wretched at being near me and not speaking to me. He had determined not to persecute me, and had resolutely kept away, but he could continue so no longer. He did not wish me to feel that a refusal would blight his life. He had felt so, but he had struggled above that,

and felt there was something even higher than his heart. If I desired it
he would give up all hope and never trouble me again. He would go
to Europe for a short time, and then return to begin life anew; but his
thoughts were all bent on an engagement, which should terminate
the moment I should desire it, but he could not help having the feeling that if he could see me often and naturally, he should be able to
win my affection. He thought it was no injury to a woman to make or
break an engagement of this kind: if it were he would never have
suggested it. He felt the power within him to become a new man if
his powers and energies had a motive to draw them into action. And
he ended by begging me to give no answer now, but think of it, if
possible uninfluenced by anyone. Once or twice his voice faltered, his
utterance was choked by emotion which I know he felt, but he held
firmly to his purpose of being calm, and when he had done tried to
speak of indifferent subjects to relieve me. I felt like one in a dream, I
not only heard him, but I observed that two men watched us with
smiling curiosity, that Miss Bigelow passed us and recognized us, and
I fear understood, as she did not bow, that the sun was bright and
spring-like, that I would give anything in the world to be at home,
alone, anywhere but there. I was moved by his feeling, was grateful
for his consideration, was full of sorrow, and yet when he had finished
I could not utter one word, could only hold down my head and gasp
out a few syllables without meaning. At length we reached Beacon
St., and, feeling dizzy, my heart beating, my breath gone, I asked
him to leave me, and rushed home.

I found Annie Loring with Mother, and the spell seemed still on
me, I felt tired and faint, but I laughed and joked, and could have
cried if I had allowed myself.

At length, after a short time of thought, I decided to tell Mother all. She was very good and kind, did not feel hurt that I had concealed it so long, and did not try to influence me in my decision. She was of course extremely surprised.

And now what to say, how to say, I think in a circle round and round.

Went in the evening to Teachers' meeting at Dr. Gannett's and then to a tea party at Aunt Anna's where I met most of the Quincy family. Mary was very considerate but my head ached, I felt worn out, and was grateful to lie down in my bed quietly and think no more.

1 April

Mother told Father this morning. He wishes me to decide quite for myself. There are great objections in family, etc., etc., but he has the highest opinion of him. I hear all these opinions, as if they could influence me, but my mind is really perfectly settled.

At a distance one may see both sides, feel doubt, but when the moment comes for saying an irrevocable yes or no, there can be no tampering with doubts. My husband! He must embody or suggest to me all that is beautiful, his faults seen through my love must have lost their edge, he must be my complement, which shall give me what I have not, and elevate and draw forth what I have. For him no sacrifice must seem great, circumstances must be nothing, my trust must be entire, my rest in his love perfect, he must be my refuge in grief, my partner in joy, for whom I can forget the universe. Am I tempted at times to think this chimerical, the belief of a dreamer? Then I feel that I have fallen below my highest ideal, and no one can do that and follow the right. If our ideal is so high that it can never be realized on earth, we may not abandon it, but rather rise to it, by patient waiting even for death. And this, I believe, as I believe in God and truth, and who dare act, in forgetting or neglecting it?

My decision is made, is firm, but to resign forever the devotion of one who comes so near our ideal, to feel that we may be neglecting, through ignorance of the real value of the gift offered, to say no to hopes founded on the very existence of another human soul, to tear away the image round which are clustered all the affections, longings, dreams, hopes of a soul struggling through this hard world, this makes one long to evade, find some crevice of escape, do anything but coldly turn away. Oh, it is hard, hard!

18 April

My cold still bad. Mother suffered all last night from a very terrible headache, so that when I saw her this morning, the blood had settled round her eyes, almost as if she had received a blow. Oh if something could be done!

Took my lesson of Dresel as usual, but an uncommonly pleasant one, partly I suppose because I played more to his satisfaction. Mary Q. wants me to have a musical party, as Dresel refuses to play on her piano or Ellen Ward's. Mary has been up to see me this week, and we had the first easy, pleasant meeting we have enjoyed together since some time. I think that J. must have asked her not to let any estrangement arise, and she is following carefully his wishes. It is very kind and very comforting to me.

I have been looking over a private memoir of Anne Everett who died at eighteen when in England. It is chiefly her journal and letters; but though the whole gives you the impression of a very pure, high-principled, cultivated person, still I must say that the diary is very dry and poor. She makes it a rule to mention nothing which might not be known about other people, and also to give no detailed account of thoughts and feelings. Her father advises it, and it may be very right, but it leaves a very meager skeleton.

It worries me a little sometimes to think what will become of all the trash I have written if I suddenly die. I should be very reluctant to have it read for many reasons. It does my intellect little credit I know, for a long time it is mere facts; often the sentiments would seem high-flown, or morbid, or affected; and of course so many daily thoughts and sensations are omitted, that the few mentioned seem all the more unworthy. Latterly I have rather overcome my extreme prudence, and many things are mentioned connected with others which ought not to be known; and lastly I have tried to be so frank in putting down feelings which I knew to be silly and wrong, as well as those which would do me credit, that I fear the most indulgent reader would think them very bad when stated so clearly in black and white.

1 May

A fine May day as a variety. Mother and I, however, did not indulge in any festivities. Went with Ellen Ward to see Page's picture of Venus rising from the sea. I decidedly do not like it.[49] No doubt the painting is fine, and it has great beauties. The coloring is certainly rich and rare too, but I was shocked by the want of refinement, and rather surprised at the want of beauty to my eyes. Not that the entire want of drapery seems to me so bad, for there need be nothing revolting in the human figure; but it can be treated in a refined and spiritual way, or in a coarse way. Then the attitude seemed to me artificial and impossible. It was a fat handsome woman, not a spiritual goddess. To be sure Venus was not of that type, but I think it should have been so in such a picture.

John Higginson came this evening with a bunch of violets instead of the wild flowers which he offered to find for me. Oh dear, dear, dear! What shall I do? It seems as if I could not have another dreadful time, and yet I have a presentiment.

24 May

The last day of Sunday school, and candor obliges me to confess to great lightness of heart in consequence. The Old Testament, my subject this winter, was as unknown to me as to them. And though now the names and incidents are familiar, it is a mystery. I do not know what to make of it, how to understand it, how to read or teach it. I cannot believe in it as many, or most people I believe do, and yet I cannot give my doubts to the children. It has been a perplexity to me all winter, and therefore, I feel that my teaching has been most unsatisfactory. If I could only get at the children, their true lives and feelings a little more, but I find it absolutely hopeless.[50]

31 May

Poor Mother has been sick all day with another violent headache, and feeling very depressed and nervous. I have been longing to do something, but could find nothing. How hard it is even for mother and daughter to open their hearts, but tonight even we met in a communion and sympathy very precious to me and very rare. Oh how I long to put my arms round her, and bear the blows of life in her stead! They seem harder than she can endure. Yet I can do so little, and she will let me do so little. I thank God that I can still devote my life to her, before it is too late. How selfish and untender and unskillful I am, how all-sustaining and all-cheering I might be. God help me.

Went in the latter part of the evening to the Quincys' to bid them Goodbye. They go on Tuesday to Stockbridge for a week, and then move immediately to Quincy. Partings even for a summer are saddening, and this year I shall not go to Quincy. Mary is very warm and has changed so much I can hardly account for it. Her old caprice has gone, which used to pain me so often. Randolph Coolidge was at the house. He goes this summer to Europe—James Savage too, who is alone at home, the family having moved to Lunenberg. Mr. Baldwin, Dr. Solger, Mr. Stickney, Mr. Dana were all paying their last visit. Mary and I went over the times when we were children, the ball and hoop delights, the tag on the State House steps—the present is almost as much a dream as the past.

2 June

I have done considerable work today, rejected an offer of hand and heart, had a tooth pulled, finished my shopping, and taken a drive!

I joke but it is with a sad face, sad for myself and for others. I search longingly for a soul that shall be my support, my joy always, but I look in vain. Others do the same, and when they find what they desire, I ruthlessly deny it to them. It seems like the freaks of capricious fortune but I *will* not believe it. I was called down after breakfast to see Mr. Higginson, who had come to ask me to ride: I could not go. He asked to speak to me a moment, and then I knew it must all come. It was very short, he said but little, except that he was in fault, he had been a fool. I told him I had not expected it as I thought he felt for another person. I should have said had not suspected it until within a short time, but I am so confused, and frightened, I lose my wits. He wished to know if waiting would do anything, he would wait any time; whether anyone else was more happy, whether there was any hope, and finally whether I would still consider him a friend, to which he received the first yes, and so he rushed off. I am very, very, very sorry for him. Mother thinks he cannot feel very deeply as he changed so quickly from Laura to me, and thinks it no great compliment; but I do not feel so, I think disappointment leaves a dreadful void which demands satisfaction. I have faith in people's feeling, though I think the object is of less importance than we imagine. Others besides Titania have a love strong enough in itself to blind the eyes to the ass's ears. Everyone has it latent, they meet something which calls it into action, and when once roused it is not easily quieted. Mr. Higginson was fearfully nervous, his hands and feet and face twitching in a way that makes me smile almost as I remember it. I am grateful that I am not a man after all.

Rode out in our own carriage this afternoon. Stopped at Emily Appleton's. She is in possession of the old place, and looks very pleasant, but it is too circumscribed to please me much. She has a saddle-horse I covet immensely.

6 June

Had a letter from Powell today, wishing to remain a year longer. I have always expected it, but it will be very hard to spare him.

Rode out to see Mrs. Crowninshield. Received a note this evening from John Higginson. I do not understand exactly his feeling in writing it; for he asks for nothing excepting that I will not think his feelings were of very sudden growth, and that I will continue our friendship as it existed before. Certainly it is dictated by the most gentlemanly and considerate feelings, but it is very formal and reserved, and expressly disclaims any desire for an answer. For which I am very glad, for though I have perfect confidence in him, I should not know what to say. I cannot tell if he thinks I have done quite right always, or whether he feels that I ought to have perceived his feelings before and warned him by my manner. At any rate he is too generous to say so. It must be hard to bear a second time, and leave a bitter distrust of himself. If sorrow would do people good, how many wounds I would heal, but everyone must bear their own burdens almost alone, sometimes I think quite alone. He says two years ago he first knew me and liked me: that was the summer I was at Nahant, that was the spring he offered himself to Laura. "This last year our intercourse has been his chief pleasure." He is content with crumbs indeed, and he seems to dwell very much on a continuance of our intercourse as friends. If we can meet again on familiar terms and he will give up all other ideas, I think possibly I might be a pleasure to him, and he to me. I have read in novels of these sort of intimacies, and always imagined that they might be much more natural than any other intercourse between men and women, but perhaps it can only take place in novels. I pity a man like Mr. Higginson, who feels the emptiness of a solitary life; for he has not the resources of a woman, cannot surround himself with home occupations or the ties from loving services, that only women can render, and has no friends and sympathizers as women have, for it seems to me that it is only women who can be real sympathizers. Men are so busy in their own objects, so full of business, that their time and thoughts are none too much for themselves; but a woman's life is in others, and her nature makes it easy and natural to be interested in their affairs. Not that I do this, but I see how it might be done, and try to come nearer to my ideal. A true woman lives for herself only in others—a difficult attainment, but we *can* be even perfect.

Beverly   10 August

Father has not been very well for a day or two.

Nellie Hooper and Sadie Cabot came over in a wagon after breakfast, to ask me to dine, which I did, and had a *right jolly day.*[51] We sat until dinner in S.'s room, which is charming, filled with prints and tasteful things, and opening on to a balcony, perfectly shaded in vines, from which the view of the water is beautiful. We worked rug work,

and discussed the affairs of the nation as only girls can do I believe; for
men do not seem to have this tranquil yet delightful social intercourse, the fingers busy, the mind and affections in full play. Even
women only have rare and small tastes of it, in perfection, with
congenial people and circumstances. After dinner we three girls and
Louis C. rode to the Essex woods, making the most of our time for
fun and talk. S. and Nellie are both good hands at either. I expected
to remain to tea and Louis drive me home, but it looked like rain,
and Mother appeared in the carriage before tea.

On my return found H. Amory was with the John Lowells and had
been to see me.

1 October

Mother's cold seems worse. Jenny and I after breakfast walked to
Anna Loring's to walk with her, but we had spent too long a time at
the piano, and after waiting for us, she had gone out. Last evening
she and Joe Quincy passed with us, Mother having asked them in the
morning. I had met them before for a minute on our return from
walking. He looked very handsome and very well, having more flesh
than usual, a very great improvement, he talked very well and stut-
tered less than usual. But he of course as in all such cases got fastened
in a seat between Mother and Father, and I and Jenny talked with
Anna L. on the other side of the room; so I could only speak to him
across the others, and of course in a very restrained way.

It made me feel sorry and disappointed. It is best for him, and
pleasanter for me that we should not meet often; but when we do I
long very much that we should see each other in true relations, in a
simple way. Surface intercourse after so much far different is very
painful.

Jenny and I like two school girls—as we are *not*—wasted our precious hours of sleep last night in talk. I spoke with her for the first time freely on all subjects, and though I have so long controlled my desire to do so, I do not regret my broken determination as I feared. God knows if I have done wrong, in showing sacred things to the eyes even of a true friend; but it all came out, without my thought or intention, and it has relieved me so much. Not that any one can do much for me; but talking of trials seems to put them in a new light, shifts the burden from a place it has made tender from longer pressure, on to a stronger and healthier spot. I dwell on things so much, that I become uncertain whether they really exist except in my diseased imagination, or at any rate, whether I do not see them through a magnifying glass. Jenny has told me too a great deal about herself, more than I ever knew. She is blinded in some ways, but a more earnest true-hearted woman does not exist.

After strolling about in the woods this morning, we returned to dress and dine with Sarah Cary. All the family but her brother and grandmother are in town. She read us some of Fanny's letters.

Boston   17 October

Our evening passed as usual, Ned was at home, but was tired, and having nothing to do but read or go to sleep chose the latter. Mother knitted, I sewed, and Father slept, waking every five minutes to ask what we said, or to criticize a remark. It makes me heavy of heart. If Powell returns to live at home, how can he stand such a home, where the intervals are small between dead silence and restraint, or self-control under irritability? How can Ned feel it too, but as a place of stupidity, how can Mother, longing for rest and cheerfulness, but as a place of trial? My God, can I do anything? I say it twenty times a day. I can learn to bear better, to forgive and forget quicker, to love on and overlook, but can I never make it brighter, easier. Oh God help me!

I went down to ask Father to drive Mother out in the morning. I said it pleasantly, feeling so, but Father thought I took a great deal on myself, thought I knew best, was always in opposition to him, and seemed to feel that he cared nothing for Mother or her health. I did not mind much the complaint of me, for it was very likely merely temporary feeling; but it showed me how hopelessly blind habit has rendered him, as to what he might do for her health, and for her pleasure. It showed me besides that he had seen my growing perception of this, which I ought to subdue more carefully, lest it may hurt him, and do no good. I would not in aiding her oppose him, I know that often I do not feel lovingly as I ought, do not keep the perfect respect in my manner I might; but it is very, very hard, my only excuse, which so help me God, I will not make use of long. If all my life and energies can avail they shall be given to this service, though I say it in bitter weeping, for my hope is small. Again I cry, God help me!

Boston   6 December

Have been to Winchester, staying with Carrie Curtis since Wednesday. It is always pleasant to me to go there, the repose is so perfect, and Carrie such a rare example of cheerfulness and contentment. I like it but I do not feel as if I could ever become sufficiently self-sustained, or unambitious, to bear it as my lot for life. I look on her entire satisfaction with amazement.

We talked and sewed. One morning I took a most exquisite walk to Mystic Pond and on to the hills that overlook it, where, the weather was so mild, I sat down, and imagined summer returning. A day or two in the country, as secluded as this, has the same effect as going to the top of a hill, it lays out your life in full view before you, maps it in its true proportions, undistorted by a half-view or the more immediate nearness of parts of it.

I was sorry to lose Dr. Bellows's last lecture. The last I heard on Tuesday was glorious, on the effects and glories of liberty, ending by an earnest recommendation of enthusiasm, to the young, sadly needed. It was original, sound, brilliant and eloquent, a splendid lecture, the most so I ever heard. He excites me as no other man ever did. He satisfies my intellect, rouses my energies, nerves my enthusiasm, excites my loftiest aspirations. He is splendid. He dined with us on Monday, and was very agreeable. I would give a great deal that I value, to hear him often, have him within reach. He provides just the external stimulus I need. I could not help feeling, that there was the man, the type I mean, I could marry; and is not the great secret of love, the meeting something in others, that has the power to stimulate and develop our higher nature? Many people have little faith in him as a man, and perhaps it is so. Many a man is nobler as a teacher, than an individual soul, and lacks the forces to carry out his own ideal.

17 *December*

Today is with me one of the days that ought to be marked, and is as much an epoch in my spiritual world, as any great temporal change would be in my physical world. Who can say what influences cause the mind at times to arise and live, the soul to throw off its lethargy of habit, and rise to a new level of feeling? Life today seems to me sad in its earnestness, its realities, its pathos. I weep for myself and my race and I rejoice through my tears, for is not the end glorious, though the way dark?

Last evening I went to a hard times party at Fanny Huntington's, that is to say a multitude fed on cake and tea, but my mental food was much richer than usual.[52] Generally a crowd of my fellows hardens me, I smile and turn inwardly to stone, but last night I could have wept for the miserable, or rejoiced with the happy. Why my sympathies remained untrammeled I am sure I cannot say. One reason was perhaps that I stood side by side with Joe Quincy and John Higginson, and knew that to them the world seemed a hard and a solitary dwelling-place. Were we not all, every man and woman there, pining for what we had not, longing for the unattained, and often the unattainable? Not all, or at least it seemed so, a few had gained what they felt the highest gift of earth, a resting-place for their souls. But I was a wanderer still, and saw no light, no end. Walter Cabot, of whom I have heard so much, stood near me, and I liked his face much more than any other in the room, no doubt because it was the only one I did not know.[53] I invested him with all the charms of my ideal, I welcomed him as my great good, the longed-for, the satisfier. I pictured the future, the blessed sympathy, the great rest, no more uncertainty, no more hopes and fears, my life until now in the bud had flowered, the crisis had come, I was face to face with its glories, its duties. The world faded, what to me were men's smiles or frowns, had I not found what I sought, was not my bark so long tempest-tossed, the toy of the waves, now moored in the bay, and prepared to sail on the straight voyage of life? Sunshine was in my soul, God seemed near me, I loved each tried human soul around me, *they* still wandered, *I* had found my home. Alas! alas! the awakening comes to show that it was but a dream, I am still buffeted by the waves of doubt, I am still lured by false lights, my way is lost, I long and get not, I am weary and find not rest, I am alone, alone, and the black waters surge and seem as if they would overwhelm my soul. And yet, Oh my God, there is a light burning bright and strong, if I would raise my eyes to see, tears make it dim to my eyes but it will not fail to guide me, and if I would trust it, I should forget all greater joys. Oh my soul, poor, weak, wandering, why do you not look to the glories of the skies, why do you not see the arm stretched out to cheer and sustain, why do you not believe? Be truthful, be humble, be loving, be true to God and thyself, and oh do not forget thy brother, who may not see yet even the brightness your poor eyes can catch, and who would fain have help from thee.

Walter Cabot, Jenny says, feels all for Loulie G. Of course she knows nothing, but she thinks so, and *she* will never answer his call. She has had her disappointment, her bitter bitter trial, and she is God's own. How unworthy I feel beside her, for the earth earthy; and will I refuse the bitter draught which will purify my soul? We are weak and erring, we are blind and earthy, but the heavens lie above us, and the way up though steep and full of thorns, has been worn by the feet of saints.

Will years roll on and bring me peace, shall I read this with eyes that have seen into the heavens, and forgot the gilding of earth, and shall I perhaps gently smile as I recall my youth's struggles and doubts, its faltering faith and vain longings, and thank God that His Providence led me to heaven, instead of leaving me satisfied with earth? Oh life, great mystery, thy stings are sharp, thy meshes strong but thy teaching none can resist, and oh my soul, have faith, look up, the heavens are eternal, and full of light, and God sits on His glorious throne, stretching His loving arms to thee! Shall earth blind thy eyes, or weakness check thy way to the everlasting joys? Live and love, be strong and endure unto the end! He is thy friend, thy aid, thy end, thy love. Is He not enough, canst thy mind compass His glories, His powers, and He is thine if thou wilt seek Him?

CHAPTER FIVE

1858 – 1860

These two and a half years of Elizabeth's life are dominated by Walter Cabot. She engages in the social round. She still thinks of some of the other men in her life—Josiah Quincy, through her surprise, shock, and indignation at his early engagement, all the way to the day of his wedding. But, having recognized Walter as measuring up to her ideal of a man, within a year and a half she admits to her diary that she loves him. At first she thinks him committed to another woman—and of course everyone is a member of the same social circle. Sometimes she thinks him indifferent, or no more than friendly, and argues with herself that her contrary impressions are mistaken. Sometimes she thinks him lacking in self-confidence, sometimes uncertain of his economic future. She wonders whether she has shown her own feelings too much. Month after month, he is absent or, when meeting her, fails to make any declaration. She tries to understand. She struggles to reach a condition of resignation, even resignation to single life. Often she sinks into despair. Then, one more encounter causes him to change. He takes the vital step. At once her mood swings into exultation.

With a decision so central to her life, with feelings so intense that a single hopeful meeting with Walter can change her view of everyone she meets that day, this period calls for the printing of the highest proportion of the original diary. Yet so nearly single is the story that very few problems of identification or explanation arise.

1858

Boston   13 February

Went out last evening to perhaps the dullest party I ever was at, at Mrs. Sargent's in Brookline, though personally I was in good spirits, and therefore enjoyed myself. The difficulty was the scarcity of gentlemen. I talked with Miss Higginson most of the evening. It was only surpassed by a ball the night before at Mrs. Paiges's, which was worse, because I was very tired.

This morning a large party went in the ten o'clock cars to Dedham to skate. Walking a little way along the railroad, we put on our skates on a little pond by the side, and then skating up a brook running through the woods, emerged on Wiggam Pond, a sheet of ice clear as unfrozen water, and embosomed in woods. Nothing could be prettier, nothing more delightful. The party twenty or thirty dotted over various parts, their shadows following them as they glided about, and the grass and trees looking almost green and spring-like under the bright sun, though the thermometer had fallen to 3° above zero the night before. My skating has come to a stand, as far as progress goes, but I suppose I shall take a start again. At any rate I can glide about independently, and enjoy myself more than in almost anything else I do. The open air, invigorating exercise and country scene give just the excitement to make one thoroughly enjoy the pleasant natural companionship.

But there is a tinge of sadness to the gayest song, an imperfection in the greatest pleasures of *this* life, and the old sad longings, made a running undertoned accompaniment to all my enjoyment. Why? Because two of my fellow mortals were tasting the bliss I pray for but touch not. Oh the selfishness of our souls, the weakness of our best purposes, the feebleness of our faith! Walter Cabot is devoted to Nellie Hooper, and before many weeks are passed they will be bound for life, or my eyes tell false tales. Indeed, indeed I am not sunk so low yet as to begrudge their bliss; if it broke my heart I would bless her and wish her well; and it will not break my heart, for it is tough and can bear many a throb. Nellie of all people I would wish well to, she has struggled courageously through many hard trials, and her triumph has made her no less kind and genial. She has an honesty and straightforwardness and fearlessness of the truth few women possess, and she has an affectionate kind nature. If this great happiness comes to her she deserves it, as far as any of us can deserve our blessings. Walter C. comes nearer my ideal than any man I know. I am sure from what I hear from his family and friends that he is affectionate and sunny-tempered, and I know that he unites refinement of taste and intellect with great manliness. He has a quiet dignity and reserve of manner, which always make the reserved riches below more charming when shown; and an occasional glimpse of enthusiasm, and of tenderness even, show what he is capable of. Nellie was quiet and much as usual, but something in her face told me all. How easily I could have burst into tears and prayed her to let me get a glimpse of what it was to taste the longed-for joy; those know only who have felt so—and their name is legion. I have reasoned and reasoned and reasoned, I have looked to Heaven and to Earth, but found no peace. Why am I to be cut off from life's crowning blessing, why all the world pass on, and the gate closed to me? Why, my soul big with a world of love and aspiration, and hidden life, why should it rest unappreciated, unknown, unused, only to feed on itself? Why? But hush, I am ashamed, I would not complain, I will not sin, God wills that it should be so, and in His goodness He will make the way clear.

I need not search for the cause nor the effect; it is the way my feet must go, and I will try to remember it is my Father who orders. I sometimes feel, I do today, that there is a deep selfishness of soul in me, that only the necessity which a solitary life gives, of finding all one's joys in those of others, can ever eradicate; that God sees that and is training me. Will I then resist? If I could see this to be clearly so, and could choose, should I doubt? Oh thank God that it is not left to me to have the added pain of deciding!

16 February

A slight fall of snow has spoiled the skating I suppose. Rode out this evening to the Cabots' to theatricals. They had a very large and rather fashionable party. I talked to Peter Brooks, and Edmund Dwight and Walter Cabot, then sat side with Harriet at the theater, and passed a very calm nice evening. The house is a model one for a country home, and the little greenhouse which serves as a passage way to the theater, enchanting, full of drooping vines and beautiful flowers, and lighted by colored lanterns. The plays were excellent, as a whole, several of the parts being wonderfully good, and several overacted, or hardly at all, but none bad. Clover Hooper sat in from of me, but Nellie had already been, and was not asked. Walter was very polite, and carried me into the supper room, etc. I still like him extremely, but am very calm. My furores are of short duration, luckily for me.

13 March

Went out today to Fresh Pond to skate, I fear for the very last time, and did not do much skating, as the wind was like a roaring lion. However, Mr. Savage and I sat considerably on the lee side of a boat in the sun, and I made little excursions up the pond to be blown down again, and it was very pleasant. H. A., G. Curtis, Mr. Higginson and Mr. Curtis's sister were our party.

An awful accident has just happened to the George Barnards, enough to make one's hair turn gray. This afternoon Mrs. B. was at the fair, where she was a manager, and Mr. Barnard and the children were at the theater; while Sarah had returned home to dress, etc., and had promised to return to the fair at three o'clock, with Hollis Hunnewell. While waiting for him, she sat down before the fire in the parlor, her bonnet and cloak being on the table. Her grandmother went into the upper room for some object, and was recalled by dreadful screams, and rushing down, found Sarah enveloped in flames. She tried to raise the large Persian mat, but being very small could do little with it, and Sarah, perfectly wild with fright, broke from her, and rushed down to the kitchen. Here was only the cook, who tried to throw over her a coat, but she was so surrounded by flames that it was of no kind of avail; as she came in she exclaimed that she was burning to death, and after rushing to the door to call the manservant, fell. The woman rushed into the next house, Mr. Sturgis's. Miss Sarah Howe the Reveres' cousin was on the doorstep, and went in immediately. The scene she describes seems too awful for reality. Crouched in one corner of the room was a black mass, but for the general outlines indistinguishable for a human figure. She was on her knees, her arms crossed, her hands rigidly drawn or clenched, her head bowed down, no hair, no trace of garments, no color of humanity left, and enveloped in the densest smoke. Even the ear-rings in her ears were melted, the steel hoops of her skirt so hot that they burned rings on the floor as they fell, the door sill on which she had stood for a moment burned, the door she had fled through scorched all up and down. A martyr's death in its agony. The agony of suffering seems almost beyond comprehension, in those few minutes, the terror, the utter loneliness and absence of help, the terrific bodily pain.

Just 21 with everything gay around her and in the future, every little want indulged, with her family doting on this one daughter, many friends, paid servants, all that could be provided to shield her from every rough wind, and afford her gratification; and yet her destiny was to burn to death in broad day in a crowded city, surrounded by friends—alone, unaided, by slow torture.[1]

Had an extra rehearsal of club tonight, but few could think of anything but Sarah Barnard.

17 April

Went to bed sick last night so could not write my journal. By it I escaped a lancer party at Mrs. Davis Sears' which I did not care for.[2]

In the morning went to Jenny's for German, which as a matter of course we did little of; then James Savage came in, and walked home with me, and we had a very nice little talk. After dinner, with a bad headache, I went to call on Miss Taylor, and then to Mary Q's, who is lame—sprained her ankle, but has driven out today. Feeling sick I left soon, but met Joe at the door, who asked me to walk down the mall with him. He said he went to church Sunday to tell me what he wanted to say now, which was that he thought it would be better for him and me both not to think of seeing more of each other than politeness demanded at present. He hoped that I would not consider it any want of feeling, any change. On the contrary it was because there was no change; and that though he hoped and believed that if our way separated more definitely, we might become true friends to each other, he did not think it possible or best now. He gave up all hope of any change in me. If there could be, he thought he might ask me to trust in his honor and delicacy and show him first; but of course there was little hope, and if I heard of him at the Huntingtons' and in various ways, and saw that he was cold in his manner to me, I must understand the cause. If there were ever a time when a man, a young man, could be of any use to me, he prayed me to think of him first as ready to do anything he could; and so after a little formal talk I reached home sick mentally and physically. But untouched—my heart instead of beating, was cold as ice. What is it that chills and stiffens me so? I think if he could show one spark of emotion, I should melt, but though I know he is feeling acutely, I can see nothing. He speaks like an automaton who has learned his part, and I connect as much meaning to his words. I could only say, after a long pause, that I was sorry, I had hoped it might be otherwise, but I felt unable as a little child to judge, and I trusted to him. And I shook hands and said a goodbye, which I feel is final. Henceforth Joe Quincy will be a stranger, whom I shall care to know about very much, and shall be interested in his fate, but whom I never hope to meet again on any but the most outside and formal footing. Oh it is hard to give up people who have acted in your real life, who have cared for you with their whole souls, and it is hard to break the cord with your own hands! But though he has a great many things that I most prize, a great many things most rare in men, though I long for one to care for, and here is one of singular purity and elevation, and mind, yet he has not touched my heart, he has no power over my soul. I cannot care for him, and so perchance I write the fiat which is to condemn me to life-long solitude and loneliness. I try to see the right and follow it—God's will be done.

3 May

Have returned from a Reynolds gathering at the Reveres'—one of those trying evenings, when [one] seems a spectator of life and happiness, merely, aloof, shut out. As I sat in the corner, watching Jenny and Annie Torrey, as one would regard little children, busy with experiences we had outgrown, the bitter thoughts would overwhelm me. Have I come to this, is here the end of all my dreams of love and life, I the one put aside, the bystander? But thanks be to God I could be very sad, and yet rejoice in their happiness. As John and Mr. Loring came into the room, the beaming on their faces, answered by loving looks, gave me a thrill of joy too, and I thanked Heaven for this gift to my dear friend. Why do I say thanked Heaven—I dislike the word used so—I thanked my Father, who is tender and loving, who strengthens my soul, and teaches me holy lessons. Dear Jenny, she is very tender, very thoughtful. Would I could let her see, how her tender words and love, drive out the black loneliness of my heart! And sometimes I am tempted to ask, why am I lonely? I have a heart, pure and fine, all my own, why should I thus put it aside, as if necessarily worthless, and ask another? I have at times a feeling of presentiment that Joe Quincy is my fate, and it is less impossible to me than it once was. I never felt it to be a thing to dislike, or dread, but simply a thing impossible. Now again and again rises the question, why? Has he not what I most prize, intellectually and morally, may I not be throwing away my life's happiness from mere fear and indecision? If I settle into an old maid—and is not the probability on that side—I know from my character and tastes that it is settling to a life of endurance, of struggle with myself. I may become peaceful through discipline, blessed by rising above the world, but not happy or satisfied. My happiness will be beyond and above life, life itself trodden as the road to Heaven. One must tremble and doubt, ere they choose such a life. I think I never should fall in love quickly or easily, nor any one else fall in love with me: it must be the growth of time. I cannot help feeling that it accords with my character and experience, to take a great step as this, after much delay, and doubt. And yet, oh my God, the other side rises before me, and I feel as if on the very brink of a precipice. Is this the way in which one should marry? Is it noble or worthy? Am I not driven to it by fear and policy and weakness, rather than by feeling, and nobleness? I would marry, my chance is fading, I will grasp ere it is too late. It may turn out well. Will this stand in presence of my highest and best feelings? Is it not worldliness in a disguise, weakness under the mask of common sense? Oh God and Father, help me, help me, for I am blind, and weak, and foolish. If I could only know him! Sometimes I believe him a god shut in by weak flesh; then I change, and he seems the weak, cold, dreaming mortal, with a little intellect to deceive short-sighted fellow men. And how can I ever know more? Well *L'homme propose, Dieu dispose*; the years will come and go; and I shall grow old, and die, according to His will who made me. I can submit, if I cannot choose.

14 May

This evening received a long letter from Mr. Higginson, asking what he had done to make me so cold suddenly in my manner, and what he could do to change it again. I am very glad that we should under-stand each other, as I now shall have no fear of my conduct being mis-understood by him; and he knows exactly how I feel, for I wrote an answer which I shall send tomorrow. He does not speak of any other relation between us, than the frankest friendship; and though I think it is impossible for a young woman to see much of a man, without exciting very disagreeable observation, I am sure I shall be very glad to do all I can to make his life brighter, for it seems now very forlorn. There must be something wrong, morbidness, want of force, that should cause such a state of feeling; but it is the case, and he does not suffer the less because it is a constitutional infirmity, as I believe it must be. I wrote him as kindly as I could; but I did not conceal the truth that it would be very hard for us to be much at present to one another. If Father were a different person, it would be easier; because at home I could see him a great deal, but it makes Father uneasy always to have any drop in, he cannot comprehend the kind of relation, and I have no peace at all. Poor Mr. Higginson, I am ashamed of myself, that the silly feeling of his being a young man, should influence my sympathy and kind feeling for him.

Father tonight found fault with Mother and me, for not courting the world more, on my account. He feels that I am rather dropping out of fashionable life, and I daresay thinks too that my chance of marrying in it is diminishing. This is not the only time that he has showed this feeling; and tonight I tried as far as I could to show him how I felt, how much less I valued the world of fashion, than the society of literary and high-minded though retired people. I feel that Father ought to know that I can never marry for wealth of position or eligibility in any way. I must care for my husband, and to care I must find in him what will satisfy my highest nature. Father's intellect makes him see things at their true value, and yet his early education and habits are so strong that he often is blinded to what he really believes. He was so good about it. After I came up to bed he followed, and as I passed through the entry, he stopped me, and kissed me, and said perhaps he had spoken more strongly than he intended. I could only say that I had thought nothing of it, and kiss him with true affection; but oh that I had thrown my arms round his neck and shown him how I really cared for him, for I think from the reserve in which we live, he sometimes disbelieves affection. Why are we not warmer, why not oftener draw to the surface those deep feelings of love, which become stiff from lying packed away out of sight always? Life would be so much sweeter, little trials be so much sooner forgotten if the tender love of those around us was oftener manifested to our weak human eyes.

Beverly   14 July

The girls and myself took "the doctor" this morning in the open wagon and drove to Miss Cunningham's; but she was out, and we then paid a visit to Kitty Lowell, and I to Mrs. Dexter. The latter was very cordial and agreeable. I think she is thankful to see a young face near her. People find great fault with her for her unsocial feelings; but I do not know if I can understand people remarkably or not, yet it seems to me as if I understood her from the very little I have seen of her better than her so-called friends. This sounds certainly cool and conceited!

Charles L. brought Dr. Brace of Catskill down with him to add another occupant of this elastic mansion. As we were all seated in the parlor awaiting dinner, he gave me a note from Mary Quincy which startled me almost out of my self-possession. It began, "I write to announce," and I exclaimed at what I thought to be the news of her own engagement. But another line made me see that it was the engagement of her brother Joe—and to Fanny Huntington! If I had been struck violently on the chest, I could not have felt more faint for a moment; and weak as I felt it to be, I could only restrain my tears long enough to go upstairs without attracting notice. Why should I care? Indeed why should I not rejoice, no longer to be a source of pain? Oh man, man, fickleness should be inscribed on thy brow, change on thy forehead! I returned to the parlor, and I have laughed more than usual. The afternoon has been passed in frolicking like children in the barn, but an undertone sounds ever from my heart, unloved, uncared for. It appears to me in a hundred different lights as I think of it. How can a man love a woman for six years and then offer his heart to an acquaintance of as many months? When was the turn of feeling? How long has he spoken truth, and when first deceived me. In April he told me—unless I dreamed it—that he thought he could not yet bear to see too much of me. He *meant* that he did not *want* to see too much of me I presume, for I hope he cared for Fanny then for her sake. And this is the love that to poor Fanny is life and happiness. What would she say, were I to tell her all? What does it mean? What can it mean? Do all men say one thing to mean another? Is all love a pretense? Or is constancy a young girl's dream? I did not expect, certainly not desire that he should pass his life mourning for me, but I did think that his desperate despair would need a *little* more time before it could turn to bliss. Oh it is hard; for I must either believe that he is unworthy, or that all human love is words, words. I dare say I may be uncharitable. I am willing to think that he may have had a genuine feeling for me, and may now have a genuine feeling for her, but it is in a way I cannot understand or imagine.

The surprise was equally great to me on Fanny's side; for we discussed the Quincys very fully before her visit to them and afterwards, Joe included. We both declared our expectation of never being married, and she was as frank and natural as usual.

I have thought for some months that it was a thing that might happen in the course of time. But now—well I will never believe in appearances or assurances again. I could never have married Joe Quincy, our natures were not suited to each other, and I cannot but be glad to see the disappointment of a human being turned to gladness. Therefore it is all as it should be; but I cannot drive from my heart a deserted feeling. I suppose I have depended more than I knew, on the knowledge that I was loved, and it is better for me that such an equivocal support should fall away; but I feel its loss. Now no one beyond my own looks to me for hope or love. My time is going, I can help and cheer, a little longer a Mother and Father will look upon me as first, in love and help. But after that I must be content to live in a world of human souls, and be second everywhere, living on and for myself as first.

Blue Hill   *18 October*

Aunt P. moved today. Mother well enough to take a drive round the hill—the woods more changed than before, and very brilliant. I had a long talk with her instead of Father. I cannot alter much; but I can relieve her from some care, and I have determined to take the house-keeping. I found her more willing than I feared. She feels so feeble this autumn that it seems less possible to her to go on as she has. One great step seems gained. She has agreed to let me undertake the whole responsibility but I know what this means, and that really to take on myself the care, I shall have to struggle for each step. She is willing to give up; but she has little faith in my powers, and she cannot be decided sufficiently to feel that for the sake of making a change and trying an experiment, she will overlook many things. But it must be done. I feel strong and brave though anything but sanguine; but I can do my very best, and leave the rest in faith. How hard it is to get people out of the old rut of habit first, and then to keep them out! After all this, should I succeed, I expect hard work, for I am a novice. The work to be done is considerable. Mother has been a hard worker, almost a drudge. Therefore I can never slight, and I hate it, I think it wrong, this sacrificing life and almost happiness to little niceties and little economies; but in this case it must be for the present. I shall have to give up reading, much social pleasure, skating often and other amusements and all else, also learn to reprimand, manage, order, as is especially difficult for me, and never say a word. It will not be easy, and I wish to look it fairly in the face, that the trial of finding it worse than I feared may not be added. But if I can only see that it relieves Mother in the least degree, it will be a constant pleasure. Nothing is worse than feeling the bitterness of an evil, and being able to do nothing to cure it. I feel invigorated already in the thought. What I need most is patience to wait as well as work on, and I *will* have it—God help me!

Aunt P. and Powell went in at three o'clock.

Boston   19 October

Came to town with my bag at nine, to get a chambermaid and arrange the house a little. This one step in the right direction. Have worked very hard all day.[3] The weather very hot and beautiful, nearly 80° but scorching on the bricks. Mother told me yesterday of a long conversation she had with Father about herself and me a few days since. He is very fond of Louise, she is so gay and affectionate and unaffected, and feels in strong contrast our habitual silence and coldness and rigidity. I feel it all, I see her charm, I see bitterly Mother's silence and melancholy and coldness of manner, but still more bitterly my own. No one can see more clearly than I do my utter unfitness to please, my constraint of manner, my silence and extreme reserve and repression of feeling, my solemn-ness and constant proper sensibleness. But no one can see as I do how impossible it is for me to change it. No one can know how an utter bitterness of heart, a sort of hopelessness, subdues every impulse, and makes all laughter unnatural, impossible. How often a determination to bear patiently and gently covers over with a still outside, a sense of injustice and indignation that burns my life away! No one can know how the living from infancy in the consciousness that every movement will be criticized, every impulse moderated, every strong feeling and desire repressed to the level of perfect propriety, has made me shut from sight all emotion gay or warm, and made it wear away imprisoned, destroying my vitality with it. Now the spring, the elasticity of spirit, the lightness of heart, the simplicity of unconsciousness of self is gone; and any attempt to recover them on my part, would be an artificial absurd imitation. My nature is quiet, my spirits even, not gay, and the result of nature and education can never be changed, but by a course of education and influences of an opposite tendency. If Father knew how intensely I longed for someone to draw me out of myself, someone so gentle and tender, so full of faith in me as to inspire me with the confidence to open my whole heart, and give out with trustful unfearing freedom some of the deep love and tenderness within me, he would be more thoughtful of his treatment of me. For he has the power to do it. If he knew how an affectionate word, the least little thoughtful attention, the least opening of his own heart, opened mine, he would do it oftener. For it is impossible for the daughter to begin, at least for me, awkward and sensitive as I am.

1859

Boston   12 February

Anna Loring came last evening to tell me bad news, yet not altogether unexpected. Mary Q's engagement to Dr. Minot is broken off.[4]

I went down to see her, poor child, this morning and she is suffering a great deal and has suffered more. Their mutual unfitness for each other has been realized by both for months, I should imagine almost from the first. His smallness of mind has oppressed her like a nightmare. I can understand it all, excepting why she was ever engaged. The only reasons I can understand are, that her mother never allowed a day to pass, without impressing on her the necessity of marrying, till she began to feel as if it were a necessity too. She was fond of Frank as a brother, she respected his noble character, his principles, disinterestedness, and high aims; she was at Lenox where everyone worshipped him; his devotion to her touched her heart; and the very contrast he afforded to all that she had been used to from childhood made her feel as if this would be the right thing for her, that once bound together they should sympathize more entirely, and she should find rest to her soul—rest from worldliness, constant excitement, and the consequent emptiness of her life. But alas, brought nearer to each other, his wants were more oppressive. Used to constant intellectual interest and activity, she could not enter into his absorption in little every-day matters, he could not follow her into her wider sphere of thought. She talked, and saw that he did not understand her; she let him talk, and was infinitely bored, and to go on so for life—she could not bear it. But it is a dreadful thing for her, not a favorite in Boston at any time, and he so much esteemed. She will be severely blamed, and coldly treated. It will be difficult for any man to approach her again; and it is no slight thing to lose the devotion of a human being, whose every thought was for her happiness. After such excitement too comes a reaction, and everything must be vapid, objectless, life empty and hopeless. Then for poor Mary her home is a place of trial, not of rest.

1 March

Went to the exhibition of fencing tonight with Ned and Harriet Amory, at Papanti's. I enjoy it. It gives the manly side of men, which women seldom see in the same way. Tom Perkins was the handsomest man, Dr. Coolidge the prettiest fencer, a fencing-master from New York seemed to me the best fighter, and the match between Walter and Edward Cabot was one of the best because they were nearly matched, and both very good. W. looked superbly, and it was pleasant to see him roused from his usually dormant state.[5]

20 March

The spring has opened unusually early; but after some lovely days, a terrific wind, cold as if blowing from icebergs, reminds one of the second winter to come, before summer shows itself.

Have just come from hearing Dr. Dewey at his own church, one of the splendid sermons, by which he lifts you beyond all small, low and temporary things into realms that seem beyond the reach of our everyday grovelling souls. It was the clearest statement I ever heard of the testimony in favor of Christ, His existence, divinity and mission, and a striking argument of His fitness and our need, drawn from the great capacities of human nature, and its actual state of depravity.

Our own church we quitted with many ceremonies last Sunday, and though I passed seven hours in trying hard with the various ministers I heard, to feel sorry, I did not succeed.[6] I never liked the church, never felt at home there, never associated with it feelings of peculiar rest, or spiritual elevation; in fact on the contrary it is connected with conscientious struggles to find satisfying what was not, and stimulating what was depressing. Nor is this the fault of Dr. Gannett. The institution of church-going is to my experience a most faulty one; and the only reason for continuing it seems to me that I

see just now no better way of putting in practice the ideas and principles on which it is founded, and which are as worthy as the practice
of them is imperfect. Today we meet at the Lowell Institute, but
Mother and I thought we would take the opportunity to hear Dr.
Dewey.

Have passed a good part of this week past, in making collars and
sleeves for the fair, and looking for a present for Jenny.

Paul Revere was married on Thursday.[7] Jenny wrote me a note
which made me suddenly feel how seldom I thanked God for the
great blessing of a friend—a friend tender and true, a friend to help
me upwards, always ready to cheer and sympathize, a friend between
whom and me there are no gulfs of experience. For we have grown up
friends, and with hearts and lives mutually laid open, as far as human
hearts can be; for there is a holy of holies in every breast, which no eye
but God ever sees, I suppose.

Spring has come, and already the people who have been my world,
for six months, have faded away from my life, like the figures on a
vanishing picture. They hold no true place in my life, their places are
filled up, but how unsatisfactory this artificial intercourse.

Every year my experience brings up the same problem, never
solved; where the fault lies in the intercourse now carried on in civi-
lized society between young men and women? And it is not of
theoretical interest alone. Each spring I pass through the same trial of
disappointment, bitterness and struggle, each summer I recover, each
autumn feel strong and self-dependent, each winter gradually lose my
equilibrium, to suffer for it again in the spring. This afternoon met
Mary Parkman and walked home with her. She breathes a new air
into my lungs, gives a new impetus to my energies, invigorates my
whole being in the most wonderful manner. Life, before empty and

dark, suddenly seems precious, full of great opportunities, great interests.

8 May

A summer's day in heat and in beauty. I have given up going to church until this afternoon; and am passing the morning in writing and trying anew to settle life and my soul, adjust them one to the other, a task never finished, ever to be begun anew. Facts are but small things in their own importance; but they are the landmarks of life, therefore I am scrupulous as I can be, to note them here; and how big with influence to us are some, which in themselves seem small and commonplace!

Jenny's wedding would have left a heavy blank on my heart but that the blessed manual occupations, that press on us, came rushing in, and I did not stop to feel or think. Dress, visits, the hundred details necessary to be executed in preparing for leaving town have filled every moment. Two new engagements equally surprising to me have come out: Martha Rogers and John Perry, a fortnight ago, and this last week Willy Amory and Nellie Brewer. Powell writes us that he is decidedly on his way home, and I think he may be here in a month or six weeks.[8] I am beginning to realize what it will be to me. I have been afraid to dwell on it, and have turned my mind from it always; but now when we begin to prepare for him, to count the days, Oh God Thou art very gracious to me. What dost Thou not give me?

And a new interest has taken possession of my life. I never thought I could care for any one, but I have seen him. Does he love me? I cannot know, I dare not hope, I cannot despair. I try to wait with patience and faith, but oh how hard it is. If he does not—and I cannot but feel that I have too many blessings to receive this also—if he does not it may become a *more* precious and blessed thing to me, for I know that this is the crisis of my life. After this I shall no longer search for what I know I cannot find on earth, one more tie to earthly things will be severed. Oh what a wonderful, what a blessed thing is life; sorrow is but an aid, and leaves a happiness which is divine, a happiness of heaven which we can never even imagine until earthly pleasures begin to fail to please! I write as if tired of earth, as if a long life of suffering had deprived me of every worldly blessing; and in fact I have every good gift, but thanks be to God, and His blessed influences, I have still more. I begin to see also the heavens, and before their glory, earth pales. On the contrary I can enter upon life now with tenfold vigor and interest. It is our present sphere, rich with opportunities, gifts, pleasures, discipline, to be developed by never-ceasing endeavor and activity; but if its happiness were all, we should have a pain in the soul which would weaken every faculty, dull every feeling. If our souls have tasted of immortal happiness, then is a disappointment like the prick of a pin, so small in the comparison. And yet, Oh God, if it be possible let this cup pass from me. It is so sweet to be beloved, to be ever with one whose inner life answers feeling for feeling with one's own. I know and try to realize that feeling paints but with bright colors, that the reality brings into the picture many sombre hues and deep shadows. I see that many things I now hardly value they have become so natural a part of life, would cause much suffering if relinquished. I know that many habits and privileges, much freedom I now prize, I could never carry with me into married life; but it is of no use, still one thing seems to me the greatest good, the highest happiness, and I can only control myself by bowing down to God's will. I know that it is right. If He can so order the universe that from the worlds, to the smallest atom, law shall govern and harmonize all, will He allow chance or disorder in the spiritual world, will He leave His children made in His likeness to the influence of chance?

How eagerly we all demand happiness! How we seek it as itself an end, and thus miss it, forgetting that to live, to live the life God means for us, to make the highest use of His precious gifts the soul, its powers and the opportunities of life, this is our high our glorious end, and that happiness is the result of the harmony, order and fullness we may attain. And yet we struggle after some circumstance, as if that could give us this blessing. Will not a tumultuous soul turn it to bitterness in our hands, will not inward peace and order make our very trials helps and blessings? Oh, unbelievers that we are! We say we believe: we know that we do not. If I truly believed that God worked always for my highest happiness, and if I heartily desired and loved that highest happiness, should I have a doubt or a moment's reluctance in accepting His will? And am I thus ready and trusting? We do not throw ourselves into our faith with enthusiasm. We do not look at each event in its highest relations, and try to make clear to ourselves that it is best. But we are told it is best, we see it is inevitable, we say that we submit, as of course we must; and then we dwell on all the disappointment it is to our worldly hopes, our low-minded desires, and think we have truly chosen God's will to our own. What an unwilling sacrifice, what a blind and forced selection of the highest good! No wonder life is better to us at the end as well as at the beginning. I used to feel sad at the coming of spring; the return of each birthday was an increasing trial to me; I seemed to be losing from my grasp all the glow, the enchantment that belong to youth, and found loss, disappointment, emptiness, joylessness the only prospect opening for the coming years. Oh how blind! And if, though with eyes dim and weak, yet now I can catch indistinct glimpses of a glory and blessedness undreamed of before, filling my soul with peace, my limbs with new vigor, my life with fresh interest, shall I not thank God with my whole heart, shall not this so overbalance every little disappointment in its great blessedness, that I shall hardly feel it? To live for God, to be allowed to perceive a little of the glory and beauty of His spirit, me, so near the brutes, to be gifted with a nature that I may train to His likeness; to be permitted to overcome trial and temptation, and so strengthen and purify myself to enter His presence; to be able to work for the world, to bless other souls, help and cheer them, to join in this stupendous and glorious scheme of the universe; to be enabled to train myself to unite with the great company of noble men and women who have made the world luminous, and be beloved by them: Oh sometimes this so comes before me in its real strength and glory that I tremble for joy. What words can express it? What trial, suffering, working, patient waiting, can seem hard for such an end, and how do the little ends of most men, the little pleasures, the little desires, sink into nothingness before it. My mortal weakness, my untrained vision will not allow me to be awake to the glorious truth but at times, and thus I suffer doubt and fear with the rest of mankind. But are not these moments of greater strength given us to encourage us, that in our times of trial we may remember them and believe in what we cannot for the moment see? And this I think is the secret (which so many never discover) of uniting our aspirations with our practical life. When the world and our mortality has shut out the heavens from our sight, we must remember that we have seen, and act with fidelity to the higher vision, not sink at once to a level with our present blindness. This is the great work of faith by which we are to guide our steps, when the light is turned from them. And now let me use this truth. Let me take my present trial as a discipline, and careful guide and control each feeling to the obedience of God's will, to trust in His loving kindness. I will try. Endeavor is the necessity, the law of progress; progress is the blessed law of life, constant, watchful, unwearied. God help me!

22 May

The rain falls as heavily as if it had had no chance of breaking loose before for weeks, instead of which it has done so most of the week. But I like it, there is a strange peacefulness in being shut into the house on a Sunday, with time to think and read calmly, when life is full; but if life seems empty, nothing is more oppressive. To me life is full, crowded, overflowing. My whole being seems in full play, and brought in closer contact with the world around. It seems strange to me to feel peaceful as I do today, when one week ago the struggle was very very bitter. How I can feel now the soreness that repressed tears had made, as if they had all accumulated and laid heavily on my very heart! I did not know before that I could feel so much physically, as a result of mental excitement. It was a new experience. But on Monday God reached out His hand to me and said you have tried to trust in me, and submit, I will show you how I watch and care for all things. If He had by a visible miracle spoken to me, I could not have had a more real sense of Him and His power.

Loulie Gardner wrote to me on Saturday to say that her saddle-horse was a very nice one that she was unwilling to sell, and she wished I would keep it with a buggy and harness, during the time she was in Europe some 18 months. Father agreed to it, if I would make all the arrangements properly, and therefore I determined on Monday to go out to Brookline to see her. After several changes and some uncertainty, I decided to take the quarter-past two cars and then walk from the depot to her house, and back again in the afternoon. The chance of meeting him was ever in my thoughts, and I had almost determined to give it up, I hated so the double-dealing with myself, of pretending to go for one reason, and really caring to go for another; but Father thought I had better see Loulie personally, so I shut all the hope I could out of my heart. It seemed so unlikely, and yet I longed to meet him once more. In the morning John Reynolds left a note from Jeanette, and my heart sank, for I thought Loulie was to be in town; but no, it was merely to ask me to take a note to her.[9] I went out early with Emily Greenough to help her buy a habit, did some more shopping, came home, ate a luncheon, and started off. The day was lovely, spring in every tree, in the air, in the sky, but the weight and struggle within me took up my thoughts. At the Common I met Jeanette waiting for her husband to join her; dear soul, she was happy at least. I hurried on to the depot, bought my ticket and entered the cars. Turning from one which seemed full, I took another, entered, and he was there. For a moment my breath was gone, the blood seemed all at my heart then all in my head, but a moment more and I was seated in an empty seat in front of him, and he was talking to me. Wm. Dexter and Miss Lizzie Guild came in, the latter stopped to speak, and I feebly offered her a seat by my side; but she said no and went in front, and I did not care. She might think what she chose, this was life or death for me. Always quiet, he seemed glad to see me, and said that usually he went out in the later cars.

At the Brookline depot we got out, and walked on, two miles and a half to his house. The birds sang, the grass seemed springing under our feet. We talked little, why talk? If he had anything to say, here was a time when he could say it. I felt no anxiety, no sorrow. As we walked on, and the way shortened, and he still spoke as he might to a friend of yesterday, I realized more and more that it was all over, that he felt nothing more, that I had but dreamed, but this was God's will, this was as unchangeable as the hills. I did not care to try to please him and win him: my love rested on the unchangeable sympathies of the soul itself. If he did not feel them so, nothing I could do could alter it. It was the nature of things. Now all accidental obstacles of time and opportunity were removed, we could act each, ourselves, and all regret left my soul. I thanked God as I walked on at his side, that He had given me this great blessing, a time when we could calmly see into each other's hearts, and then part satisfied that I had known the truth. At his house he made me enter through their grounds. He showed me his brother's house building, and the fine trees round his own home, which I never had seen well before. He stopped half-way to the garden before a bed filled with pansies and, making me sit down on a bench under the trees, picked a bunch for me, culling here and there the most beautiful. Oh what words could describe those moments, with the real world around me, near to him for the last time in this world? And yet truly was it hearts-ease that he gave me. Though I never see him again, he is as real to me henceforth, as much a part of my life, as if I passed each day with him. My life is richer, fuller for the influence, the feeling I have given him is never lost, he cannot throw away, it returns on me bringing a deeper life with it. After this we walked through the garden, through the greenhouses, along the hedge and a beautiful meadow, and turned into a little wood path. Here we soon came upon the house, and he stopped, saying he must say good-morning. I said, "and we must say goodbye too must I not?" His face became very serious and grave and he said no, he did not go until the first of June, he had wanted to call and see me, but he did not know when to find me at home. I said "in the evening we should be glad to see him"—shook hands and then turned. He was gone. But what a change this made, I could not stop to think; but I should see him again, and he cared enough to see me, he so shy, so quiet, to wish to come to my house, when he could have said goodbye then so well, so satisfactorily. Oh one word, how it lifted the great burden from my heart, which freed from such a weight bounded beyond my control, leaped to all kinds of possibilities of joys. I went in to Loulie's, saw her and the horse and said goodbye, then returned through the same grounds, my feet springing over the earth with a new energy.[10] Everything seemed to smile and bless me, the world of spirit, of beauty, of joy seemed all around me. The old world of man, with its artificial existence, its trouble and vexations, its meanness and its miserable empty pleasures, seemed to have faded like a dream. Everything took a new color, duty and pleasure and people. I met Ellen Amory and Miss Bowditch, and I longed to stop and chat with them, and be glad or sorry with them as they needed it. I met Joe Gardner, and I longed to stop and ask him how he felt, if I could not help him in the way that seemed rather hard to him. I met Gardner Hammond and Lizzie; and even they seemed invested with a new interest, and new demand on my sympathies, for my heart was so free to feel for others. I was early at the depot, and sitting down on a trunk in the sun, I had time to calm myself a little, to think as well as feel. How wonderful it had all been: how, I a young lady, he a young gentleman, acquaintances of a ballroom, how we had met as old tried friends, how all conventionalities, all stiffness had slipped away, and we had met with as much ease as if we were brother and sister! What wonderful confidence I had in him, and he in me, that we had made no pretences, said nothing for talking's sake, but just lived and acted truly! How I had disregarded proprieties, and when he said will you walk up with me, had left Miss Guild and gone with him; when he had said, sit under the trees while I pick some flowers, had sat down and forgotten time; had wandered round the grounds and through the greenhouses, and should have felt that all was natural and right if I had met the family, or any one else! I seemed to belong to him and he to me. I know full well that my confidence and joy are built on a very fragile foundation. He may like me, and have said and done all that he has, without ever dreaming of anything more than a simple sincere friendliness; but I had schooled my heart to feel that all was hopelessly over, and it is not over, and no power of mine could keep my soul in bonds longer. I had risen and broken them.

And now today I have a rest of soul from the same small cause, nothing more has happened since then. My heart has been in my mouth with every ring at the doorbell, but he has not come. One evening I heard the bell, and being upstairs I looked down. It was he. I went down, and it proved to be Caleb Curtis.

Mother has had a bad cold and been sick in her room. We have had a sewing-machine going, and I have been all the week busy as I could be, and it has been the best thing for me possible. I go round the streets insanely smiling, as if I had just heard some wonderful piece of good news; and I check myself with the thought of what a trial and disappointment may still lie before me, and how much harder to bear from the change, but it is of no use. Smile I must, until a bitter reality has chilled me forever.

I dwell on the future as little as I can. Who knows better than I should, what a change of my whole life, a day, an hour, a moment

may bring? If it is the joy I long for, do I not know too that this will
have its dark side, and if a trial I hardly dare think of is waiting for
me, God will help me, and it too has its blessedness. Jeanette is more
to me than words could ever tell. When my heart is overflowing, I
run down to her, and there is no effort in our sympathy now, for it is
all explored ground to her; and this has given me a new light to her
life, so that we meet without concealment, or regrets that we cannot
do more.

Yesterday I was to have gone to Milton to pass Sunday with Fanny
Cunningham, but the rain prevented; and now I shall not leave home
in the evening until he has gone. This week I am 25 years old, this
week will be I think the crisis of my fate. I may still be left to uncertainty all summer, indeed it seems to me probable, and I dread it
very much. Uncertainty, hope and fear contrasted are so hard to deal
with or bear; but I will wait, not speculate. I do not attempt to study
his feelings or motives. Men are so different from women, men differ
so in expressiveness themselves, that I dare not judge by appearances.
He is very shy, very deep and calm, very distrustful of himself. He
may be doubtful of my feeling, he may think that he has not known
me long or intimately enough to authorize his speaking now. He may
think it better, as he must go away, to wait until his return. I have
faith in him.

Sometimes as I write this I fear that I ought to be shocked at
feeling so, before he has given me the right to, but I am sure this is
the false propriety of the world. I am not ashamed to lay it before the
Father. I know that it is connected with the purest and best part of
my nature, unworldly, unselfish. What will the issue be? How our
hearts ache for the answer to this question!

1 June

After coming to town I went to see Jenny. He goes Friday, one day more and he is gone, gone. What does it mean? I feel at times as if I cared for nothing but to know this, what it meant. Certainly my eyes nor my ears have not deceived me; I am not dreaming when I say that he has treated me a whole winter as if he cared for me. Why did he come to call.[11] It could not be for fun, for it must have been very unpleasant fun. Has he been playing with me, as he did with Nellie Hooper? How I long to ask her the facts! Or has he never realized that talking to one person a whole evening, many times successively, implied a preference. Is he so modest as to believe it no harm for him to do anything, or has he thought me a good match? I am good-looking and well-educated, well-mannered, and of good moral character; my father is rich, and I should be willing to indulge his fondness for the country and a quiet life, and could gain for him a good luxurious home, where he could have his own way. But he could not bring his mind to marry entirely for the sake of marrying, and love did not come with his wishing, and so he thinks he will wait awhile at least. No harm to lay an anchor to the windward by calling, and then on his return he can take me up, or leave me alone as he fancies. Oh God, am I indeed saved from a fate like this? But then I hear his voice in my ears, I see his manly face, his kind smile, his tender, frank, truthful eyes; and I believe in my inmost soul that he is true and noble and good, and then what does it mean? Have I appeared so cold that he has no hope? Has his shyness and self-distrustfulness blinded him, or does he think that he will wait until some position of his own making, will allow him next fall to return, and see me more intimately, and offer me more? I dare not believe the latter, I dare not trust my hopes and until I have proved it, I will not believe the first. The little intermixing of doubt and hope make it ten times harder to bear. I start at every door-bell, I am disappointed at every note. For he cometh not, I am aweary, aweary. Enjoyment in any and everything seems to have faded out of my heart, and it is aching and empty. And so I write this story of my life, a starved heart, for my hopes are all delusions. It would be too much joy if they were fulfilled.

Mother said last night with tears in her eyes, that she had thought I was unhappy for two months past. What could I say, I turned it off, she must not know, it would weigh on her more than on me, and she has had enough gloom; but I was surprised, for I have made such effort to be gay. How I longed to tell her, and have a pitying word, how near I came to speaking; but I choked it down, and shut it up far down, down, to gnaw unseen.

5 June

It is all over. I suppose he went on Friday, as he intended—Jeanette came to see me Friday evening and said she believed he was gone, and so this chapter of my life is ended. This part of my life is to be laid away in some inner closet of my heart, and the door locked. Well, it is hard, but it is so much easier to bear when all hope is gone. Satisfied as we may be of probabilities, as long as a chance remains, human strength is not equal to closing the heart entirely to every ray of hope, and so disappointment is renewed over and over again until it seems as if our lives could not bear it; but this is impossible, and we begin to look about us for comfort elsewhere, our eyes, dazzled before, can now see the brighter side of the cloud. "Blessed are they who mourn, for they shall be comforted." These words have blazed forth to me in letters of gold, with so many other passages that before seemed merely beautiful, and are now meat and drink to me, life-giving. I have not quite yet settled myself and my future. I have been living (I see now) so many years, counting on the future, its possibilities, that I hardly take in the fact that a single life, such as I lead now, with the same trials and advantages, is now my certain lot. Perhaps this is a part of the bitterness of the trial, that it not only is actual loss, but also the destroying of all dreams, possibilities, longings. But it is necessary to bear it, and I *will* meet it strongly, God helping me. It may be to me so rich in blessings, I can already see. It seems to me nothing can so throw us entirely on the love of God as this, nothing help us so to look to Him as our guide, our dependence, our joy, and as for work, oh there is enough to be done. All have their cross. I will take up mine courageously, trustfully.

I pray for him with all my heart. I cannot understand him, I long to know how he has felt, that I may justify him, for I cannot now see how he can have done rightly; but I am willing to leave it, and pray that he may be happy and led in the right way. It sometimes comes over me that in the eyes of the world, I have not kept in the bounds fixed for women's feelings; but I cannot feel that I have done anything for which I should blush. God knows that never by word look or deed have I tried to win, what was not freely offered; and if I have loved what was noble and beautiful, it is my misfortune, not my fault, that I was deceived in thinking I had a right to.

6 October

The weather is very beautiful today, but for an excessively high wind. Mother and Father went to Blue Hill to pass the day, and I walked down Heath St. to see Sadie Cabot. I have thought it over and over a great deal, and as she is sick, and I know I ought to go, I have decided to put away an unwillingness which seems to me foolish, and undignified. The country was exquisite. The barberry bushes were covered with their little crimson fruit, and with the brilliant scarlet Virginia creeper. The sky spoke of autumn and its glorious spirit, everything was gay and beautiful and I walked with my eyes filled with earth's tears, my spirit crushed at the contrast between the gaiety without, the hopelessness within; and yet I tried to be courageous, to be faithful, to look up. As I came to Theodore Lyman's avenue, with the midday sun throwing the branching shadows of the trees over the road, and pictured my aunts and uncles as children, vigorous and hopeful, playing there, I could but wish that I too had fought the hard fight, and was going down the hill to rest. But only for a moment. I dare not be so cowardly. Shall I ever forget this walk, or how each stone and twig looked, for every sense was strained, my brain on fire, and my limbs and heart, they seemed paralyzed. Yet I wondered if other people had felt before as I did. I speculated on my feelings when a few hours after I should be going home instead of coming. I had time and to spare to turn every probability in my mind, and measure its consequences, so fast did my ideas rush. Well, I went on and I faced the house, and my heart gave one choking leap, and then stood calm and cool. He was there on the doorstep smiling his smile. Whose is like it? It seems to me the soul's smile showing through, and so sweet, yet so almost shy. I had trained myself not to blush, not to stammer, but my pains were lost, for I was too peaceful to do either.

Sadie was at home, and really glad at seeing me. All my doubting and wondering why she had never been to see me was gone. We sat down in her room, and talked. Mr. Cabot came in, and seeing me was unexpectedly kind and expressive. Then Walter came, he said to show me the crystals he had collected in the mines this summer; then we looked over some of his photographs from drawings, and he asked if he might make the ones I liked best for me. We talked of Powell's future and his own, the difficulties in finding work. He said he had not been willing to stoop low enough, he was ready to take now what at first he had despised, and he had faith that it would come by patient waiting. I saw all. He has nothing to offer; and he waits and hopes, little thinking in his modesty, that I too may hope and suffer. At last Sadie said frankly and simply, that they were going to Cambridge before dinner, and I therefore came away; but she promised to come Saturday morning to see me. I went to the garden, and what fullness of joy filled earth and sky! What sunshine! What richness of flowers! What images of happiness and rest! I met Franky Lee and after a ramble round the greenhouses and garden, we walked home with the other children, as merry as any crickets that sing all the day long.

In the evening Powell and I drove to Waltham to drink tea with the Lymans.

4 December

Oh time, what a myth thou art! Have I not lived whole months of suffering and hope since last Wednesday! Months, it seems as if years of life had been crushed into three days. I dreaded the Amorys' party, but if I could have foreseen the agony that it would bring me, I could never have faced it—agony I did not know was in me, and yet was not God leading me by the hand even through that time? Oh the blessedness of being allowed to see that He was, to learn a lesson which cannot be forgotten, a lesson of faith and patient waiting.

It was not large, but pretty and gay. Isabella, Alice, Arthur's wife and several married ladies remained in the front parlor, and I with them. Dancing went on in the front, but had little to do with me. He came into the room, and, after a few moments, seeing me came up. In ten more Horatio Whitwell came up, I had to see him, to bow to him. Mr. Cabot left me; and though, if I could have called him back at the sacrifice of my life, it seems to me I should have snatched at it, I did not call him back but went on smiling, talking, joking, laughing loud as if my heart were light, and Mr. W. filled my mind, and so the evening went on. Mr. Joe Gardner relieved Mr. W. Arthur came up, and took me in to supper, Peter Brooks talked to me, I came back and sat 20 minutes on the sofa alone, and he stood opposite and talked gaily to Lizzie Hammond. I could hear him laugh; then Greely Curtis came up, and I began to feel that I was giving way, that my attention could not bear the strain much longer. [12] While Greely C. was with me, he came over and talked to someone just at my side; then Gus. Peabody came to me, and Greely C. and he went off together, I suppose to supper. Mr. Peabody was kind and charming. I longed to thank him, for I had taken no notice of him once in the evening when he came up to me, and he had overlooked that, and now told me about his journey to South America so pleasantly. His manner was so kind and gentlemanly that I could have blessed him, but oh how my brain and heart were working! It seemed to me as if I could think, feel, do, say everything at once. I went over the ten minutes Mr. Cabot was with me, many many times, every word, expression of face, tone of voice, and each in turn stabbed me, crushed me; and I laughed and said to Mr. Peabody, how funny, oh it must have been delightful, how beautiful, how you must have enjoyed it! And I saw him too talking before me, heard Alice Crowninshield's joke as they watched the German, and his responsive laugh, and did not die, did not shriek. But why? I think it was because it seemed to me like a nightmare, and that it was too horrible to be. Mr. C. had said that he had met all his friends in the street—where had I been—very indifferently; and I said that I never seemed to meet anyone, though I was always out, and that I walked to Cambridge a great deal. He asked me if Miss Hooper went with me, and I said no, she never walked. Then I asked about Sadie, who was not well, and Louis who had a headache and preferred skating to parties. Then I said I had heard from Powell that he was going to Europe; and he said very abruptly that not until the spring at least, so that he might unite pleasure to business. And he asked how I liked Mrs. Lowell's parties, and I said I had only been once, when I had victimized Ned, and had not been able to get him again; and he said he thought I often seemed to victimize him, as in dancing last year. And then I said no and that he was now in Cambridge and liked his life so well he would not come to parties; and he said the life abroad in the universities was very delightful in appearance—and Mr. Whitwell came up and he moved off instantly.

Changed as all is now to me, the struggling agony, as one can imagine a drowning man to feel who catches at straws to save life still dear to him, gives me now a shudder of terror and distress. I went over this, weighing, measuring, testing, again, again, again. I had ordered my carriage at one, would it never come? Sidney Bartlett was saying something to me, about my pretty wreath, and somebody's dress, and my father's billiards, but I did not even attend. He was standing now close by talking to Powell, but as pleasantly, as calmly, as Powell himself. The last ray of hope, that he had ever cared a straw for me, went out, a dull settled fact seemed to close over, and grind into my soul. It had all been a mistake from beginning to end. It was all my imagination, of course he had done no more than many others whom I had never dreamed of reproaching. I had imagined, twisted, made up, painted every little word and action; and a shame that seemed the last drop in my cup of woe, woe unutterable, crept into my very blood, made it curdle. Powell looked at the clock and said five minutes to wait. I waited stiff and cold, half asleep it seemed, then went up for my cloak, spoke to Miss Mifflin something about her dress, came down and waited on the stairs. He was in the entry; I tried to smile, but I think I must have looked as if mesmerized. He went, I hardly saw when, without even a bow. I got into the carriage, Powell took me out, I came up, took off my dress, put it all away, and went to bed. But then I began to wake again, and sleeping and dreaming at intervals, and mingling the reality and the nightmare, I hardly knew where I was, whether this earth could still be my abiding place.

Thursday was a miserable day. What words can describe passive suffering, the weight of something which seems slowly destroying all we feel to be life? I told Mother a little what I felt; I say a little, for who feels that they really represent by words joy or sorrow? Then I, feeling very tired, lay down, and hurried to dress to call on Mrs. Wm. Mackay, at her wedding reception. I wondered if I seemed to everyone natural, and happy as usual—I suppose so. After dinner I went out to walk round the Common to cool my head. Even the weather seemed unnatural. It was as hot as June, so that the air was full of damp, and yet I could hardly wear a thin cloak. I went in to see Aunt P. who had a bad cold. Nellie and Harry were there and said their mother had a bad cold. That moment the determination came over me to go to see her the next day, and tell her all, or rather to ask her about Nellie Hooper's previous experience, and try to bring my mind to anchor somewhere. For it was already afloat again since last evening, and I felt even that misery was more bearable than when alternating with doubt. I have tried a great while and very hard to pretend to myself that I was not suffering so much, that it was after all my imagination, which I had let slip from my control, and it was mere self-indulgence and want of firmness which allowed such a morbid state of feeling. But I felt now that, however morbid, I was beyond my own reach, and it was time I should obtain aid from without. That evening I was unable to conceal myself even by silence from Mother, and for the first time on my account in my life, we cried together hopeless.

Friday Mother came to breakfast sick, sleepless, her eyes swollen; and I felt like a criminal. After breakfast I went to see Fanny Cunningham and her baby at her mother's. I looked upon her, her husband smiling at her side, her child in her arms, like some blessed being made of different clay from me. I should never feel as she did in this world. Her loving pride, her gay tenderness for child and husband, seemed to me like blessings reserved for angels; and oh what pleasure it gave me to see such joy, still left on earth. I prayed for her as if she had been my sister. After this I walked down to Mary Parkman's. The weather was wonderfully lovely, though enervating— damp, hot, like spring. I would not stop to decide now whether to go on or not. I felt as in going to the dentist's that if I stopped to reconsider I was lost. I had decided to go and however hard, I would tell all. Mary was at home teaching Nellie. In ten minutes she joined me in the parlor, and after the first bursting words, how relieved I felt; for I found with her no doubts, but strength, decision, and intense, understanding sympathy.

She told me that about Nellie she had no right to speak, excepting that he had done perfectly right. If there was fault, it was on her side; and she told me that Mrs. Cabot had known that he felt drawn towards me, had ardently desired that I might answer to it, and had asked me to Beverly to show me, as far as she had a right to, that she felt so. Oh what can I call the certainty, that I had not been dreaming, nor imagining, that something real had been felt and done? It seemed to change the world from a land of shadows to one of real hearts and lives at one stroke. I know that I have been cold, that I have pretended indifference, played the hypocrite, tried to make Sadie and even him believe that I was cold, happy and indifferent; for I was so torn by hopes and fears, by distrust, shame and strong feeling, that I could only act with decency, by covering all up under a shell of polished indifference. Dear, dear Mary! I told her how I suffered, how I had tried to bear, how often the heavens seemed closed against me, life itself a dream; and her heart could beat an answer to each word. She told me too how she had suffered, even last summer, when sick, and it seemed to her as if God, her husband had ceased to love her, sinner as she was; I could hardly bear to feel glad.

And here I am. My thoughts are like unruly horses, I cannot control them, they will rush forward to the future, they will go over the past. I try to remember what I have suffered, and that tomorrow, the next hour, may bring it back; but I do not believe it. The certainty, oh that word, the certainty, that at least he has cared, that I have been worthy to appear to him lovely and lovable; I say the certainty of this is as much as I can realize now, and as for not hoping, it is terribly impossible. For it is terrible. So much may yet happen. And when shall I see him again? Can it be that both feeling so we may wander about for weeks blinded by a few miles of earth to each other's presence? I can only clench my hands and entreat God to forgive this tumult, to help me to find trust, and give room in my soul for thankfulness for His providence. To put my hand in His, and watch His face, if I may rejoice, or be patient.

21 December

I have only time to write a few lines. Life has been such a tumult that I could not write before and I would not wait longer. A new heaven and a new earth have been created for me, unworthy, and the Father has lifted me from intense suffering to all the brightest happiness He gives on earth. I feel too much and also realize too little to write. A man saved from drowning could not give description of his feelings in being snatched back to life; neither can I. God is too good to me. I am poor, ungrateful, all unworthy, these fill my soul.

Saturday 10th I went out to Ward's Pond to skate with Nellie Hooper—how I remember each detail! Alice went with us. We found the ice creaking, and covered with a thin layer of snow, and only three men on it at the further end, instead of a party as we expected. One of these three turned out to be Louis Cabot. After a time Walter came. He seemed more quiet than usual and after being driven to despair I said, Are you afraid of me, your manner has so changed I thought you were annoyed. He said, oh no, and left me soon, quitting the pond without even a goodbye. Grace Heath came, I skated with her cold and still as if frozen through, my very teeth chattered. Finally we left the pond. I was late to dinner, and ate it alone, swallowed it. Then Mother said, "There is a note in your room, Mr. Cabot left it."

Captain Dumaresque and Millicent Dublois drank tea with us that night. After they had gone I told Father, he was kind and pleased, and I lay down that night not to sleep, but to thank God for His unutterable blessing.

Sunday I went to Sunday school as usual. Dear Powell took a note for me to Brookline; and I waited all day anxious, happy.

Monday he, Walter, my Walter came, and it is all settled, mine for life, if it please God mine forever.

Tuesday I wrote or told Jeanette, Aunt P, Annie; but it seemed a dream, and I myself a shadow. Ned has not been well since Thursday; and Sunday Dr. Warren pronounced him sick with varioloid, and shut him up in his room, where no one is allowed to go near him, and he makes his own fire and bed, and takes in his dinner from a chair at the door. But he has never suffered anything but headache and heaviness, and Monday went out. Wednesday I wrote and sent innumerable notes. Thursday my own friends came to see me, or wrote me the kindest notes. How my heart beat for them all, and someone from John Higginson who sent me a brooch that I might possess something from him—I shall keep as treasures that rarely fall to the lot of woman. Such feeling, such generosity, such delicacy, more precious than the world and its contents, and Walter was so generous, so trusting. That afternoon we took our first ride in his sleigh. Was the earth really brighter than ever before?

Friday we walked out, I dined with Jeanette, and our evening— it was a time worthy of paradise. Saturday he came in the morning, dined, and drove me out over Cambridge bridge after dinner. Mr. and Mrs. Cabot came to see me Friday.

Sunday was a heavy south rain. The excitement of the week which I had hardly realized entirely exhausted me, and I took a long nap. After dinner he came, and as it stopped raining, we walked over Cambridge bridge.

Monday Harry Lee came to see me. His wife is sick, and all have a dread of the varioloid. Saturday before Edward and his wife and Elliot and his wife came and were *very* kind. Sam and his wife came Friday the day before. Monday Walter drove me out in the afternoon. Tuesday Louis came, and we went to see Church's *Heart of the Andes* and walked about. [13]

Today we went early to see the picture again, and walked; then went at three to the picture and went to look for some books, and dined at six with Mary Davis, a long happy day. My heart is too full to write, to think.

1860

Boston   1 January

A New Year indeed has begun for me. Ten days more of happiness since I last wrote, pure, unclouded, no doubts, fears, disappointments, no anything but joy and peace. My only surprise is at my incapacity of feeling. It seems as if I must, ought, to be in rapture all night and all day, when for a moment it flashes over me what has been given me, how I might have been; but here we come on the limits of human nature, and I cannot take in the whole amount of my blessedness. My one prayer is to cling to God, to never forget Him for one moment, and to try to settle in my own mind my new relations to life and to Him, and to remember that this is all His gift, which He may see it best to lend but for a little while. One so soon becomes used to happiness, it so blinds the eyes to all else, that there is something almost awful in the blind way in which we may be rushing unprepared on a precipice. Walter has been with me every day but Friday—then it snowed, and he tried to come in in the horse-cars and could not. How fearfully he seemed to be vanishing as the hours went by, and my old life closing round me again; but Saturday brought him early, and I could breathe peacefully.

Christmas was Sunday. Saturday, Mother and Father dined at Aunt Grant's, and we passed the evening there. Walter gave me that night my ring, a single emerald. Sunday, he and Annie Webber dined with us. Annie brought me a manuscript translation of an Italian book called *Marguerita Posterla*, which she told me about a year ago, and which she has been at work on ever since, a most herculean task. Oh my friends! Shall I ever forget their sympathy? Powell Parkman astonished me by his feeling, he kissed me, he walked up and down the room overcome. Such moments make life precious, and balance years of indifference and trifling.

Monday evening we went to a Christmas party at Mrs. Appleton's, very trying for Walter, he was introduced to all sorts of relations he had never seen before.

Week before last we had two days of most perfect skating, [after] one of which I dined with Mrs. Cabot. This week has been stormy, and bitterly cold.

Today I went, after my Sunday school, with Walter to Mr. Freeman Clarke's chapel.[14] The sermon was fine, and I like very much the whole service, very simple and hearty.

Today is the first of the New Year, and I would offer up myself a sacrifice to God. Oh that I may choose Him, and never wander! My happiness makes me fearful, fearful of myself above all. Walter talks now of going to Europe in February instead of the spring, to be gone three months. It seems to me very, very hard to bear, very, very hard to put all in God's hand, myself and him; but I will try with my whole soul. Oh when I think where I should be without him, and remember that God has seen fit to try other souls as dependent as mine, I shudder at my own weakness to endure, at the thought of the great abyss yawning around us. I can but cry Help, help, oh my Father in heaven.

14 January

Came home today from a visit to Lizzie Cabot in Brookline. Monday, Walter drove me out after dinner. The house is very comfortable and convenient, though not to my uncultivated eyes very tasteful. They live in it exactly according to my ideas. Everything is very simple; but each room up stairs and down has a fire, they keep four women, they send for a carriage to the stable whenever they want one, which is often, the express man comes to the house every day; and they manage to have all the substance with none of the show instead of all the show and no substance, the common mode of using an income not very large.

Tuesday was one of those days, so beautiful in the country, when everything seems to burst its bonds and smile, a regular thaw, making one delightfully impressed with the idea that spring was come. Walter took me a long drive all round the old way I went so often alone last summer, by the Worcester Turnpike and Puttenham woods. Existence seems a new gift such a day, the heart sings with the rest of nature. We dined late. The baby comes down after breakfast and after dinner, and is the most delightful playmate, a great rosy restless boy, who seems to grow visibly in mind and body. Wednesday, I had an engagement at the dentist's and Walter drove me in in the morning. We dined at three at Mrs. Cabot's and passed the evening with Mrs. Edward C. Sadie has a bad cold. She feels pretty badly still about Walter's engagement, and is very cold to me, but I can forgive her—the loss must be very hard to bear, and he was everything to her.[15] I long to be a great deal to her, for I think she needs change and help very much; but I hope for very little. She seems very noble in some ways, but very undisciplined, and I almost fear sometimes whether I shall get along with her at all, except in an outside way. I feel as if I rubbed her the wrong way all the time. Mrs. C. is lovely, so motherly and kind. Mr. C. is very kind and pleasant, but I feel rather ill at ease with him.[16] The whole family have treated me in the warmest and pleasantest way. All call me Lillie, and treat me like one of themselves. They are not critical either, and expect you to be different from them, and follow your own ideas.

Thursday, the snow fell fast and was quite deep; but towards noon notwithstanding Lizzie furnished me with snow boots that came up to my knees, and Walter and I waded through the garden out into the woods, and to what they call Trowbridge's field, where in winter there is water and skating. While we were out the sun came out, and everything looked as exquisitely pure and brilliant as it does after new-fallen snow. I got thoroughly wet, but had a glorious walk, and took no cold. Mr. and Mrs. Edw. C. came to dinner and passed the evening.

Friday was very cold. The house, however, seems so well built that you do not feel the changes. Lizzie's little dressing-room, where we sit after breakfast, is delightfully sunny and cosy.

Lizzie Lee, Mrs. Harry, came to see me after breakfast and was very kind and cordial. She is a great invalid, especially just now, and I have never been able to see her before. She is still lovely though thin and pale, most graceful in her motions and with a most lovable angelic expression. After she had gone Lizzie took me over to see Mrs. Follen and Miss Cabot, Pattie going with us. There I met Mrs. Fred Cabot. Miss Susan has been sick for some weeks, and looks miserably. A person of her temperament is very much affected by illness, and she was so quiet and changed, as to seem hardly like the same person as before. Mrs. Follen was charming as ever, full of fun and kindness. After our return Walter took me a long sleigh ride by Mrs. Ripley's old place, the stock farm, but it was terribly cold. He came back to dine, and Sadie and Louis came over in the evening.

Lizzie and I had a little talk over my fire in the evening, which was a great comfort to me. I could not help saying, that it was trying to me to see Walter at home. He seemed to draw into a shell, to become more strongly tinctured with the family traits of inexpressiveness and apathy of manner, and that I sometimes could not help the feeling, does he love me so very much after all? And yet I felt it was wrong to have such a thought, not to be able to understand his manner and go behind it, for I was sure in my heart that he did love me. But Lizzie said she had often had the same feeling with Elliot before they were married. She thought engagements a trying time, and that she used sometimes to ask him over and over again, do you love me, until he was really troubled at being so doubted. Then she told me a little of her life and how happy she is now, and if ever a woman looked like an angel she did that night. Her character shows itself in the most beautiful way through her plain features, and makes them lovely. She has lived all her life for others, and forgotten herself. Oh that I could drink in her spirit! I feel so earthly, so selfish and mean beside her, that I could bow my head in the dust before her.

Elliot is very kind and though cold in his manner, you never feel for a moment that he is cold. I do not feel at ease with him yet, or even with Lizzie, but I think I shall. Walter drove me in this morning, and I found Mother sick on her sofa, where she has been since Wednesday, so I was very thankful I came back.

21 January

This week has been passed in a hubbub about a fancy ball at Mrs. Charles Amory's on Thursday night. I did not expect to go, but Mrs. Eustis offered me a dress that she had worn, and so I thought it would be a pity to miss it. It was a skirt of Moorish silk, scarlet and white stripes with a broad band of scarlet at the bottom, made short, and covered with black lace. The bodice was black velvet, with a low necked chemisette of white, and my hair was dressed with the very high Spanish comb on top of my head, and a black lace Spanish mantilla, falling behind from it, my front hair was braided and coiled round in two little rolls at the sides of my face, and a red camelia and gold pins fastened on the veil. My feet were dressed in silk stockings with red clocks worked at the sides; and I put scarlet bows to some satin slippers I bought in Paris, and covered the heels which were high with scarlet silk. Aunt Anna lent me a beautiful necklace and earrings of coral, and I completed my costume by wearing on my wrists some black velvet and gold Venetian wristlets, and any number of bracelets. Every one thought is a very pretty dress at home, but of course there it was lost in the general splendor. Walter wore a Turkish dress quite handsome in itself, but his face was painted and the turban changed him so that I could not think it becoming to him. Ned and Powell hired two stage dresses, very handsome in themselves, but I thought not showing them off to advantage. P's was black velvet and steel, Ned's scarlet and gold with a long curling wig and a great hat and plumes, that half buried him.

The ball was superb, many of the dresses, especially the gentle-men's, very rich and perfect. I was desperately tired, and looking and admiring so much is very fatiguing; but it was a sight I should have been sorry to lose. Mr. Wm. Saltonstall, a friend of Walter's, was introduced to me. It was something new and delightful to wander about, and feel unconcerned as to who spoke or if any did; to go off to dance and have him wait for me, impatient for me to return; to see his eyes dilate with vexation when anyone came up to take me away, and smile when he could have me all to himself.

Oh wonderful, how wonderful, that I should be all this to any-one—and to him!

25 March

I find by my dates that I have skipped even more time than usual in my journal, but my days are too full to leave any extra minutes.

Since January a good deal has been decided upon, and our way has opened before us as we dare not even hope. Money seemed to Walter a hopeless difficulty, as his father could not do for him what he ex-pected; but Father and Mr. Cabot met and had a long talk, which resulted in the latter promising to give us $2,000 a year and Father to furnish a house and contents, and $1,000 a year, so that we are started without any necessary dependence on Walter's business. Then came a few weeks of uncertainty and debate about a house. Father was very anxious I should occupy a stone house belonging to him on the Mill Dam; and I felt that it was too large and too far off from Mother, besides which Mr. Chickering had the lease of it for two years more, and it was difficult to provide for the interim. Just then John Jeffries' house in Chestnut St. offered. Father wanted us to live with him next winter, but I did not feel it prudent or wise or pleasant, and therefore he gave that up. We had one rainy afternoon to see the Jeffries' house in, and decide on it, and as I was pleased, Father bought. He has been *very, very* kind and considerate to us. This is all I could wish; the position is pleasant, and sunny, and near Mother, the house small but convenient and in perfect order, cosy, all that I like, and the price, $20,000, not extravagently out of proportion to our means, as are the establishments of most young people. We can live in it quietly, and comfortably, without show and with everything pleasant. Being near Mother, however, is the great point to me. I can come up for ten minutes, at any time of day or evening, with a hood and shawl on, and as many times a day as I choose. If Mother is sick I can hear of her before breakfast, and see that she is cared for the last thing at night. Every time I go out I can look up at her windows, and every time she is out, she can drop in to see me without going out of her way. It has really changed her feeling about my being married, and going away, for such a step seems hardly like leaving home. After this was settled we decided definitely to be married this spring, and now I am in the full tide of preparation. Probably if it ever happens—which seems to me all unlikely, so strange is it—we shall be married the last of May, pass a week or two at Chestnut Hill, perhaps take a little journey, then go to Mrs. Cabot's, and when she goes to Beverly remain in her house in Brookline. Mother will be at Chestnut Hill, and I shall be preparing my house in the summer to move into late in the autumn. These are our plans, but it is all unreal to me still. I live but in the day. The reality, that in two months I shall have left home forever, that I shall no longer be Lillie Mason, that Walter will be mine, that I shall have started beyond possibility of return on a new and untried road, which looks now all sunlight, but which I know must be check-ered with many a black cloud: all this is words to me only, and I

laugh as freely and talk on as little anxious, as if I could see no change.
It is wonderful how gently we are led up to these great things, and
what in speculating upon seems sufficient to overwhelm one with its
momentous importance, in experience steals softly upon us like the
yearly recurring seasons, or daily duties. But yet the change is no less
great. I feel as if I had gained new senses, new perceptions, new
powers, a new life. What was barren seems filled up: empty, satisfied.
The present is sufficient, and I can look, need to look, neither before
nor behind. If I can only remain faithful, not forget heaven now that
earth is so sweet, not seek less the love of God, now that I receive so
freely from a human soul! And I have dreadful moments of fear sometimes, when the possibility of losing all that I have found seems
almost to make me regret that I have known how much there is to
lose. But happiness is my rule, my lot, filling, overflowing happiness; and I can usually thank God for it trustfully.

Harriet's engagement has been a rather painful interest to me
lately, though not unexpected wholly, but I cannot feel satisfied for
her, though I think he is kind and well-meaning; and I fear it divides
us with a glass barrier imperceptible but impassable.[17]

Jenny is soon to be confined, and I cannot but be a little anxious
until it is over. We have been together constantly all winter, and
she has known every interest of mine, I all her's. Sympathy, what a
blessed thing it is, how it binds souls together! I thank God for it
more than for almost any other gift.

Chestnut Hill   11 June

Time sweeps us on past trouble, anxieties and joys, and we may vainly
pray it to pause even to take breath; on it rushes and we with it, all
our powers needed to keep from upsetting as we swing hither and

thither in the current. I wrote the last two pages and looked forward
to last Tuesday, my wedding day (June 5th) as in the dim future,
too far off to be realized; and now, already, it is gliding away into
the past.

Oh life, what more will you unfold as you come, of joy of sorrow of
mystery? It makes one faint with pressure. I cannot paint even in my
memory all that has been in my life for the last six weeks. It seems to
me as if years of feeling, thought, knowledge were crowded into these
days, and I wonder that I have lived through it. But we walk blind-
folded, and only realize in looking back what we have passed through.

I am no longer Lillie Mason, with her life mapped out, her hopes
and fears and trials and joys marked and well known; but that woman
has gone and in her place has come Lillie Cabot, with such new feelings, such a new experience, that even her home, herself, all that is
still unchanged, looks no longer the same to her eyes, but bathed in a
new light seen from a new world of thought. Shall I say I am happy?
The word used for past enjoyment seems weak and faded, for this life
grown bright, out of an unutterable misery. It is a change like passing
from this world to another, or rather like gaining eyes and ears a
dozen senses after living in this world in unconsciousness that we
were without them. I was tired mentally and physically before my
marriage to a very great degree, though I strove hard not to be; but
the excitement kept me up, and there seemed no possibility of stopping. Hurry, anxious looking forward to a new life, bitter regrets and
loving reminiscences of a past life to be quitted forever, unavoidable
anxieties, and above all intense sorrow and pity for the suffering necessarily to come to Mother: all these seemed feeding on my very life's
blood, and I felt my strength shrink daily. I had many presents, over
70 I believe; and among my small trials was the necessity of writing

70 notes of thanks, when my brain was too tired to think, my heart to feel. But Tuesday June 5th came, and the notes and cards, nearly 500, had been written and sent, the thousand details of preparation accomplished; and I had only to go through the work of the day with courage and then be at rest. My dress, white silk with tulle flounce and trimmings, was very simple but very pretty. Mrs. Capen put on my tulle veil with natural flowers and trimmed the skirt; and my bright color made it even in the day-time becoming. Annie Webber passed the night and day with us, and Grace Heath came in early to help me; but I had no hurry, and dressed quietly and otherwise alone. Walter came at 11. At 12 we were standing in front of the minister. People say it is over in a few moments: to me it seemed endless. We stood with our backs to the people so that as I hoped I hardly realized their presence, and only saw Mother who was in front of me. But at first my knees shook so violently that I was frightened, and could think of nothing but not to fall; this passed off partially, and then I could feel the service with my whole soul. Dr. Gannett was very solemn but also not too long, just as I liked. For a few moments after it was over I almost lost my self-control; but Mrs. Cabot, dear old lady, came and stood right in front of me, and in a few moments I was safe. Everyone kissed or shook hands. I seemed a sight set up for the entertainment of the company, but it never occurred to me to be embarrassed or annoyed. At half past twelve and one some of the visitors began to arrive; but it rained in torrents, and many, most who had cards, did not come. I rather preferred it, as it made less of a rush and confined it to my real friends. I felt gay, at my ease and cordial in a way that astonished myself. All went well. Dear Jeanette was like a pillar to lean on at my side, Sadie and Laura both stood near, and Walter not far off. Three o'clock arrived. I put on my little old black

silk to please Walter, and ate a piece of meat, at the end of a table of flowers, ices, all sorts of delicacies that looked now rather forlorn.

Mother, dear, dear, dearest Mother, what courage and determination she has! She was composed, often smiling, and to the very last. The rest of my things were packed, the last directions given, Goodbye, the word that seems to crush us, said, and at six I was crossing the Mill Dam alone with my husband.

Chestnut Hill is a cosy little place, and we have been much favored in the weather. Wednesday rained all day, and I was very grateful to pass it in entire rest. Walter read to me, and the peace and quiet seemed heavenly. Since, we have had rain at night and showers, making the country radiant, the air delicious as that of paradise. We have Charley and a wagon, we walk, we read aloud, we talk, we take deep draughts of rich heavenly life and joy and love.

Today is more beautiful than any yet. Walter has gone to town for a few hours; and I have passed the time in trying to understand what I have, where I am, and to thank the Father, who it seems to me must have blessed me far above all women. Mrs. Cabot is already sounding natural to me. My past life seems a dream—not that I cease to love it—and the friends who belong to it are more precious than ever. But a new heaven and a new earth are indeed created for me, and they fill my soul.

CHAPTER SIX

1860–1896

No doubt because her duties are more pressing, though also because she experiences less emotional turmoil than when she was a young woman, once married Elizabeth keeps her diary in a form far less consistently full. Special circumstances may bring back detail and eloquence. But many entries are now brief, and fewer lend themselves to quotation. Readers may find this disappointing; but they are assured that what is printed here reflects what Elizabeth was able, or cared, to say.

Many of the entries treat problems of running homes and managing servants, facing pregnancy and childbirth, depending on wet-nurses after the severe difficulties encountered in trying to breast-feed her first child, coping with the frequent illnesses of husband and children.

Four times the Cabots visit Europe: once for two and a half years, once for fifteen months, briefly in 1881 for Mabel's operation in London, and again briefly in 1894 to visit Venice. Their journeys include visits to places not much frequented by Americans: the south-west of England, the coast of Normandy, even Pau near the Pyrenees was not crowded with compatriots. During the third of her tours,

Elizabeth hears *Parsiphal* at Bayreuth, only two years after its first
performance. In America, she goes to Florida alone in 1873. Most
summers are spent on the North Shore, at Manchester-by-the-Sea.
But increasingly the Cabots go to Maine, not so much the fashionable
Bar Harbor as Castine or Rockland, on their way to islands. They are
helped, from 1890, by having some sort of steam yacht, presumably a
very small one since no crew is mentioned beyond a skilled engineer.
Like the Brookline receptions, and the Paris wedding dress for Ruth
in 1890, such details suggest a more opulent lifestyle than before;
but no explanation is ever provided.

By the 1890s, with some of her children independent, Elizabeth
takes on more public work. She helps raise funds for Radcliffe,
though she is never satisfied with its relationship with Harvard. The
Schlesinger volumes suggest how important to her is her work for the
Children's Aid Society; and the annual reports at the Boston Athenaeum provide more substantial proof. Often she gives $200 or $300
in addition to her small annual membership subscription. She is a
director and sits on the society's General Council. More important,
she is a member of the committee that screens applicants, determin-
ing whether they need only advice or supervision while in parental
homes or placement with other families. Her daughter Elise, too, appears as a visitor, supervising the small libraries deposited in private
homes, for the use of neighboring children.

1862

Lenox   4 October

Sickness and various occupations have caused a large gap in my journal, and today I take it up; but what changes have intervened, what experiences have I been through since I wrote the opposite page! Then I was looking forward only to a child, as a wonderful dream; now today, he has been a reality for 19 months, and what a lovely blessed little fellow he is! Since then I have been through months of sickness from which I came near never emerging, suffering which had its pleasures and joys, for they showed Walter, and my friends, as I should never otherwise have known them. Then Walter's long illness, which has only lately lifted its heavy weight. Then in addition Father's long illness and wonderful restoration. And last this terrible war, and the experience of this summer, which seems like a long life of anxiety— and an anxiety a weight to which at present we can see no ending— 18 months of fighting, millions of money, thousands and tens of thousands of lives, and still but begun. And with all this teaching, I sometimes feel as if my soul stood still, that my faith is no firmer, my life no purer.

I have lately been reading Emerson's *Essays*, and am now reading a *History of Methodism*, two books strikingly contrasted to each other.[1] The latter is very fascinating, and it would be pleasant to accept it; but I cannot believe its faith any more than I can believe black is white. I think I have learned a little in one way, that it is wrong to dwell enough on oneself to worry about one's state. I have wasted too much time so, and try to stop it.

Powell is still with us; but we break up soon, and the probabilities,

if looked at fairly, are against our ever being together again. With
such bloodshed as we have there seems little hope of escape. When
one counts those who have been killed—Jimmy Putnam, Jimmy
Lowell, Stephen Perkins, Dick Cary, Edward Revere, Sam Quincy a
prisoner, James Savage probably dead in a prison alone, Frank Palfrey
dying, Major Sedgwick buried here today—it seems as if another year
could leave none; and these are only a few of those even I know.[2] And
but for selfish aggrandizement, party passions, the blood already shed
would probably have been all. Now it has been shed in vain, as far as
physical effects go. But I am convinced that the duty of women is as
definite as well as arduous in this struggle for liberty, as the duty of
men. Their patriotism must enable them to give all they hold dear in
the cause of freedom; they must keep up the courage of the nation by
their cheerfulness and firmness; and being away from the actual scene,
they must use all their influence to preserve as far as may be the laws
of humanity, of justice, of moderation, of Christianity, which are in
such terrible danger of being forgotten in the excitement. But oh! to
what a future must we look forward, and prepare ourselves for, for
this generation is to be suffering, and struggle to the end. I can remember when a girl, and looking forward to life, with the intense
egoism of youth, I often wondered if I was to live through the world
the every day prosaic, uneventful career that I saw all around me.
Most childish feeling, for what life is really uneventful, or unimportant, viewed in the true spirit?

But I should have trembled and drawn back, if I could have seen
what the years held in their arms.

Ned is again in Fort Albany, after having been away a few days,
taken prisoner and returned. The two armies look at each other, on

each side the Potomac. Powell, too weak still to go back this month as he intended, will return the first of November. The "Emancipation Act" is being discussed everywhere, but as yet with more moderation than expected; but in the rebel congress it has been proposed to hoist the black flag, and no one can foretell to what extremities they may go.

1863

Blue Hill   5 July

Here is a gap to be sure, eight months. How strange, how impressive it is to read what one thought and looked forward to months before, and then compare it with the reality, as it has slowly unfolded itself. It teaches, at least, that there is no wisdom in looking forward to either the joys or sorrows to come. We were meant to work and live in the present, and to profit by the past. We are at Mrs. Davenport's since the 13th of last month. The last time I saw Blue Hill was five summers ago, when Walter was only an acquaintance, and I had quite made up my mind to single blessedness. Since that how much have we all lived through! Walter—for I must take up the loose ends of our lives—has, by the aid of his horse, been well all winter, and this spring accomplished a good deal of architectural drawing for Elliot; but was rather overworked, and soon after our move to Mrs. Cabot's on the 23rd of May, undertook to be sick again. But the attack, though on the bowels, was not the same thickening he had had before, and he recovered so well, that I feel really encouraged about his general strength. He is very thin, and looks very delicate still, and the stoop he always had, and which was much increased by his illness, makes him look more sick than he really is. But there is some comfort in this, for it makes it quite clear to every one, as well as himself, that he cannot go to the war; and though I hope if he were really strong, that I could do my part with courage, it is a great comfort, to have all doubts out of the question, for I am sure that his constitution at any time would not stand a soldier's life.

Harry is hearty as a little buck, full of spirits, sweet-tempered and lovely. He is backward in talking and we considered it a great achievement this morning for him to say Peas mama Harry in— papa's room—with a great reduction of the r's and s's; but he is not wanting in spirit or intelligence, and the timidity I thought he inherited from me seems to have disappeared as the *boy* appeared, much to my pleasure. The dog walks by and knocks him down, then sits on him, and Harry laughs. He wishes to mount Dick, and feeds the little calf without the least regard to teeth or tongue. I try not to spoil him, but can't tell how much a mother's eyes may overlook. He ought to have a brother or playmate soon; and I have so changed, that I long for another little one. I begin to feel really well, better than I have been for many long years; for I have found out that I was by no means well before I was married, even when I was strong enough to do a great deal. Last winter I hope was the finishing up of this term of sickness, and a trying ending it was; from November to almost April I had an eruption, which hardly left me a comfortable hour, and sometimes so affected my nerves, that I had no control over my tears, but was a perfect baby. I lived in poultices for a fortnight at a time, and tried all the salves and applications ever heard. At last, after growing thin and miserable, I suppose it wore itself out, for a simple salve prescribed by Dr. Warren stopped it at once. Since then I have felt, with of course days of fatigue, and very slight dyspepsia, perfectly well—as well as I ever hope to be, for I think my organization is naturally a delicate one. Just as I had got well, while Sam was down at New Bern, Sunday afternoon the 20th of April, I found that Harry had some trouble, and in sending for Mason Warren, discovered it was a rupture. It was a dreadful thing to us then, the idea that our little boy was not sound, and might be delicate all his life, and now it is a matter of anxiety, but has turned out so much less of a calamity than we feared, that our feelings are quite changed. The truss he wears seems to give him no trouble of any kind; and he moves as freely as ever, and has gained in strength and health so that it cannot affect him in that way. I cannot but hope that with care and watchfulness he may become as strong and sound there as any other boy. Sam believes so. In the meantime I never leave him for more than a few hours, and always see to him myself, and so far have had no accident or difficulty. So trial sometimes becomes smooth to us.

1864

Boston   18 February
Thermometer 6° below zero! Have a cold on my chest, the first of this winter. Went over to see Olivia Lothrop—could not see her—

and the Browns. Should have done better to stay at home. Parlor very cold, notwithstanding furnace and roaring fire.

Had a note from Rev. Edward Hale about my employment office plan.[3] There is something wanting in me to make the true philanthropist. My enthusiasm does not keep up to the right pitch. I see too many difficulties.

4 May

Dined at Mother's. Went in morning to third Women's League meeting at Mrs. Quincy's, very large and earnest.[4] Settled by vote of 46 to 23 on Hannah's memorial as re-written by Miss Lowell. Appointed as committee H, Mrs. Loring, Huntington, and I to confer with the committees in New York and Washington. The country seems everywhere aroused. In evening, Marianne asked if a cook had been to see me, if so she should look for a place.

2 June

Cooler. Very heavy rain last night and this morning. Trying to teach my new cook, who knows how to make bread, and that is all, not even how to broil a chop, but is very willing and pleasant. I heard of Mrs. Felton's death from diphtheria.

4 August

W. woke up with a sore throat, and feels poorly. I have a more difficult time than ever before in managing Harry. His new nurse, Jessie, is good and faithful, but afraid of not pleasing him; and it is wonderful how soon he has found out and acted on it.

22 November

H. went to school! at <u>Lucy Codman</u>'s, with Guy and Godfrey, Eddie
Reynolds, and Charles Codman, from half past nine to eleven.[5]
Brought home ticket of *excellent*. Passed the morning at Powell's
again. Has got a wet nurse. F. doing well. Baby asleep all day.
Wanted to sit up with Fanny, but W. after considerable entreaty
would not let me.

1865

Boston   14 January

Rainy. <u>Read to old Colored Women.</u>[6] Came home and made Charlotte Russe. Gave H. his dinner. Went down to see Fanny, who seems
miserably. Annie Webber and Julia Bryant to dine, and Powell.

20 January

W. had a linseed poultice on when he went to bed; but at 12 he woke
me, with quite sharp pain in his side, more severe than he ever had;
and I was up all night putting on hot water baths every 20 minutes.
Relieved towards morning, but in bed. Busy all day <u>nailing up curtains in my back room</u> and arranging flowers and showing Christina
how <u>to cook</u> oysters and make chocolate, etc. Lizzie and Elliot came
to dine. At seven to tea came Mr. Van Brunt, Mr. Wm. Ware, Sadie,
Nellie Hooper, and Nina Lowell. W. of course not down. Played
parlor croquet. Ate constantly and played bezique. Went off very
pleasantly.

15 April

Exquisite day. I heard the rumor of President's assassination, then waited for paper—news confirmed. A terrible cloud on our joy. Poor man! It seems like the loss of a personal friend besides that of the nation. Seward too. He has finished his glorious mission, the President; but what shall we do without him? Who can take his place? The ways of God are not our ways. Concert for Chicago fair given up. Great excitement and sorrow everywhere. Took Mother and H. and drove with W. to Mrs. Cabot's—dined. Drank tea with Mother. Everyone feels thunderstruck and indignant. Assassin of President is Wilkes Booth, the actor.

Blue Hill   11 August

W. has gone to Boston, Harry to walk with Katy his nurse. It is a regular dog day, and I feel more debilitated and uncomfortable than I have yet; but I do not mean to utter the least word of complaint, for I do not believe anyone ever brought a child into the world, with less suffering than I have, and it is a blessing I have longed for so much, for my own sake and Walter's, and Harry's too. It cannot be long now before the end, or the beginning, and I hourly look at the hills and woods, the beautiful earth and the beautiful sky, and think these may be my last glimpses of them, for I suppose there is always danger. But I do feel that God has the care of me, and that He loves me, very deeply. Then too I do not suppose I realize what it would be at the last to leave all I love and enjoy, and go to unknown scenes. As for quitting Walter, putting the silence between this life and the next between us, and causing the suffering to him I know it would be, I cannot think of it. I can only say over and over to myself, God is good, I will trust Him, His arms will protect and comfort my be-loved one, better than I could. My love for Walter is so intense, every hope and fear in this life is so centered in him, that life without him seems to me as impossible and unnatural, as life would be without a body, without a world. And yet separation has come to many whom I must believe loved and depended on each other as we do. And I can bear hardly better to think of Mother's suffering, who has had so much, but I will not think of it, if it comes it is arranged by Our Father, the good, the all-powerful, the all-seeing.

Beyond these three none would lose much from life, in my depar-ture, though, thank God, there are many dear ones who love me, oh so much better than they could if they knew me as I know myself. Darling little Harry would soon forget "mama" and God would take care of him, God through his father, whose loving pure example must lead a child aright. I would gladly say goodbye and God bless you for your loving-kindness to me, to many, how many, friends of my youth and friends who have come to me at my marriage, and taken this new, reserved, unloving, faulty stranger into their hearts. Mrs. Cabot has been a loving mother, a constant friend, and from the gifts of her nature in such contrast to mine, a most deep and blessed ex-ample and influence in my life. But I cannot name the many friends, whom I shall wait for in heaven, if I go there first, though if goodness has a rank and a dwelling-place, most of them must be far above me. I speak of going to Heaven, but what is it, and why, if it is the haven of pure and perfected souls, should I think of being there? Even to my own clouded and biased vision, I must go through many series of teach-ing and struggling, before anything better than this earth is fit for me. Oh God! How much self-satisfaction, blindness, want of zeal and selfishness must I get beyond, to take even the first steps in a holy life!

And now, dear friends, if such is God's will, farewell. Think gently of me and my faults.

And Walter, husband, who lovest me with the love of an angel— not that of mortal man—you whose great heart can see no blemish in me, whose eyes, blind to all faults, can see the smallest feeblest sparks of virtue in me, there is nothing I can say to you but that I love you wholly and utterly, that there is no secret corner of my being, that is not wholly given to you, that you have been to me a joy, a rest, a blessing such as I did not believe God gave his creatures in this world, before I knew you. I see your failings, I know you to be an erring im- perfect man; but no revelations of another world, no closer inspection of your soul, can change my loyalty, my love. It is not your virtues I love, it is you, you as you are, imperfect I know but perfect to me, loving, generous, unselfish, as only I can know in this life, excepting Our Father. I hope, if I do leave you, this may be a daily pleasure to you, as the expression of my inmost soul; and that you will feel as assured as I do, that two souls the Father has brought together, and who are fitted to each other by eternal laws of nature, as we have felt ours to be every day that we have been together, cannot be separated. The more spiritual the existence, the more certain our being one. It will be time and matter only, that can come between us. Trust in God, darling. Live and enjoy for Harry's sake, and perhaps for an- other little one who may be given us, and believe that I love and watch you wherever I am, that my heart is true to you, wherever that heart exists. And should you even seem to forget me, cease to love me as you do now—impossible as it is for me to think of it, for I should lose my all—I shall love on. For I well know that the affections in this world are bound by many cords of flesh—God made them so.

Oh! how hard it is to say good bye, even in imagination on these pages! How I long in advance to stave off, to bear some of the suffering you will go through if you part from me; but such will not be God's will, and He will care for you, dearest, dearest, dearest.—And one word more: I leave my mother to you, the dearest being in the world to me, after you and Harry. If you love me still, love her for my sake, be *tender*, be true to her through everything, take my place to her as far as you can, make her feel that all of me has not gone, that my husband loves and values her, that he knows what my feelings were for her, and would help her in this life of many trials. And let Father and Powell know that I loved them dearly and truly, that notwithstanding my reserve, my harsh criticism, my want of tenderness, I love them and believe we shall meet in a world where the flesh is less of a barrier, and where we shall each see each more truly.

Goodbye, goodbye, I have often longed to talk with you, to prepare you for the possibility of my death; but it made you suffer so much, and perhaps without need, that I could not do it. I leave all to Our Father in Heaven. If God does give me more years of happiness, it seems to me as if I should be almost overwhelmed by blessings, and yet, alas, I shall forget to be grateful.

Walter, my very own dearest husband Walter, mine now and forever, if God so wills, goodbye. Love me, Oh love me always; I would not think of myself, and yet the possibility of your loving me one shade less entirely than now, seems to me impossible to bear.

27 *August*

Awake all night with pains, but not violent and did not wake Walter. Called Miss W. early. I got up, put on dressing gown and fussed around and read. Pains subsided—then began. W. went for Sam after breakfast.[7] Got to me at 9. I pretty well tired. I had gone to bed. Had 3 regular pains, then he gave me ether. Baby, a girl, born at 10 of 10, weighed 8 lbs. 15 ½ oz. with clothes, 7 lbs. 8 oz. without. I knew when she was born. O! what happiness. Feel peaceful, and no aches or pains after the first hour.

12 September

Very hot and muggy, rain all round but not a drop for us. I feel the heat more than any day yet. The baby slept in my room and was wide awake after 1 in the night, not crying, but needing constant tending. Mosquito tormented me. A fire down at Readville. Today sat up in bed several times without support and ate my meals upright. Cannot use my eyes much. Learned some poetry, a hymn, and revised Bryant's *Waterfowl* and *The death of the flowers*. Baby asleep a good deal in afternoon. Does not digest very well since Margaret's return. My digestion perfect—for breakfast ate 2 peaches, 2 rolls and oatmeal. Dinner, chop, potato, tomato, gingerbread, and little bread. Tea, oatmeal and gingerbread. Think of eating all day.

26 September

Colder and very clear. Baby had a worse discharge than I have seen for some days. Did my best to prevent her nursing, and went once 3 ½ hours. Have made Margaret to promise to diet rigorously. Katy and Miss W. carried me down on their crossed arms and I sat a good while on the piazza, holding the baby part of the time, and I dined downstairs and passed afternoon in parlor with a little fire. Walter shingling his cowshed. Mother and Father came in in afternoon a little while.

7 October

Dressed and came down to breakfast. Sat on piazza an hour and dined downstairs. Feel better though every muscle in my body lame. Weather exquisite, notwithstanding the intense drouth.

Sadie came to pass a week at Hannah's.

17 October

Beautiful day. Out most all the morning. Feel better and stronger. W. went to Boston. Before dinner drove up to farm, sat under the lee of a stone wall. Went in to see Hannah. Lydia and Helen better.

Christina came to say, that she could get three dollars, and wished to leave unless I would give it to her. This is the reward for teaching a person. Cannot go to town, so agreed to pay $2.75. Do not feel charitable.

Baby had hard crying spells and vomits often. Seems starved the moment she stops nursing. Only sleeps soundly 6 or 7 hours at night and not at all in day, except dozing. Wakes with a start.

1866

Boston   23 January

Fine day. Up earlier than usual, breakfasted at ¼ of 8. Hurried about but did not get to Mother's until 10. She is better. Dorcas is going to leave and wants to go at once. Took H. down in town. He tired and cold, and I sorry I tried to do errands with him. Brought him home, and made 3 calls. Saw to his dinner. Dressed, read an hour, tried to take a nap before dinner, but Miss Brown came in. After dinner played with H., then went up to see him in bed, tuck him up and hear his prayer.

Blue Hill   13 September

Exquisite day. Baby and H. out. I rode on horseback to farm. Tried to make Mother's old saddle go, but too bad. Put up 26 cans of tomatoes. Hard work and very tired. In afternoon, Mother and I and W. drove round Ponkapog Pond and went to Great Pond, very lovely.[8] Mrs. Parker and Charles in evening.

1867

Boston   30 January

Powell came up in morning to say that Fanny had felt pain since midnight. I took my work and went down there soon after 11. Soon the pains increased. She went to bed and Dr. came. I did not intend to remain, but waited for a time, then when Sam gave ether found I was needed. Suffered terribly, beyond my power to imagine before. Tried ether twice and had to give it up. Baby, a boy, was born about 7 after 5 or 6 hours of the severest labor pains. Fanny's courage wonderful. Went home, and Mother stayed until 10.

31 January

Fanny had a good night. I awake most of the night, happy to think of her at rest, but with an awful impression of mortal agony, which seems to increase now the excitement of keeping calm and doing is past. Fanny Crowinshield and little Ellie came in at 12 to stay a few days.

Fanny's boy weighed 11 lbs. with clothes on.

I feel as if no pain I ever had could be thought of after such long agony. I do not feel as if I *could* support such pain.

Annie Hinckley and Hannah and Annie Webber came in this morning. Jenny R. and Loulie Gardner came to tea. Had a nice evening.

24 March

Harry been vomiting, etc., as usual. I went down to talk with Fanny and Powell about Europe. They surprised but advised going. Then made up my mind to tell Father, which I did, and then Mother. Both feel very badly, and Mother feels a little doubtful of benefit. I miserable. Sadie arrived to dine and spend the night, and I went to practice *Elijah.*[9]

Blue Hill   *21 May*

Went to Boston. Few errands down in town, and then to Mother's. Her foot troubles her. Met Annette there to say goodbye. She very anxious that Mother and Father should go to Europe too. It brings back to me with a rush all my doubts and misgivings, my intense longing to take Mother. Can it be right to leave her, and to so much suffering? I feel sometimes as if I could not do it. Oh for someone to decide for me what is right, the best for all! It seems so selfish to think of enjoyment in connection with going.

28 May

Changed the trimming of my bonnet, and put on a black ribbon, and at 12 went to Mrs. Gardner's funeral. Dined with Mother. Her foot again painful, not able to use it—the trouble is in the joint of heel and ankle.

Had a long talk with dear W. in evening about my morbidness. He cannot understand it; but he believes in me and is an angel of sympathy, yet does not encourage any indulgence of it. What a loving soul he has.

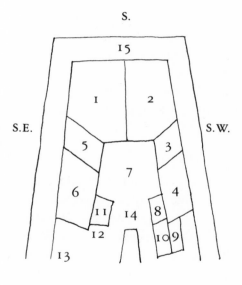

S.

S.E.

S.W.

Rome   14 December

1. parlor
2. my chamber
3. W.'s room
4. Cousin Nancy's
5. a small chamber where we take lunch
6. chamber unoccupied now
7. salle à manger, don't use it
8. ante-room
9. ante-room
10. a servant's chamber
11. small room
12. smaller room
13. kitchen
14. balcony on courtyard
15. balcony all around the house

Up 4 long flights and called 4th étage.

25 December

Fine day, then 46° in evening. W., H. and I went, after carrying some presents to Hunt children and Grace Kuhn's little boy, to St.

Peter's where we arrived just as the Pope was being carried up the nave in his chair.[10] Had a fine view of him. Heard the silver trumpets, then moved about the church and heard Mass in a side chapel, and then came home. Spent some time in shortening my dress. Wrote a letter to Godfrey from Harry. Thought of home. So passed Christmas. Cousin Nancy dined at Mrs. Tom Cary's.

1868

Rome   29 *January*

Another splendid day. Had letters from Powell and Fanny yesterday. The former says that our income this year is about $14,000, though that seems to me unduly small and I imagine is a very moderate statement.[11] Went with W. to see W. W. Story's studio. The *Sappho* struck me particularly, though the *Saul*, *Cleopatra*, statue of *Quincy*, and others were to me very fine indeed. Came home and took up H. and Cousin N. and went to the Rospigliosi Palace to see the *Aurora*.[12] Wonderfully beautiful. The garden very pretty, camellia and hyacinths in full bloom. Home and sat still until 4, and then walked with H. to have a double strap fitted. In evening kept myself awake by sewing.

30 *January*

Fine day again. Started off at 10 for the hunt, out the Porta San Giovanni, and then to the left, a most lovely road and most beautiful view. The hills exquisite. Several dozen carriages, 40 or 50 horsemen, several in scarlet coats, the whole very picturesque.

Naples   8 April

Went with W. to bankers to sign some orders for money. Received there a letter from Powell, one from Miss E. Grant, one from Mrs. Cabot and Sadie, the latter all agog about our living in Brookline. Don't feel well and H. don't feel well: both took some magnesia and lemon.

Had a long and painful talk with W. about money.[13] It is our one point of difference, the result both of temperament and education. How I long to do exactly what he says, but I do not think it right. Went to bed early. Weather cloudy. Vesuvius buried apparently in a cloud of smoke, but can see no fire.

Lynton[14]   *30 July*

The sun out bright, and the place perfectly lovely. Our hotel backs on a very tiny little village, with the picturesque church and churchyard at the side. The other side looks right down a sloping hillside on to the sea. On the right runs a lane shaded by trees and hedges going down very steeply to the beach, and village of Lynmouth below. Round the house are a few shrubs, vines and flowers, and the green-est, thickest bits of lawn I ever saw; and a gate leads on to a path along the hillside with some seats and fine trees. Stretching off to the right are wonderful cliffs, painted in the deepest colors, red, purple and green, and the valley of the Lyn thickly wooded. Altogether I think it is the prettiest place I ever saw. Our parlor has a large bay window opening on to a little piazza overlooking all this beauty, and, to add to the pleasure, the sun after the early morning goes around the house, and leaves us in perfect shade. Nothing could be more delightful. A fine bracing day. After breakfast we took a horse and donkey, and walked to what they call the castle, some high hills of [?] so washed with rain etc. as to stand out like buildings.

I feel splendidly, no dyspepsia. The baby has a rash all over her face and all, does not seem very bright, and gave her some syrup of rhubarb.

In the afternoon we drove to the Watersmeet, where the Lyn and Brandon meet.

Pau[15]   *22 November*

W. stayed at home with Harry and I went to the Episcopal church behind the Grand Hotel, a Mr. Tait the clergyman. Full of English, and do not feel at home nor do I like the service. Walked home with Mrs. Baylies.

At six dined with Mrs. Baylies.

Much pain all day in my hip and leg.

7 December

Exquisite sunrise. Mother called me in to see it from her room. After this clouded up but still very pleasant, absolutely no wind and there is in our parlor no fire and windows open, 68°. Saw to washing and various things, as Katy and Mother have no tongues; then sat a little while in parlor to hear H. take his lesson.[16] Took a drive with Mother. On way home, got out and went in to see a Mrs. Fay about a teacher, and did some shopping. Home a little before two. Out again at 2 ¼ in carriage to take H. to the dancing teacher's house to learn his first steps. Then to buy a common hat, pair of kid gloves and order some boots.

Mlle. Larroque began her lessons this evening at 5—Harry rather refractory.

20 December

Lovely day again. Very warm. Mother and Katy went to church and W. and I took H. and R. in the carriage to the park. Very lovely but very warm, so that I was obliged to open Ruth's little light coat. H. complained of feeling very tired, and pain in neck and shoulder. In afternoon I went to French Protestant service in rue Servier and fell asleep. On return found Harry feverish with headache and nausea. W. very much worried, and went for a physician. In meantime H. fell asleep and got into a perspiration. Got him to bed. When Dr. Bagnell the English physician arrived I had quite decided it was nothing but a bad cold.[17] He prescribed an emetic if he was restless and more feverish. A young girl of fourteen on the story below us, a Miss Bloode, is dangerously sick with brain fever begun by sunstroke. In evening sat up until after midnight watching the burning of a house near us. Very magnificent.

25 December

A most perfect day, a little cooler. Waked by Harry before five whistling and exclaiming over his tool box, his purse, marbles, stamp book, and crayons. All entirely satisfactory. Ruth waked up in the middle of the night to talk about Santa Claus. Her doll's carriage and teacups also filled her soul.

After breakfast went with Mother to hear the music at St Martin's—poor.[18] Sent the children off to dine at Baylies' and then walked with Mother to the Place Royale—music and quite gay and the view most lovely. For dinner a regular plum pudding. The children came home with doll and paintbox; and the day ended most happily. Dressed our room with some very beautiful holly, and mistletoe. Began giving Harry cod-liver oil.

1869

Pau   20 *January*

Beautiful day, though cool. Walter and H. wanted to go to the stee-plechase, so we gave them the carriage, and they took Arthur and Amelia, and Mother and I walked down to the Place Royale and the Park. [19] The Mountains covered with snow and most exquisite. I find owing to practice I can walk much better than I could a month ago. Not home till after three. H. much excited over an accident at the chase, and also the fall of his riding teacher just as he was winning the race. Miss Upton and Mr. Shields and Miss Stewart called. Baylies and Masons came to dinner. I very sleepy, for first time for a long while.

7 *February*

Most perfect and exquisite day. Fresher than it has been, but could sit with the windows open all day. I started little after ten, and took Ruth and H. to the Park, where we passed over two hours most de-liciously. The birds were as jubilant as with us in early June, a little squirrel threw down moss and bits of wood on us. The Mountains were like a dream of heaven. The children were as gay and as good as they could be, running about picking flowers, running down the banks together, rustling the leaves, or sitting with me on the seat listening to the birds. What can be greater happiness than this? I have felt very well all day, and but little tired when I got home, the children always walk tediously slow. Laid down and read. Mother and Walter went to a service at the Grand Hotel, read by Arthur.

Mother not well, has headache and dyspepsia. W. went to ride in afternoon, Mother took R. and Katy to drive, and H. and I went at 4 to church. Then came home and sang hymns. After dinner read aloud some poetry. A Sunday spent after my heart—peaceful, quiet and happy.

Paris   23 March

Still very cold and cloudy. At 12 went out with Mother in carriage and gone 5 hours, for teapot, egg spoons, gloves, and every variety of odds and ends. H. and W. took a short ride on horseback. My saddle and H's come from England and look very nice.

Dined downstairs. Am fairly unpacked; only half my things on sofa, as my armoire is locked and no key.

24 May

Over six weeks since the last lines were written; and I now have a fat, well, dear little daughter added to my treasures. Three children, a son and two daughters. How nice it sounds. How delightful it is. My confinement was all over by twelve o'clock the night of April 9th; and though I took more ether I think than Sam would have given me, and came to several times before it was ended, I have rather less dread than more than I felt before, of the suffering. After this I did wonderfully, astonishing nurse and Dr. for a week, and then had an attack of inflammation of the bowels, which scared us all, and then slight inflammation of the veins of my right leg, which carried me back to bed after being up, so that I did not sit up until the baby was 5 weeks old, nor ride out till a week ago last Saturday, over five weeks. But today I have been out to ride twice with the carriage open. Can eat what I like, and can slowly get up and down the one flight of stairs to the court, though my legs are pretty weak and lame.

The baby had a troublous time for the first three weeks, as Mrs. Munroe's nurse did not write, nor send her address, as the telegram did not reach her; and I had to get another, whose milk left her entirely, and after trying to get along, the poor baby growing thin and having diarrhoea badly, we had to send her home, take another for two days, and then fortunately could have the nurse I had lost, Mrs. Munroe's, Reine Hortense as she is named, Non Non as we called her. And the baby slowly, in ten days perhaps, got into order, and has gained flesh, till she is as fat and well as any baby could be. She is larger than Ruth in every way, and looks about very knowingly for a child of six weeks. She was carried out when five days old, and is now out pretty much all day. Non Non whom I dreaded, thought from her letters was very *exigeante*, and when she first came would be discontented, is bright and pleasant, takes good care of baby, and has given me a good lesson not to judge by appearances, nor borrow trouble. Ruth and Harry are finely. Katy has decided to remain another year. Louis was married the 22nd of April. Mrs. Cabot and all are well. The Baylies are here, and quite near in the Avenue Joséphine; and Lincoln and Walter have gone to Étretat and Dieppe to look for houses for the summer.

I have changed cooks, and have been busy arranging dinners, as my five servants are not as easy to satisfy as three.

Mme. Chouad the monthly nurse left on Saturday to my joy, though a very good nurse and in many ways good and pleasant woman, but with her difficulties; and then I never make myself a favorite with anybody, and I always feel it. And now I have condensed the unfortunate items for the last six weeks I believe—excepting that Annie Webber left here before my confinement, and we have heard of her safe arrival in Boston and we hope soon to hear of Bessie Lee's. Also Walter has bought five pictures by modern artists. He has suffered a good deal from boils, also from [worry?], but is looking better.

Arques[20]   *3 July*

The weather has been so cold all the week that one day we gave up riding, and another I wore my winter coat, wadded jacket underneath, and waterproof over, and was cold at that. Sitting out was almost impossible. Harry is cutting two large back teeth, and has been a little feverish. Walter not quite well, and Mother complaining of neuralgia.

Yesterday I cut off Ruth's hair. I can hardly call them curls; but the color was so light and so beautiful, a golden yellow, that it was hard to part with it. But she is more comfortable, and looks pretty with her round comb above her little round face.

Have been reading a poem by George Eliot, *The Spanish Gypsy*.[21] Don't know why, but all the terrible questions of the future seem to have come to me very vividly. I feel as if living on the edge of a precipice and cannot feel at ease, though very happy in the present. Sometimes all these realities seem very much, one cannot grasp them. I hardly know which state of mind is best, for fear does not lead to much that is good. Trust is so hard for me.

14 August

Started after breakfast to take Non Non and baby to see Dieppe; but a tremendous shower came up, and so we had to turn back, then started again, leaving Non Non behind, and it became exquisite weather.

I feel rather better today, but have been pretty miserable this week, chiefly mental. Waked up one night and got into such a state of trembling and perspiration, thinking about the suffering in the world, and the mystery of life, that I could hardly lie still, and came near calling out to relieve myself. But there was dear W. so peaceful at my side, that I *must* not disturb him.

After dinner took a nice walk with the children and Non Non and baby to Château. Took a glass of lemonade, [gaseous?].

24 August

Walter has decided to go, and I hurried around to get all his things and arrange all his bottles and powders I insist he should take in case of sickness.[22] Took him to the cars, and cried my eyes out coming home. Went up nevertheless to talk French with Mrs. Eckley, and in sympathy for her constant anxiety forgot my heartache. I want him to go, but I do so miss him. In the afternoon went with Mlle. and H. down to the meadows, and got the old fisherman to pull us home in his boat.

13 September

Received at breakfast a letter from Amelia Mason telling us of a telegram from America announcing the death of Isabella Appleton. She was to be confined in November, and I suppose her death was the result of that. It is too old a story to cry. Ah, the uncertainty of life! But it becomes stamped into one's experience more deeply with every succeeding day of life. And why does it not come to us, and when, and how shall we bear the agony? Rain.

Pau   6 October

Hard at work all day going over inventories and scolding about the small supply of cooking utensils, etc. M. and Mme. Bar tough subjects. Very warm. I went to bed right after dinner, I was so tired.

Arthur Mason has been here to talk about Powell Parkman.

Bagnères-de-Bigorre[23]   7 October

The heat most oppressive. Afraid to let the children go out, and afraid of their getting sick; so after some debate decided on a second move, and managed by dint of hard work to get packed and start by two o'clock for the station, only leaving cook and man behind. The heat in station and in the cars was really very severe, and felt alarmed for baby. Train tediously slow, did not reach Bagnères-de-Bigorre till seven; and then to our horror found all the hotels full. Finally tumbled into some rooms opening on to a court, two or three only on to an entry, and went to bed wishing ourselves in our well aired rooms in Pau.

8 October

Too hot to be out but a short time. Looked for rooms and found some in the Hôtel de Paris on the Place. Tried a little walk before night, but felt very weary.

1870

Biarritz[24]   *11 February*

The ground fast becoming white with snow. Started from Pau at 12 and came in cars to Bayonne and then here by omnibus; but the weather very cold and stormy, fear we shall freeze. I am writing this however in a clean snug little chamber, with a bright fire, and feel quite like a girl of sixteen on her honeymoon, only honeymoons are dreadful, and this is very nice. An awful struggle, however, to leave the children. W. has sold his horse Nora to Mrs. Belknap for 1500 Fr. and we have heard of a possibility of selling Emir and letting the house. So we shall end off and start for Paris as soon as I get home.

London   8 May

Not out all day and spent it badly in packing. Hate the life. At half-past five drove down to Spurgeon's tabernacle, expecting little, but were deeply impressed.[25] He heavy and common looking; but preached with wonderful power on the atonement, a doctrine I could not agree to but he was very earnest and impressive. 6,000 souls hung on his words and a half were in tears. Would not have missed it for a great deal, nor the drive home across the river and by Westminster Abbey by moonlight.

Beverly   23 August

My cold, instead of giving way in a day or two of bed, has kept me there until today. Now it is hardly better, only I cannot find that bed was doing anything but weaken me. I have taken [opiate?] pills all the time. The worst cold on my chest and in my head I ever had.

Ruth has had one for some time too, and after keeping her in the house and being very careful of her diet she suddenly had regular dysentery, and has been in bed since Saturday, but is better. Mother came down from Boston yesterday and passed the night, and seemed very bright and well in spite of heat. She is arranging slowly for her move to Beacon Street. The Mount Vernon Street house is not sold yet, neither is the Chestnut Street nor the Blue Hill; and we have bought the place between here and Manchester that we looked at; so taking the White place at Brookline into account we have plenty of houses, yet are going to pass the winter at Mrs. Cabot's and Mother's and probably hire a house for next summer in Brookline.

The house here tempted us because it was so wonderfully cheap, and so wonderfully small and ugly, that it could not be counted as a *second* estate of which any care need be taken. It is too rocky to grow even grass, and the house too ugly ever to be embellished, which I count a great deal. I want all my care to go to my Brookline place, and this is to be only a camping-out place. It is cooler than almost any place on the Shore, has a lovely view, a little beach and cove of its own two steps below the house, is close to a railway station, and the house is large and commodious. I should like it a little nearer West Beach; but is only twenty minutes' walk by the railroad, 12 minutes' drive by the road, and a very short row.[26] So we *seem* to be fixed for life; and yet how these nicely arranged plans come to naught! The weather has continued very hot, and Sunday was one of the hottest.

Boston 17 *September*

Katy has come from Nova Scotia and an angel could not have been more welcome. She has agreed to come and help me in taking care

of baby; and it is time, for it is many weeks since I have had a good
night's rest. The baby is very wakeful at night and feeble in the day,
though her bowels are rather better. I have passed my time in trying
to find a wet nurse, and to persuade baby to nurse her. One woman,
an object of charity, with excellent milk, came, and I persuaded the
baby twice at night to nurse, of course with much difficulty; but the
woman disliked the care of her own baby, and entirely unconcerned
for her promise that she would stay, refused to remain in spite of
bribes and entreaties. It will be much more difficult to induce the
baby to take to another woman; but Sam thinks it so important that I
shall try. Two babies, one my own, so delicate that every mouthful
makes a difference, and [?] cares to be watched and cajoled is to say
the least troublesome.

Mother is getting her house ready. The weather is as hot almost as
August. I have put on black for Aunt Sears and consequently have
nothing to wear.

Brookline   28 September

We all moved to Brookline today.[27] Katy is coming to me for the winter, and Margaret leaves. It was a difficult business to manage; but
Margaret, though a good woman, was but little help to me. We are
delightfully settled.

Mlle. sleeps downstairs in the wing, and has the little room next as
parlor and schoolroom. This keeps the children out of sight and hearing of the rest of the house, and gives her a nice place in the evening.
The baby and Ruth have the two little rooms overhead. I am in Mrs.
Cabot's old room, and H. in a little room between, so it is all very nice.

1871

Boston (Mrs. Mason's house)   2 April

It is snowing hard, the trees and ground completely covered. As the crocuses are all in bloom, the lilacs budding, the grass green, and the frost entirely out of the ground, it is rather a violent change. But it cannot last; and we have had the most beautiful March I remember anywhere, no wind, soft and sunny, and as good walking as in June. It has been most fortunate for our house, which is now up one storey, and all the brickwork done except the chimney. It looks very nice, and is going to be very charming, I think. We have succeeded in placing it just right, and so far I see little to change. The ceilings are higher than I wanted, and I fear my dressing-room is the wrong side of the house; but some mistakes are almost inevitable. It will cost about twice what we intended, but I suppose that also is inevitable. We have decided about the Beverly house, and it is being altered; but we have not succeeded so far in letting or selling Blue Hill. Mount Vernon Street is sold, and I went there yesterday for the last time. $60,000 instead of $80,000! Selling and building are strong contrasts.

Walter and the children are very well. Mother has felt the spring a good deal as in days of yore, and I have felt something, and have a great deal of backache and pain in my legs. Still I do not feel badly; but I am trying to bring my mind to the fact that I shall never be strong or comfortable, that I shall always be nervous and find life hard, and also that, instead of arranging for this, I have built and bought two large houses to take care of, and must prepare for a life-long struggle with poor servants. So do we preach and practice. I meant to do differently: in looking back even it seems to me that I did all I could. So people always say who let circumstances mold their lives, instead of themselves molding circumstances. If we clearly saw the right path, it seems as if one could follow it; but when at each step one is uncertain which ought to be taken, one takes the one which pleases and satisfies others rather than oneself. It was not self-ishness, but I fear it was a foolish self-sacrifice, and that my husband and children will suffer more than if I had made them give up some advantages. But it is done; and I am trying now to take things as they are and do the best. But it is hard to feel that a year ago all was in your own hands and you have drifted instead of guiding. I am weak, weak, weak, and then complain and regret. Walter is very happy, and that is the best thing; and what if I do pass my life in drudgery, if I do it for him and for God. Perhaps it is as good a life as I can have. For I suppose bearing with servants, bearing with your own miserableness, if borne heroically, is as noble a fight as any that can be fought—all the more because no one sees that it is any fight at all, even the nearest and dearest.

14 June

Moved to our new house, West Manchester, in the eleven o'clock train.

It has been very warm in Brookline, and Mrs. Cabot was anxious to come down earlier than usual, so of course we could not be in her way, and have hurried down pell-mell. H. and I came down last to place the furniture, which I expected to find all here; but it had come by car, and we met the carts just beginning to bring it. W. went up fagged out in the middle of the day. Barney and I stayed until five, and then missed the *last* train, and had to race over in a hired wagon to Beverly, where we found the cars had changed, and we waited an hour and a half. Drank tea at Mother's, and drove out in evening after a long day's work.

Brookline   26 December

Today is the day fixed for the grand event, our move to the hill. This morning, last things have gone, and I went up to the house, in spite of a drizzle which at night increased to a pour. The avenue, never properly laid, is so deep that one has to get along on floating boards, and the dirt and nastiness are beyond belief; but after dinner, up we came, and are really in the house.

1872

Brookline   1 January

A fine day, and Mother came out to dine with us. Mr. Leighton and his carpenters have been here until Saturday night, hammering, planing, and stepping round everywhere, but are really gone. The weather has been most dismal and unusual, a dense mist most of the time, shutting out all view, damp and gloomy. Saturday I went to Boston, and did a quantity of pressing errands. Ruth took a bad cold, and is in her bed. Mother seemed very bright and well, and brought little Fanny with her; and I sent them after a three o'clock dinner to town, and brought out Harry from dancing.

11 February

The weeks roll on, and my time shortens. Sometimes I am full of dread; then the reward, and the thought that what I have borne I can bear again, gives me courage, and I think of other things. But it seems to me harder to look forward to each time, rather than easier.

Mother has had a series of colds in her head, though not sick; and I have driven to town twice a week to dine. *(while pregnant)*

I have plenty to do, as I have two or three rooms and an attic full of unassorted goods and chattels and rubbish; but all essentials are arranged, and I feel comparatively at leisure.

The children have had a great time this week, coasting on the crust, Walter going from top of hill to bottom with Ruth and baby in front; but we are again getting to bare ground. I have had two delightful sleigh rides and beautiful weather. Lizzie C. is still obliged to go often to Cambridge where things are worse rather than better. She is a saint.

21 April

Who can begin their daily life again, after the birth of a sound child, themselves well, and not feel full of gratitude to the great Creator, full of wonder at this great miracle, no less wonderful a miracle because so many times repeated? There is something very beautiful to me in having this new life begin with the revival of nature, the birth of the whole vegetable world. Many things have happened, too, to stir all my deepest emotions. Lizzie Lee has lost her two daughters, just as I was rejoicing in my added child, and under such trying circumstances.

Mother too is and has been sick for 5 weeks, and been very lonely and depressed; and I feel very far away from her. The problem is never to be solved, to try to do away practically with this distance.

12 June

Very warm, and Mother carried downstairs for first time, but it was on a bed by six men, and she dozed a good deal. Powell came from Walpole, but she said but little to him.

Our house is full of paperers and painters. It is very painful; and yet, as it does not incommode her, I let it go on.

15 June

My wet nurse left the baby under a tree and went off, saying nothing to anyone. The baby will not feed, and it is hard to get one immediately. I feel sometimes as if I could not hold out any longer, I am so tired and so tried.

19 June

Mother died this morning at about eight o'clock, as peacefully as a little child, 65 years old next December. She had been unconscious for some days, and though she has asked for me once or twice, I do not think she knew me. She seemed to suffer less. Margaret has been her devoted servant and friend, and feels her loss like a mother's. [28] She looks very peacefully. Oh, is it possible? Dead—dead—what does it mean?

West Manchester   17 July

Went to Boston, and brought down my new Swedish wet-nurse and her baby. She promises well; and Jane, who is very good, unfortunately does not suit the baby at all, nurses him all day long. He has been in a very bad state, and I felt he might be very sick any moment. But I have had so much disappointment that I hardly like to expect much from this nurse, though she appears well. Ruth has been sick, a bilious attack; but excepting that, we have all been well.

9 September

Came home from Walpole today, after a visit full of sadness, but also full of pleasure. Every stone remained in the spot it was 17 years ago, which as far as I can reckon is the last time I was there apart from a day with Walter.[29]

Its loveliness is more exquisite than I painted it even in my memory. We walked up on to the hills where I used to go to dream as a girl; and it seemed like returning to a former world peopled by shadows. Almost all gone from my present life, who surrounded me then. How one's own being seems changed, though still the same; and what a wonderful train of blessings have followed my steps! What wildest dream could have pictured the future then to me half as bright as at the living present it is now, with a husband beyond all ideal because breathing reality, the mother of four darling beings, with houses and lands, friends, and other gifts too many to count! Why is it we must come up to the [mts?] of life realize the blessedness of our surroundings, and walk our daily path with closed eyes to its delights?

I never saw Walpole so rich at this season. The incessant rains have filled the river and made everything wonderfully luxuriant. I enjoyed it very much, too, Fanny and the children. I went to see several old friends—the Haywards, Miss Williams, and Hattie Dorr—and also engaged a most delightful housekeeper.

Found the children all nicely. The baby is certainly splendid.

Brookline   13 September

Moved up from Manchester, as Walter is very anxious to begin on his barn. Very hot day, and a pouring rain in afternoon, in the midst of which W. and Barney arrived, driving the two carriages.

24 November

Thursday, went to Boston to see about moving some things from house, which I wish I had never done, also about dear Margaret's present, and to see Aunt Parkman, who arrived on Thursday. She is bent with rheumatism, but otherwise looks well and very lively. Is at Tremont House. Today drove into town in afternoon to Catholic church, to see Margaret and Patrick married.

Thursday my two Swedish servants arrived, healthy strapping wenches. Bridget stayed to show them till Saturday. How I hate the exchange.

8 December

Not much to be told of the past fortnight, except unmitigated bother. My housekeeper departed indignant, and leaving me with no one in her place. The laundress has been in bed three days with face-ache, used up all the wood and nearly all the water in the house, and tore the clothes. The cook don't know how to boil a potato nor light a fire, and yesterday was sent to the hospital on account of a sore and varicose veins! I all the time feeling so wretched that I ought to have been in bed.

15 December

Have passed a very wretched and unhappy week, from the discovery of what is again before me. "I pray for patience, but it cometh not." I have had countless blessings and few great griefs, and yet rest, for which my very soul thirsteth, is denied me. I have ceased to believe in it for now or the future; and yet when one is hungry can they do anything but make believe that they do not pant for food.

Elliot was attacked on Monday with lung fever, and it has been a week full of anxiety on his account and Lizzie's; but today he seems decidedly better, and the attack a light one.

Smallpox is everywhere; and according to orders from the town, all the servants have been vaccinated today.

Christmas is coming; but I have made no preparations for it, nor can I, it is too fatiguing. I have a temporary cook now; but soon this peace must pass, and I start on a new era of worry.

1873

Brookline   19 January

A week of bad weather, melting, freezing, blowing, and the most slippery walking that was ever seen, so that for me the use of my feet has entirely stopped and indeed I have hardly been out. Still at working clearing up, and have finally got the spare chambers on this floor cleared up and pleasant looking. Yesterday passed the day in moving everything out of the trunk room, preparatory to having drawers put in; so clothes, books, knickknacks, linen, etc., etc., were packed and re-packed and changed about for the tenth time at least. Now all un-arranged articles are massed in one big room, so gradually the limits narrow, and I hope this winter to see all put in their proper resting places; but the amount of work is incalculable until one has done it. Children all well. I cross and dyspeptic as can be and not drive out of the house all the other members of the family. Grumble, grumble, find fault, from morning till night, bitterly regret it, determine to do differently, think I cannot be quite so bad again, and then repeat the program exactly.

Louis and Amy are staying at Mrs. C.'s and are very anxious I should devote myself and Walter to driving, resting, and nursing generally;

but I don't see the way for many reasons, and fancy my status is to be much the same as long as I live. I dread death, and yet feel at times it would be better for the children—excepting their bodies—and better even for Walter that I should leave them. It is so bad for them, a constant atmosphere of discontent and complaint, dullness and hardness. I am fond of Mlle., but her boisterousness, and want of tact, are so irritating to one, that I do not [word omitted] I could have her remain, if it were not for the gay, light-hearted atmosphere she makes for the children.

27 April

Very busy again, though I try hard not to be, and have given up the dinner to Walter and old Bridget. Have engaged an American woman at $7 a week, to take the place of Miss Coffin, the baby's nurse. Also passed Thursday night at Powell's, and divided with him Mother's silver-plated ware, linen, etc. A good deal of inevitable shopping for the children. Went this week and took Mlle. to see some theatricals in the town hall.

4 May

The ground this morning covered with several inches of snow, trees and everything white! Walter has just succeeded, too, with great exertion, in planting some hundred trees and shrubs received from England. New nurse has come, and Miss [Craigie?] the housekeeper and Miss Coffin gone. Matilda the laundress, Swedish, went to town Thursday, taking $15 I loaned her, and has not returned. Tuesday took Harry to hear the negroes sing in town hall. Friday went to a meeting of executive committee of Woman's Education Association, poured buckets.[30] Yesterday took children to the dentist, getting tired in spite of the best I can do. May Day was a warm and lovely day, and Ruth and Elise had a picnic with Charley and the Frank Cabot girls, all under the trees at the head of Mr. Lyman's avenue under the lookout.

1874

8 January

Aunt Parkman died today at half past ten. She had been almost a mother to me, and is one of the last links connecting me intimately with Boston, or my unmarried life. For weeks she has been unable to speak plainly; but I think she knew me until almost the last, and said I was her greatest comfort, though I could do nothing but feel for her. Her sickness has been a very painless one.

6 March

I am for the first time since September shut up in my room—in fact have been in bed for two days. The winter has been the happiest time I can remember, partly from my better health which has made me feel as if the world was a new and better place, and more still from the health of Walter and the children which has been almost unbroken, and from my gradually settling down in my new home and home cares which become much easier by practice. I am very busy, but not driven—a great difference. The baby is a perfect delight, the gayest and most active of all the children; and Marianne and Bridget—nurse

and wet-nurse—have been so faithful and amicable, as to relieve one
of all anxiety. Harry is growing a big boy and a strong one, and has
taken hold of his lessons in a way to give me great satisfaction. I have
finally achieved really clearing up all the "clutter" left from moving,
and have arranged and overlooked vast piles of old letters, giving me
a comfortable sense of not being in arrears.

1881

Brookline   22 March

Went over before dinner to say goodbye to Mrs. Cabot. Lizzie C. has
been with me all day. Mabel went down in middle of day to receive a
watch from her grandmother, Mimi Lyman sent her a ring with a
little sapphire, and Walter a travelling bag.[31] Louis sent me a chair.
We have been overwhelmed with kindness and expressions of feeling.

London   7 April

Read our second batch of letters received last evening, dated 25
March. Mr. C. went off to an appointment with Mr. Ben Crowninshield. I took Mlle. and the children down to hunt up a fur store in
Watling Street which Fanny gave me, but which turned out whole-
sale after all. Saw the Thames Embankment and St. Paul's inside and
out, and got Walter measured for some clothes at Nicholls, and just
got home in time for lunch. Wrote in afternoon and shivered with
dread. Mr. C. took the children for an hour's walk. At 5, Mr. Spencer

Wells, Sir James Paget, Mr. Thornton and Meredith arrived.[32] Mabel agreed to see the latter without much discomfort; and when I told her that I wanted her to smell something which I had taken, and would do her no harm, she put her little hand into mine and never hesitated. Mr. M. administered the bichloride of methylene which they use instead of ether.

I remained in the room. The needle seemed as if going through soft bone. Mabel came out from ether very quietly, with no nausea. Physicians decided that it was ovarian in character but might also be malignant, and unanimously and decidedly advised an exploratory opening. Give no hope otherwise of life longer than for 6 months, and probably attended with much suffering. Mabel ate some bread and milk, but did not go to sleep until 9.30 as the Dr. wanted her to lie still on her back. Had to turn her on side. Heard from Lizzie that Perry Winsor is dead and Guy has gone to [Louisiana?].

10 April

Mabel slept from soon after seven last evening to eight this morning, as peacefully as a little lamb.

The weather has been steadily growing milder. It was very damp and chilly early in the week; but the sun has been out in its dim misty London style every day, and yesterday and today are very soft and mild. The streets are full of daffodils, primroses and gilly flowers, to sell for a penny a bunch, and the peach trees are in blossom, the green leaves coming out on the bushes in the parks.

Mlle. and Rose went at ten to a Catholic chapel, and Mr. C. and I are sitting with Mabel who is gay and chirrups like a bird. She looks plump and rosy, and very hungry. How will it be next Sunday? Is it I who have to face such a dreadful future? Oh, my courage seems to flow away, and I feel helplessly weak. Walter keeps up most of the time, but sometimes it is impossible.

This evening before dinner Mr. J. Charles Potter came, our shipboard friend. Mr. Cabot and Mr. Meredith went out hunting for rooms, in vain. At 8.30, Mr. Thornton arrived for a last talk. He considered it absolutely sure that this is a solid tumor. He came across substances with the needle that could not be pierced. He considered it equally sure that it will enlarge. If left to itself it causes death by disturbance of all the organs, a slow and very suffering death, the worst, so he thought, of all deaths. If it is malignant, death may ensue at any moment by piercing of the bowels or similar injury elsewhere. His diagnosis is that it is a dermoid ovarian tumor, ovarian from the position as first observed by me, dermoid from its hardness (bone, hair, teeth, etc. being often found). He thinks the fall may have twisted it on its pedicle in such a way as to stop the passage of blood, and so arrested the growth. The renewed growth would come from new attachments. These are at first very delicate, and removable by the finger, afterwards become more tough and must be parted with scissors and tied, later on much harder. He proposes making a small opening in the flesh outside the tumor sufficient to insert the finger, and lay bare the surface of the tumor. If he discovers the tumor (and he expects to be able to ascertain) to be malignant, the wound is easily healed and becomes as sound as before with no painful consequences. If he finds no proof of its being malignant, he will make a larger opening, sufficient to insert the hand and ascertain if the attachments are such as can be dealt with with any hope of success. This involves some risk; but the tumor will not be pierced except by an accident, and the wound will probably heal well. If however the attachments would give any ground for hope of a successful removal, he would complete the operation at once. Danger would then be from death at the time from the great shock to the system or from bleeding. If she lived through the operation, there would be good chance for recovery, and she might be well in three weeks. Mr. C. and I both said that we wished the operation proceeded with if there was *any* hope of success. We should rather she died in the operation rather than to recover to die by inches.

He told us of a nurse and lodgings and we talked over further arrangements. Did not leave until after ten, and refused a fee. Very gentlemanly and very sympathetic.

13 April

Very lovely day, only too warm, heat oppressive, sun would be bright but for the haze or smoke or whatever it is.[33] Out with Miss Matthews to buy blankets, flannel, feeding cup, etc. At 12, Mr. C., Mlle. and I took Mabel in a brougham to buy presents.[34] Got a brooch for Ruth, [silver?] buttons for Harry, pencil for Elise, brooch for Miss Holman, and cross for Marianne. She wanted to get a cream pitcher for Aunt Lizzie and a handbag for Uncle Elliot, but had not quite time. Was out two hours. Ate a hearty breakfast of chops, etc., buttered bread at 11, chicken and baked apple at 2.30. Wanted to go out to Hyde Park again; but the wind has changed to east, and it is colder, sun gone in, and we persuaded her to play cards instead.

Miss Matthews, Walter and I took the brougham and went for a screen and some shoes for Walter. My nettle rash better. Walter has a good deal of cold, and Mabel a frog in her throat; but I think it is the heavy atmosphere and debilitating warmth.

Mr. Thornton came at 6.30. Played High Low Jack until eight. Then Mabel went to bed. I wanted try the temperature after she was in bed, and she begged that her father would come up again. She has been looking over her presents and rejoicing in them. Whispered to me that she wanted to carry a present to Barney, Maggie, Katy, and all. We decided on a knife for Barney and brooches for the women. She very happy and gay. She kept saying "see little Ma, she's too cunning," and hugging and kissing us. Then she wanted Mamadelly to sit close by her. Her love is overflowing. Oh how can I live through tomorrow, and what it will probably bring; for our brightest hope is that the doctors will be willing to go on, and that she will die under their hands. That she should a second time get well only to die in long drawn-out torments seems too awful, and yet it is probable. The doctors and the nurse think it probable. I hear the verdict ringing in my ears: if she could have come to us sooner, we could have cured her, but it has gone too far, too far.

14 April

Rain. This made it easy to keep Mabel contented in not going out. Had her breakfast, of fish and bread and butter, and milk at 8, and at 11 some beef tea and toast. Dressed her, etc., and took her after her lunch into the dining room downstairs. Walter had been out early and bought a bag for Elliot and some breastpins for the women. She busied herself writing the names and hers on all the boxes. Miss Matthews hard at work arranging the room upstairs, the curtains, the beds, the fire, the table and carpets, etc.

Sent Rose out for a knit jacket. Got home just in time to send her and Mlle. and Walter off in a brougham at 25 minutes after one, as Mr. Thornton arrived, he in his shirtsleeves with carbolic acid, boiling water, etc., etc.

At two Meredith arrived. I told her he wanted to see her upstairs, and she without hesitation or objection went up with me into the back room and was undressed. Put her on the bed. When she saw him come in with the bottle and tube for giving the methylene hung round his neck, she looked a little wistful, but said nothing and put her hand in mine. In a few moments she was unconscious, and he took her up and carried her to the other room and put her on the table. There were Sir James Paget, Mr. Spencer Wells, Mr. Thornton, Mr. Meredith, an assistant, and the nurse. I came downstairs at ten minutes after two. At twenty minutes of three Sir James P. came down to say that a large dermoid ovarian tumor had been perfectly and beautifully removed with very slight loss of blood, nothing malignant, nothing extraordinarily difficult. I don't know what I felt, for when I heard his descending steps so soon, all my worst fears I suppose realized, and that he had come to say nothing could be done. He was wonderfully kind. Sir James Paget and Mr. Wells drove off with their carriages and pairs at 4, the whole being completed. They said they thought the chances were ten to one in her favor.

Mr. Thornton went home to dinner, but before going asked us to see the tumor. It is as large and unyielding as her own head, of an irregular oval shape, with a new growth, softer, projecting from one end. He showed us the pedicle where it was attached to the right ovary, the place at the side where it was probably injured last autumn and found new connections with the walls of the abdomen, also attachments to the bowels, the place where he inserted the needle, and the place he first punctured today, to let out the liquid. It contained large pieces of bone, human hair, besides semi-solid and liquid substances. The opening to take out tumor was about 5 inches long.

After his dinner, Mr. Thornton returned and Mr. Meredith went home. Mr. Meredith called me to come into the room where I found

Mabel very restless and excited, complaining much of the tightness of the band round her body, of general uneasiness, and of nausea. They gave her beef tea, laudanum and digitalis by the rectum. The nausea came to vomiting several times, which was very distressing. At times she quieted down for some time, but not sleeping more than a short time at once. She had two very restless and excited turns during the night, accompanied in the latter with a collection of phlegm in the throat which troubled her very much. Very thirsty. Mr. Meredith sat up all night, most of the time near her. He tried her temperature and pulse every hour. I watched her closely. The nurse sat on one side of the bed, I on the other, saying as little as possible and fanning and holding a little bowl when sick. The doctor put her pillows very high and gave her ammonia and water to clear the chest, as there is great fear of lung trouble. Her knees were over two little pillows, and we kept them as still as possible, but she wanted to move them constantly. I put three chairs in a row by her bedside and a cushion against the wall at the head. I dozed a little. Towards morning I got a little nap on the sofa, and then came down to breakfast. Mr. Thornton took Mr. Meredith's place at 9.30. He brought her a delicious rose. Told me to go down and get a nap; and when he left at 11 sent word that I had better not go back, in which judgment I agreed from what I saw.

15 April

Temperature 101 ½, pulse 120. Doing fairly well, not as much nausea and vomiting as usual after methylene. Mr. Meredith comes when Mr. Thornton goes, the latter back at one and again at five. Her temperature raised a degree towards five, her chest better, but her skin not acting very well, and does not sleep, only short naps. Gave her bromide of potash. Determined not to cable until tomorrow. Mr.

Potter called and very kind. Mr. Meredith back at eight, Mr. Thornton at 10 for the night. Walter and Mlle. went to Hyde Park, a beautiful day and very quiet. Neighbors kind and interested, and street owing to Good Friday unusually quiet. Mr. Thornton came into parlor and stayed until after midnight, telling us his experiences and all about Mabel.[35]

24 April

Found that some of what seemed nettle rash was caused by a very active flea; and as I slept better, and my tooth and throat are both better, I am decidedly more cheerful. Mr. C. went to hear Mr. Stopford Brooke preach.[36] I stayed with Mabel, as Mr. Thornton and Meredith came at eleven, to take the stitches out of her wound. She bore the lifting of the great mass of plaster which stuck very tight, and the cutting and drawing out of the silk threads, with the greatest patience, though I saw the color come into her face; but she said not a word, and smiled as brightly as ever. They praised her pluck most highly. They said the wound had healed unusually well; but she is to keep even more still than before for a few days, and they covered her again with the carbolized muslin and great strips of plaster.

At a little after two, Walter and I set off in a hansom to St. Paul's, where though about three-quarters of an hour before service, there was already a great crowd. Canon Liddon preached, who is considered an unusually fine speaker.[37] He was certainly elegant, and his pronunciation most clear and delicate. It was what seemed to us mincing; he raised his left arm only, and kept his voice *up* at the end of his sentences.

His language was very good and choice. The ideas did not seem to me to abound, that it was a kind of amplification of Christ's walk to

Emmaus with two apostles, and a moral drawn. There was also a reference to Lord Beaconsfield, nothing that I could not have said, only
not so well expressed.[38] The music was very impressive in the grand
church, though you cannot hear it as perfectly as in a smaller building. A fine anthem by Mendelssohn was sung by male and boys' voices.
The intoning I hate. We had been invited by Mrs. Potter, who made
us a little visit before lunch, to take afternoon tea with her; so, though
after five, and the pavement so slippery with rain that it was hard to
go fast, we decided to drive there. It is at the opposite end of the city.

We found Mrs. Potter and a married daughter, besides her two unmarried ones. Afterwards, Mr. Potter, our friend, and a baby granddaughter came in, the latter a most charming rosy little creature.
Mrs. Potter and two of her daughters are certainly very handsome,
and the other very intelligent. In fact I like this plain daughter very
much. Mrs. P. gaped in my face, but seemed to intend politeness, so
I took it quietly.

The house where she lives, and the whole blocks beyond it, she says
were not in existence several years ago. London grows as American
cities do.

Liverpool   20 May

Sunshine. Up at 6. Mabel had a good night and looks bright, but I
fancy has done rather more than was wise these last days. She is a
most eager sightseer.[39] Breakfast at 8. Ran in to bid goodbye to Uncle
H. and Fanny. Off bag and baggage at 9.15, Sophie saying a warm
goodbye, and Miss Matthews and Annette and Bessie going to station
with us. Miss Matthews gave Mabel a locket with her hair, Mabel
gave her a brooch with her hair; and the former said goodbye with
many tears. She is a nice woman. Mr. Meredith came to the station

with a fine basket of hothouse grapes, and remained until we started, Mabel of her own accord having made a bunch of lilies of the valley for him. She admired him most heartily.

Train started at 10.10 and we had a most delightful ride to Liverpool, the sun bright, and the grass the most brilliant and tender green, the briars in blossom and the foliage about half out. Mr. Cabot looked very miserably, but had a good nap. Got to Liverpool about 3.30 and found very nice rooms at the Adelphi. Had all our trunks up, and Rose and I packed and re-packed most indefatigably until it was dark, which was near nine.

Had a delicious night on soft nice beds, Mabel in a little bed, sleeping like a lamb. On what a change since last here—not two months ago![40]

1885

Brookline   28 February

Arthur slept at his grandmother's and this morning went to town thinking his grandmother better. I went down at 9 in the morning. Sam Cabot out at 11. Thought she showed signs of blueness. She was quite drowsy. Told me to watch closely, and give ipecac and ammonia. Returned to town. At half past eleven she complained of severe pains in back and limbs. Louis came in a little after one and we went for Dr. Sabine. Got her up into a rocking chair, but still suffered much. Dr. S. advised paregoric. Telephoned Arthur, and he said no, would

send his father. The pain lessened with hot embrocations. Sam out at
3.30. He looks very poorly himself. Found her temperature 103 and
breathing 40 to 45. She did not know him and called for him, and
said if he were there she knew he would help her. Sam finally took her
hand and spoke to her and she understood him. Sadie came out.
Mrs. C. became drowsy and quieter. Lizzie C. stayed with her until
after midnight.

1 March

At 2 o'clock I went into the room; she had long quiet naps of over an
hour and between spoke, recognized me, and asked if I had been
there long. Took milk, also pills of amm, ipecac and cereum. Waked
at six as quietly as a baby and looked rested and had a good color. I
asked if she felt better and she thought she did. She remembered the
name of Miss Rice the nurse, and asked about Katy MacIntosh's cold.
Perfectly clear in her mind. Her temperature lower. Stephen C.
arrived. After breakfast I sent up for Walter and when he came in she
said, "Oh, is that you, Walter." Elliot came too, and held her hand
some time. I went home. Returned at 4 P.M., found a second nurse,
Miss Kingston, there. Mrs. C. drowsy and breathing more labored.
Lizzie C. came at 8 P.M. I slept in Katy's room.

2 March

I went into room at 2 A.M., found her breathing very labored and
sleeping but for short times. She wanted magnesia which quieted her,
but very hot, and out of the bed twice in the night. After the last
time complained of faintness and distress in stomach. She had taken
some chicken broth, refused to try ammonia. Wanted some milk and
whisky. Distress increased. I called Arthur, and later Sam. Lizzie Lee
came in at 4. Sam turned her on her side and she suddenly ceased to

groan, had a look of infinite peace come over her face, and ceased to
breathe at about 8 A.M. Lizzie Lee was kneeling, holding her hand.
Sam, Arthur and Katy at her side. Lizzie C. came in, and Willy. We
breakfasted together, Lizzie Lee, Elliot, Stephen, Sam, Arthur, and
Willy. I saw the sun rise in his glory from her dressing-room window.

Sat up in the evening with Harry, exquisite moonlight. Mrs.
Cabot would have been 94 on the 17th of this month.

Scarborough[41]   *24 September*

Fine day, cooler, air more bracing, hotel high and better air than at
York. All went out to the Spa and grounds on hill over beach. W. and
I went into town, and at 12 E. and M. took an ocean bathe. After
lunch, R. and I repacked the trunks, H. having carried off one, so
that I have my black wood trunk (Mother's), Mr. C. his with brass
corners, R. a straw trunk or basket trunk, E. and M. a large bellows-
top leather, and W. a portmanteau. Besides this we have two extra
trunks—one light wood, one basket—which we shall send forward.
Splendid moonlight night, good for the voyagers. Hear through
papers today that cholera has appeared in town just outside Paris—
bad for us.

1886

London   22 September

Shopping hard. In afternoon to see the Colonial and Indian Exhibition. Very beautiful.

23 September

W. M. suffering from nettle rash. Wonderful weather, a little cooler. Looked for furs.

24 September

Out in afternoon with Mr. C. after his nap, to look for glass, china, etc.

25 September

In afternoon went to see a Japanese village performance, of wrestlers, dancers, tightrope, and rolling balls, rings, and a square board on an umbrella. In evening R., E. and Jacksons went to *Mikado*.[42]

30 September

Shopping steadily: china, glass, shoes, dresses, shawls, etc., etc. Went to hear Irving and Miss Terry in *Faust*. He a wonderful devil and the scenery most picturesque; but the whole does not seem to me high art.[43] Weather extraordinary, every day sunny and hot. The children have all had colds, E. quite a bad one, and I fear I have taken it.

Liverpool   3 October

Surprised Dr. M[eredith], who came at 7, by having my temperature almost normal. All started in ten o'clock train in a saloon car, 15 trunks and 11 packages! I quite protected in my new fur cloak. Reached Adelphi, Liverpool, at about 4, and went to bed.

At sea   5 October

Wonderful day, really hot and like August, bright and sunny. Bundle of gloves arrived from Paris just before starting. Tapestry from Florence came yesterday. Left hotel at one, crossed to vessel on tug. *Cepha-*

lonia started at about 3. The three girls and I have again staterooms at foot of stairs, which is nearly midships and well aired, though near the screw.[44] Mr. C. and W. on other side of cabin in same situation. Mrs. Henry Abbott, son and daughter on board. Also Mr. Jack Peabody and children, and Misses Fosdick, on board. These all we know. Miss Neilson, sister of Mrs. George Warren, under Mrs. A.'s care. I remained in stateroom on account of my cold.

1890

14 *May*

Walter M. has had a long cough and cold again keeping him at home. Decided to send him and Harry to Switzerland. They sail in the *Lahn*, 2 July. Presents for Ruth still pouring in. Miss Hovey sent her a locket, yellow sapphire with diamonds. Mr. Robert Paine sent an oil picture and $1,000. Mrs. P. an inlaid writing desk, the children a Sevres tea set, also candelabras and butter dish. Mr. Charles Paine $5,000, silver pitcher and waiter from Mrs. P., silver knives from children. Powell sent a silver water pitcher and waiter.

26 *May*

Gemma Timmins died, and Fanny Mason did not want to be bridesmaid as she was a great friend. Decided to ask Lotta Lowell to take her place and her dress.

27 May

Pouring southerly rain turned to East at 10 P.M., very dark. The awnings which we had put up over the terrace to West and South of house soaked and flabby.

28 May

Most exquisite day. John Barthlome arrived, brought 16 waiters and 7 women. Table the length of dining room into bay window. Two great cakes. Bob came out at 12. Ruth's satin was very becoming, the skirt plain, embroidered round bottom and up sides in white and long train 2½ meters. Sleeves full on shoulder and high, with high standing collar embroidered, and open in front with fichu of crepe lisse. I put on her tulle veil with a wreath of myrtle and a sprig on waist and sleeves. She wore her pearl necklace, and a little white violet sent her by Ellen Coolidge. Willy came to take her photograph with no great success. Then we all, Lotta Lowell included, dined in hall. Elise and Lotta, Mabel and Ethel Paine were the bridesmaids, the two former in white crepe over pink satin, the latter same over white. I went up the aisle with Walter M. Robert came out of the little side door at 3.30 looking very white. At once came the four bridesmaids. Ruth and her father looking very serene, and 13 ushers, Henry Sedgwick from N.Y., Owen Wistar, George Morisson, James Storrow, Robert Codman, Jr., Herbert Lyman, Sumner Paine and Fred Stone who was best man, Harry, Ted, Joe, Godfrey, and George who stood at front of the steps on each side (the desk and rail were taken away). Mr. Howard Brown performed the ceremony. At 4 o'clock we had a reception, 394 people came, a few who had not been invited to the church. Mr. Phillips Brooks came. The clouds began to gather and were very splendid, but it rained hard at about 5. Ruth retired to

dress at 6, and drove off amid slippers and rice to 395 Marlborough
Street.

29 May

Ruth and Bob went up to the Wheelwrights' farm house in the
morning, where I had sent a woman to cook, and enough furnishings
to be comfortable. The house is about 2 miles above Peterboro, N.H.,
and the farm house close by, with splendid view of Monadnock.

1893

Brookline   20 February

Birthday of Walter Mason C., 21 years old. W. C. in bed with a sore
throat. Tremendous snowstorm and blizzard. Deep drifts. Went to
get gold watch and chain for Walter but only got chain. Harry came
in. We had a long, delightful and most cheering talk. He is very
happy. Meeting at Children's Aid [Society]. Discussion over funds.[45]

14 March

Important meeting in Annette's parlor about the circular printed by
the Committee to raise money for the Annex, to forward its junction
with Harvard.[46] Pres. Eliot, Prof. Goodwin, Mrs. Agassiz, Prof.
Byerly, Mr. Joe Warner, Mrs. Whitman, Fanny Morse, Marianne
Jackson, Mrs. G. Palmer.[47] Pres. Eliot said that he could not agree to
this circular, and when told that he had seen the first draft said he had

not understood it. He supposed the Annex was to take the same position as the Medical School or Law School and be under the care of
the College, but have separate teaching and only such advantages as
it could pay for by funds raised by itself. Mrs. Palmer said that she
could not keep even the $70,000 already raised, as it was given on a
different understanding. I spoke, but not to any good effect. Mrs.
Agassiz in an attitude of gratitude for smallest favors. Harvard will
be considered in 20 years to have been very "old fogy" I am sure.

5 April

M., E. and Annette have worked hard on their dresses, and tonight
went to the Artists ball which was very splendid and very crowded.
Elise wore a [low?] brown velveteen dress with long sleeves and yellow chemisette, and on her head a gold net, early Florentine. M. in
yellow with Annette's gold brocade tablecloth as cloak and a heavy
roll wound with a gold chain on her head. Walter M. as a page, in
flowing yellow wig, old gold small clothes, purple velvet cloak, and
fur collar, and velvet cap and plume, and gold chain on neck, yellow
doublet underneath.

Annette as a Dutch woman in long brown velvet cloak trimmed
with fur, close velvet cap, and ruff. W. C. and I went to Louis', to see
the girls, who were also in early Florentine dresses, very handsome,
and to see Ann and Harry. Ann in bl[ack?] velvet with full sleeves
and ruff and a piece of brocade of mine as stomacher, and hair curled.
H. in a hired dress, doublet and deep collar, not becoming. Ruth
wore Fanny M.'s red velvet brocade ruff and red velvet hat which she
wore at the first ball. Bob did not go.

1894

Brookline   12 January

I have quite a cold and could not go to meeting of Fund Committee.
Petition from men and women in N.Y. for B.A. degree for women.

18 January

Annual Meeting of Woman's Education Association. Miss L. read
her report. Mr. Warner gave an account of the new arrangements
with Annex. Mrs. Prof. Goodwin attacked the Association for un-
friendliness and unreasonableness about Radcliffe, and I like a fool
answered her.

22 January

Went to rooms, 55 Bedford St., of the Women's Relief Committee
for the Unemployed.[48] Working from 9 to 1 and 2 to 4.30 receiving
applications. Annette, Fanny Morse, Mrs. Greene, and Marianne
Jackson are the managers; but it is a difficult task.

9 March

Bob and I went to hear *Lohengrin*—Jean de Reszke, Melba, Plançon—
in Mechanics' Building, a horrid place but glorious performance.
Have seen also Calvé in *Carmen* and *Romeo and Juliet*.[49]

New York   18 July

Arrived at the wharf in N.Y. harbor, very hot and uncomfortable,
about middle of day.[50] W. C. has been more and more miserable, and
sat on deck quietly while we packed and arranged. Harry not to be
seen at first, but finally came and helped us off. Delay of course over

baggage and W. C. a good deal worried. Went to and fro several times
with inspector. Very hot. Tried to rise from a trunk on which he was
seated, staggered, and would have fallen but for H. and inspector.
Bathed his head, gave brandy, and I started in a carriage for Windsor
Hotel while H. went for a physician. Dr. Rufus Lincoln came and
pronounced it slight paralysis. Got a nurse, Miss Belt. Quiet night
after bromide. Called in Dr. Wm. R. Draper, who calls it not paralysis but failure of the circulation.

1st stroke.

19 July

We have a long suite of rooms on 47th Street off 5th Av. Heat tremendous, 92° in W's room, and incessant noise. Another nurse, Miss
Hills, came for night.

28 July

Hotter than ever. Nurse locked the door last evening. I demanded
an entrance, and passed the night on the bed in the dressing-room.
W. C. had a good night. Dr. Draper came in early. At 9.30 the porter
and another man carried W. C. downstairs in a chair. Drove a short
distance to Central Station and got him into a wheeled chair previ-
ously ordered. Stateroom very commodious with a long sofa and a
short one opposite. Carried a pail of ice with flannel to cover it, and
milk, water, brandy, and chicken sandwich. Heat intense. Got along
well until about 1.30. Then he became flushed. Had an icepail, basin
and rubber ice bag, and kept ice on his head. In Boston found our
men and a hack, and decided not to stop but to drive straight to
Brookline, but had to stop several times, get out the ice pail, and
apply ice bag. Reached home at about 4. Dr. Sabine received us at
the door, helped carry him upstairs, and gave him a good sponging.

The house deliciously cool and quiet. Said to be the hottest day this
summer.

Brookline   24 September

Hot. W. had a restless night and seems very weak. Elise gave up a
little journey with Lou Hallowell. Dr. hopes W. gain if nothing else
sets in; but considers him very weak. I am trying to face the worst. If
he can only be spared suffering. He has only 4 spots on back and one
has dried, twitching less, pain less, but only sleeps a few minutes at a
time, and his mind is bewildered.

Walter M. began his course of architecture at the School of
Technology.[51]

7 October

W. less well. Has dreadful dreams. Thinks he is in the cellar and begs
to get back. Tosses from side to side and hard to keep him in bed.
Miss Martin wonderfully skillful and Elise also. Mabel got home.

9 October

Fred Shattuck out.[52] W. talked with him quite brightly but his mind
wanders, and especially after sleep. Fred not encouraging. Thinks the
wandering, the imperfect nutrition, and unconscious urination are
signs of serious loss of power in the brain. Miss Tarleton left. W. did
not like her, and nurse came from City Hospital.

11 October

Walter had been moved in his bed near to the window and was enjoying the view. Suddenly Miss Martin called; and he had a violent chill,
his eyes became dull, he seemed dying. Miss M. most energetic and

skillful, giving whisky, rubbing, fanning with ammonia, and surrounding with hot water bottles. I believe her promptness saved him. Dr. Sabine could not come, and sent young Dr. Houghton. He remained very dull and exhausted all day.

12 October

Sabine slept here most kindly, so that I had a long sleep undisturbed. Miss Hodgkins back again to take place of Miss Martin who has been doing night work. W. C. had a quieter night, less wandering of mind, and a peaceful happy day. I read to him and his mind seemed clear—a wonderful change for the better.

1895

Brookline   1 January

Celebrated by Miss Martin, our nurse, leaving, and Miss Nettje Borgman taking her place, a Dutch woman. Opposite in looks and character as possible, but both good in their way.

6 January

Elise in bed, sore throat and fever, eyelids above and below much swollen.

W. C. gets up twice a day for 20 minutes and walks across the room 4 or 5 times. Night nurse left Friday and I feel in clover.

10 January   1895

Went to the last meeting of Committee of Harvard Annex Endowment Fund. A good deal of bother in payment of money—about $14,000 goes to Radcliffe and some to go to half-a-dozen different things, with interest on each.

Elise and Walter had planned to go on a trip to Aitken, S.C.; but W. received an invitation to dinner which he wanted to accept, so asked E. to change. Decided to go to White Mountains and E. much disappointed.

20 January

Went to church for first time since last March, and with me R., Bob and H. Harry went home. His baby gained 14 oz. in one week.

15 June

Went over to Radcliffe Commencement (the first) in Sanders. Miss Irwin the Dean not graceful but dignified and simple.[53] Mrs. Agassiz the President always good. Many *magna cum laude*'s given.

30 June

W. C. chilly and feverish with slight inflammation. Must postpone move to Dublin for which we were almost ready. He has done a little too much. Went to see F. Cabot and Lizzie Lee in one p.m. Has walked twice in one day down our avenue, and round by road up Harry's.

1896

Brookline   20 January

Great anxiety, almost panic, over the President's Message, and the jingo feeling in the West.[54]

Talk of an electric railway from Newton down old Worcester turn-pike, now Boylston Street, behind us to town. The world agog for avenues and small house lots, and turning Brookline into a suburb.[55]

5 February

Damrosch opera at Boston Theater. Vast improvement on hideous Mechanics' Hall. Went with Molly Loring to hear *Fidelio,* and passed the night.[56] First night away from W. C. for 2 years.

8 February

Great discussion at meeting of Executive Committee of Woman's Education Association on having a lecture and discussion on Woman Suffrage.

CHAPTER SEVEN

1897 – 1906

The last decade of the diary is found wholly in the Schlesinger collection. Entries remain typically brief. For the most part, they treat
domestic matters and the activities of Elizabeth's grown-up children,
like Walter Mason, expert in things oriental at the Museum of Fine
Arts. She still reads serious books—A. V. G. Allen's biography of
Phillips Brooks, for example—and she still loves opera. Mlle.
Rhode, the French governess acquired during the European tour of
1867 – 70, left the Cabots' service some time after 1881; she visited
them in 1887; and members of the family are found, in April 1906,
discussing the best ways of helping her. Interest in Maine leads, in
1901, to the purchase of a property at Pulpit Harbor, not far from
Rockland and Vinal Haven.

The Schlesinger volumes are useful, too, in elucidating aspects of
the Cabots' life in much earlier years. It becomes clear that the 1867
inheritance was in the form of a trust.[1] The scale of Walter's farming
is revealed by the statement, in 1902, that his eight cows have been
examined for tuberculosis.[2] The list of mourners at Walter's funeral
suggests that there are eight servants at the Brookline home.[3]

For much of the time, Walter is an invalid. He goes to the Athe-

naeum and the Museum of Fine Arts, takes walks and drives, and
sometimes goes in boats during vacations. But there are long spells
of severe illness, sometimes with signs of mental confusion. In May
1904 he dies, aged seventy-five. Elizabeth has to nerve herself for
widowhood, after nearly forty-four years of married life. She wishes
to commemorate Walter publicly; so she gives Harvard $50,000
to found a fellowship, the income designed to enhance the salary of
some outstanding teacher.[4]

Elizabeth begins to withdraw from her good works, pleading age
and incompetence, showing that her capacity for self-criticism is not
extinct. Her interest in Radcliffe, however, persists. In 1905 she
gives $5,000 toward the purchase of land, while still expressing—
but not fully explaining—severe criticism of its policies and status.

The approach of war with Spain, the fighting in 1898, and the
annexation of the Philippines, lead to some of her rare expressions of
political opinion.[5] She is an anti-imperialist, but not in all respects
a liberal; for in 1902 she signs a petition in favor of the literacy test,
promoted by Henry Cabot Lodge and others as the best way of reduc-
ing total immigration, while discriminating against those newer
races that were regarded as inferior to, and more of a social problem
than, their predecessors.[6]

The diary ends fourteen years before Elizabeth's death. We know
nothing of that last period, beyond the fact that she continues to live
at Brookline. Just as with Walter, local newspaper obituaries give us
no help. The *Proceedings* of the Brookline Historical Society, of which
Elizabeth has been a member, is a little better. The notice identifies
the organizations in which she has been interested. It states that she
has been in poor health for some years and that "she was well known
to the former generation . . . and a lovely lady."[7]

1898

19 February

. . . there is a strong war party at Washington and I fear that the jingoes, including Cabot Lodge, may carry the day.

1902

12 September

Ten years ago I could have undertaken it [Radcliffe fund-raising] and been full of hope, but little by little through my children and the outside world, I have learned to judge myself more carefully than I once did and to realize that I am not competent for much, that I have little ability, less tact, and that beside this I have grown older in the last year than for many previous ones. If I can keep a steady front in my own home, it is about all I can do. It is a healthy lesson to learn, if a bitter one.

1903

23 April

Radcliffe has long been in the hands of rather elderly women, most of them very conservative, very timid in meeting prejudices, and none of them with any personal connection with young girls. The President and faculty of Harvard have complete control, yet entirely as an outside body, and refuse to father the degrees they themselves give. Would anyone be willing to give a large endowment to an institution under such conditions? . . . I have given $2,000 this year . . .

1904

1 May

Wrote to W. M. as usual. Mabel drove to Milton to stay with Elise a few days. W. C. again sick and I sent for Sabine who gave him a very little dose of calomel. He dozed all the afternoon and did not get up as usual before his tea.

3 May

W. C. better. Exquisite day. Letter from W. M. in Rome.

4 May

Thermometer 80. Went to concert by Eleanor Standen (Appleton), Mrs. Frothingham and Fred Lowell. In evening W. C. complained again of his leg feeling numb. Rubbed it, but he wanted to get up and walk, and then found it give way under him.

5 May

Weather very hot. W. C. seemed to find difficulty in swallowing, but was carried downstairs in his chair by George and Withers and lay a long time on the south covered piazza on the couch. In afternoon he seemed very dull and kept his eyes shut. Dr. Sabine came and found his temperature 102. M. home at lunch. Packing to make a little visit to Stockbridge.

6 May

Fine day. W. C. had a quiet night and temperature normal, but can only swallow even water a teaspoonful at a time, and his left arm slightly paralyzed but can move his hand a little. Dr. S. advised Mabel not to give up her visit to Stockbridge. Went at 10. In evening temperature rose to 99⅗.

7 May

W. C. had a bad night. Miss Dickie, the trained nurse we have got to sit up at night, here. Paralysis is increasing and after 2 or 3 teaspoons of food, milk, vomiting sets in. Telephoned at 10 to Mabel. Difficulty in swallowing even a teaspoonful of water. Great collection of mucus in throat. Elise came over in afternoon. He knew me and squeezed my hand. Ellery and Mabel arrived before 10 in evening, and M. thinks he knew her.

8 May

Exquisite weather. Dr. S. thinks Walter failing and can only live a few days. Consulted about cable to Walter M. but have written only. Give a great deal of oxygen to breathe. At 2, Miss Dickie telephoned to Sabine, but there is nothing more to do. His eyes are shut and he seems unconscious. Ellery has been called up several times to help move him. Breathing very labored. At 7:45 P.M., with hardly a struggle, he died.

9 May

Cabled to W. M. Had Caproni to take cast of hands and face. His face full of the dignity and peace of a new life. It makes one feel left behind in a flight to purer airs. Whither! oh whither! M., R. and I arranged service, and in evening saw Mr. Tucker for music. Ralph and E. here to lunch.

10 May

Fog and rain. Many flowers came. Elise here all day and she and M., and Ellery and Ruth and Mr. Batty went to the church, decorating it with branches and big cuttings from our shrubs, and wreaths of wild flowers made by the children. Mr. Brown came to talk of the service, Mr. Lyon being in Europe.

11 May

East wind, but wonderfully beautiful clouds. The sun shone out at times and in afternoon clear and bright. Polly, Amy and Bessie Hamlen early to the church to receive and arrange flowers. The coffin was moved down in front of the window in hall after Willy had come up with his camera and taken photographs of him as he lay serene and beautiful with branches of his own shrubs around him and wild flowers brought by his grandchildren. M. went to the church early. I and Fanny M. and Ruth followed the hearse and went into the church before anyone. It looked very beautiful. Great branches of green with blossoming shrubs, largely white, stood up around pulpit and steps. Miss Belyea, Elise, I, M. and H. sat in front pew, Ruth, Nancy, Bob, Ralph, and Ellery behind us. Mr. Batty, George and Katy, Mary, Ella, Lizzie and Alice, Barney and Mrs. Cullinane in the side aisle next us. Harry and Sam, Ellie Lee and Frank Cabot, Bob,

Ralph, and Ellery brought him in and carried him out without help.
Elise and Mabel stood before him and covered the coffin with flowers
they had picked and brought with them.

At 3 o'clock the service began with "While Thee I seek, protect-
ing power," Brattle Street. Quotations, Portuguese hymn, 4 short
prayers (none voluntary), and then Federal Street, the organ playing
as they carried him out.

Mabel and Ellery and Harry drove to the crematory at Jamaica
Plain with him, and so the end.

I write this for my children and grandchildren, that the picture
may not become dimmed. For them chiefly I write this diary; for if
life continues and is renewed in death, the past will be ineffaceable—
I would say "alas" but are not the mistakes, even the sins, a ladder to
climb by if we will?

I was sorry that the roses and lovely flowers, the expression of kindness from so many friends, should have been much hidden. This was
partly by a mistake as to the position of the coffin.

12 May

I am sleeping in Walter's bed in his and my chamber. As soon as
possible I shall move all my things there and hope to live for the few
remaining years and die there. I have opened the door into Mabel's
room, that our last days may as much as possible be together.[8]

Miss Belyea went home to her mother. She has been a good friend
and most affectionate, cheerful, devoted nurse, a singularly pleasant,
refined housemate. These last years would have been very different for
Walter without her. She had a youthful enthusiasm and enjoyment of
small things, a French unconsciousness of self, and tact, a prettiness
and neatness of person, and in all she did most pleasing; and I should

find it hard, in these years she has lived with us, to fix on any fault. I could not possibly have filled her place.

1906

29 May

Drove Walter to town to take the train for New York and after seeing Mabel to sail for Europe. He leaves me, though he does not mean it, or know it, very blue about myself. I suppose it is a blow at conceit and false pride that makes me sore and discouraged.

31 May

Walter sailed in *Deutschland* for Havre. Wrote to Ruth to meet her in Havre, 9 June, when she and Bob sail for home on the *Savoy*. Wrote Mlle. and Mrs. Richardson who has been so good to her in her illness. She seems now much better. Sleeplessness gone and arm healing. H{arry?} intends to increase her income by partial life insurance, and Elise is to send her money for a journey. Mrs. William Paine has come out to Ruth's to be with children.

7 June

Physicians and surgeons here from every part of the country. Arthur Cabot and Fred Shattuck read papers, and Dr. John Rogers, son of my cousin, read a paper describing his wonderful success in curing wife, who after years of illness was dying of a form of goitre in the throat.

June has been very warm and delicious. What I have done with my days, which look so free from all duties or claims, I hardly know. It seems to me while I am still strong and well that some result of a little importance to someone ought to follow. One ought at least to have a sense of repose and leisure, of time to reflect and to read; but I think it must be a weakness in me which allows small details to crowd the leisure out of sight. {This is the last entry.}

NOTES

Preface

1. The information was supplied by Peter Drummey, now the Historical Society's librarian, who handled the transfer. For the years 1854–60 (and a few fragments to 1865), there exists a very accurate typescript, made just before World War II. It was useful, in the early stages, for rapid reading, but of course all my selections have been checked against the original manuscript. With the diary and letters are some genealogical notes by Elizabeth's daughter Ruth, who married into the Paine family, and a brief typescript based on notes by Elizabeth herself, which throws a little light on her mother and other relations.

2. The *Brookline Chronicle* (18 December 1920) says little.

3. I have used, without providing exact annotation, several familiar works of reference. Among them are standard encyclopedias, including *Larousse;* the *Dictionary of American Biography* and its British, French, and Italian equivalents (the last two still very incomplete); *Notable American Women,* ed. Edward T. James, 3 vols. (Cambridge, Mass.: Harvard University Press, 1971); the *Union Catalog;* and the catalogs of the British Library and the Bibliothèque Nationale. I have also referred to a few more specialized sources. For music, I have relied on *The New Grove Dictionary of Music and Musicians,* ed. Stanley Satie, 20 vols. (London: Macmillan, 1980); and *The Encyclopedia of Opera,* ed. Leslie Orrey (New York: Charles Scribner's Sons, 1976). For ships, the su-

preme authority is Noel R. P. Bonsor, *North Atlantic Seaway* (Prescot, Lancashire: Stephenson, 1955). For Boston, two old compilations are often useful: *Memorial History of Boston,* ed. Justin Winsor, 4 vols. (Boston: Ticknor, 1880–81); and *Commonwealth History of Massachusetts,* ed. Albert B. Hart, 5 vols. (New York: State History Co., 1927–30).

Introduction

1. Cunarders *Asia* (put into service in 1850) and *Cephalonia* (1882).

2. The *Handbook of Northern Italy* (London: John Murray, 1853), xiii, explains the system of hiring a *vetturino,* who had carriage and horses and arranged meals and accommodation along the way.

3. Nathaniel Hawthorne, *The English Notebooks,* ed. Randall Stewart (New York: Russell & Russell, 1962), 248.

4. Diary, 8 April 1868, the Cabots at Naples. See also Nathaniel Hawthorne, *The French and Italian Notebooks,* ed. Thomas Woodson (Columbus: Ohio State University Press, 1960), 62, 575, 579, 592, 617, among many references.

5. Diary, 10 November 1852. Also, 13 December 1856 saw the delivery in Boston of her brother's letter from Paris, dated 26 November.

6. Diary, 14 November 1844. Another technological landmark is recorded in her first mention of a daguerreotype, 3 February 1846.

7. Walter M. Whitehill, *Boston: A Topographical History* (Cambridge, Mass.: Harvard University Press, 1968). The 1840 census found 93,000 people in Boston, so by 1844 the city's population would have reached 100,000.

8. Bainbridge Bunting, *Houses of Boston's Back Bay: An Architectural History, 1840–1917* (Cambridge, Mass.: Harvard University Press, 1967), 277–85, is a good introduction. For sewerage defects, even many years later, see George E. Waring, *Report on the Social Statistics of Cities,* 2 vols. (New York:

Arno, 1970), 1:130–35 (the first edition was published in Washington, D.C., in 1886–87 as a supplement to the tenth census).

9. Diary, 11 July 1851.

10. Lizzie Cabot to Elizabeth, 12 April 1881, Elizabeth to Lizzie Cabot, 9 December 1894, Paine Papers, box IX, folders 14, 12; diary, 20 February 1896.

11. Elizabeth McClellan, *History of American Costume, 1607–1870* (1904; reprint, New York: Tudor, 1969).

12. In Brussels, Elizabeth and her mother went shopping, while Mr. Mason and the boys visited the Waterloo battlefield (diaries of Hannah Rogers Mason, 1 August 1853, Paine Papers, box XXI).

13. Hawthorne, *French and Italian Notebooks,* 51.

14. Diary, 24 September 1885, 3, 4 October 1886. A Customs inspector charged $40 for baggage that included "bronzes, rugs, etc." (27 May 1870).

15. Diary, 18 July 1854.

16. Diary, 21 August 1854.

17. Elizabeth's account almost fills the diary during April and May 1881. See the photograph in Helmut Gernsheim and Alison Gernsheim, *Historical Events, 1839–1939* (London: Longmans, 1969), 77.

18. The Registration Report, which appeared annually as *Doc. 1* in *Massachusetts Public Documents,* provides details of mortality, with some comparison with past years.

19. Long accounts of Edward's and Mr. Mason's final illnesses are in the diaries of Hannah Rogers Mason, 28 August–14 September 1862, 10 October–4 December 1867.

20. Similarly, in the 1850s Elizabeth could not have been reading the greatest Russian novelists, or Zola, Maupassant, James, Howells, Hardy, or Joyce.

21. Diary, 17 March 1846, shows Mr. Mason's club dinner at 4:00 P.M. Entries for 13, 20 February, 13 December 1856 have dinner at 5:30, 6:00,

and 6:30. Diary, 19 June 1854, has tea at 7:00 P.M., 3 November 1855 at 6:00, while 10 March 1856 mentions three hours of conversation between tea and a 10:00 P.M. supper.

22. See Sarah J. B. Hale, *Manners: or Happy Homes and Good Society* (Boston: Tilton, 1868). The author, long editor of *Godey's Lady's Book,* tries to relate etiquette to the domestic, and even the Christian, virtues.

23. Diary, 14 July 1850; 9 June 1854; 23 January, 3, 8, 14 November 1856; 19 February 1858. See 22 May 1859, where natural and sincere behavior is contrasted with worldly propriety.

24. Diary, 29 August 1854. For a more general condemnation of boorish behavior and slovenly dress at Newport, see 22 August.

25. Theodore Lyman, private notebooks, 19 January, 1 March 1870, Massachusetts Historical Society. Diary, 31 August 1855, shows Elizabeth's respect for Boston ladies' brains rather than their social graces; and entries for January 1857 reveal how few congressmen measured up to her standards. From time to time, the diary also touches on standards of artistic propriety: e.g., she was unable to discuss George Sand's *Consuelo* with a young man who admired it since that would reveal that she had read it—something she would not have done had she known how "coarse" some of its passages would be (3, 21 April 1856).

26. Hawthorne, *English Notebooks,* 12, 62, 88—89, 197, 225.

27. Diary, 7 October 1856.

28. Diary, 12 January 1856.

29. Diary, 29 January 1868; William Powell Mason, Jr., to Walter C. Cabot, 17 January, 1 March 1868, and to Elizabeth, 8 January, 20 March, 22 April 1868, Paine Papers, box VI, folder 1. For background information about the scale and continuity of Boston wealth, see *"Our First Men": A Calendar of Wealth, Fashion and Gentility . . . persons taxed in the city of Boston, credibly reputed to be worth over one hundred thousand dollars . . .* (Boston, 1846) (about 10 percent were widows and heiresses); Edward Pessen, *Riches, Class and Power before the Civil War* (Lexington, Mass.: Heath, 1973); Frederic C.

Jaher, *The Urban Establishment* (Urbana: University of Illinois Press, 1982); Peter D. Hall, "Family Structure and Class Consolidation among the Boston Brahmins" (Ph.D. diss., State University of New York at Stonybrook, 1973); Ronald Story, *The Forging of an Aristocracy: Harvard and the Boston Upper Class, 1800–1870* (Middletown, Conn.: Wesleyan University Press, 1980); Paul Goodman, "Ethics and Enterprise: The Values of the Boston Elite, 1800–1860," *American Quarterly* 18 (1961): 437–51.

30. Lloyd V. Briggs, *History and Genealogy of the Cabot Family,* 2 vols. (Boston: Goodspeed, 1927), 1:324–25.

31. Sidney Ratner, *New Light on the History of Great American Fortunes* (New York: Kelley, 1953), 19–21, based on *New York Tribune* estimates, 1892; Bunting, *Houses of Boston's Back Bay,* 238–39, 264–72, 341–45, including several photographs.

32. Diary, 22 February 1852, 25 March 1858. Architect's drawings, dated 1846, are in the Dexter Plans, vol. 9, Boston Athenaeum. Had all three rooms been used, the dancing area would have measured nearly eighty feet by about eighteen.

33. Diary, 21 September 1848, for Boggy Meadow; Paine Papers, box VII, folder 3, for rough drawings of Blue Hill. Chestnut Hill, where Elizabeth's parents sometimes stayed, is not identified or described.

34. The letter, 17 February 1868, is in Paine Papers, box VIII, folder 7.

35. Diary, 26 May 1874, 26 May 1896.

36. Pessen, *Riches, Class and Power,* 189–201. A map, in Walter Firey, *Land Use in Central Boston* (Cambridge, Mass.: Harvard University Press, 1947), 56, shows the great concentration on Beacon and Mount Vernon streets, each house being marked by a dot.

37. Eighth census, Suffolk County, Ward 6, p. 54, microfilm of manuscript schedule. The man's age was twenty-eight, the women ranged from twenty-four to thirty-four, and all had been born in Ireland. For deliveries, see Samuel E. Morison, *One Boy's Boston, 1887–1901* (Boston: Houghton Mifflin, 1962), 39–40. Servants' lives were of course complicated by the

labor of moving from house to house with the seasons. For this, and casual labor, see my "A Beacon Hill Domestic: The Diary of Lorenza Stevens Berbineau," *Proceedings of the Massachusetts Historical Society* 98 (1986): 97–98.

38. Firey, *Land Use*, 72, 115; *New England Magazine*, n.s., 39 (1908–9): 264–77; *Clark's Boston Blue Book, 1895*, 362. George W. Bromley and Walter S. Bromley, *Atlas of Brookline* (Philadelphia, 1893), shows the estates. See also Ronald D. Karr, "The Evolution of an Elite Suburb: Community Structure and Control in Brookline, Massachusetts, 1770–1900" (Ph.D. diss., Boston University, 1981), esp. 191–92, 255–72, 294–311, 350–54, 362n. Of all towns in Massachusetts, Brookline had the highest number of servants per household.

39. James McLachlan, *American Boarding-Schools: A Historical Study* (New York: Charles Scribner's Sons, 1970), esp. chaps. 5 and 6 on St. Paul's, and 345n showing how few Boston boys were attending even in the 1890s. On Harvard connections, see Bliss Perry, *Life and Letters of Henry Lee Higginson* (Boston: Atlantic Monthly, 1921), 21, 24, 158, and chaps. 4 and 11 passim; *Autobiography of Thomas Jefferson Coolidge* (Boston: Houghton Mifflin, 1923), 99; Theodore Lyman, private notebooks, 9 January 1865, 2, 16 September 1869, 15 January 1870.

40. Alexander W. Williams, *A Social History of the Greater Boston Clubs* (Barre, Mass.: Barre Publishers, 1970), gives the background. For the less formal clubs, see diary, 17 March 1846, 10 February 1855; Lyman, private notebooks, 28 December 1865, 21 November 1866, 9 April 1869, 3 February 1870; Edward W. Emerson, *The Early Years of the Saturday Club, 1855–1870* (1918; reprint, Freeport, N.Y.: Books for Libraries, 1967), 21–26.

41. Eugene C. Tompkins, *The History of the Boston Theatre, 1854–1901* (1909; reprint, New York: Blom, 1969); and seating plans of other theaters are in *Clark's Boston Blue Book, 1895*, 518–40; William A. Fisher, *Notes on Music in Old Boston* (Boston: Ditson, 1918), esp. 32–43; diary, 2 June 1854,

10 January 1855, 23 January 1856, 19 February 1858; for details of theatricals at the Perkins home, with elaborate scenery painted by Walter Cabot's brothers Edward C. and J. Elliot, see Carl Seaburg and Stanley Paterson, *Merchant Prince of Boston: Colonel T. H. Perkins, 1764–1854* (Cambridge, Mass.: Harvard University Press, 1971), 412–13.

42. Lyman, private notebooks, 31 August 1864; the diary confirms the presence of many familiar faces at Nahant, Beverly, and Newport, 8 July, 4 September 1854, 13 August 1855, 23 June 1857; for background, see Joseph E. Garland, *Boston's North Shore* (Boston: Little, Brown, 1978), with many photographs.

43. Spacious apartments in Rome, diary, 14 December 1867, and in Paris, 19, 20 March 1869, and villa at Pau, Elizabeth to old Mrs. Cabot, 3 October 1869, Paine Papers, box VIII, folder 9. Diaries of Hannah Rogers Mason, 17, 30 April 1853, show Mr. Mason buying a Poussin and a Guido Reni.

44. Diary, 19 June 1854. For background, see Paul R. Baker, *The Fortunate Pilgrims: Americans in Italy, 1800–1860* (Cambridge, Mass.: Harvard University Press, 1964), 20–21 (an estimated 1,200 in Rome in 1868). William L. Vance, *America's Rome* (2 vols.; New Haven, Conn.: Yale University Press, 1989) appeared too late to be used here, but its focus is on creative artists and writers, not travelers.

45. Diary, 26 April, 1 September 1845.

46. Diary, 16 December 1849, 29 December 1850. An entry on 21 April 1850 shows Elizabeth reading Anna Jackson Cabot Lowell's *Theory of Teaching* (Boston: Peabody, 1841), written in the form of letters, applying to a governess in a prosperous and enlightened household.

47. The published version, *Seed-Grain for Thought and Discussion,* 2 vols. (Boston: Ticknor & Fields, 1856), contains the excerpts only, not the commentary.

48. Compare diary, 2 May 1852, with Samuel E. Morison, *Three Centuries of Harvard* (Cambridge, Mass.: Harvard University Press, 1936), 344–47.

49. Diary, 30 November, shows sermon summaries required; comparison of 11 June 1854 with vol. 3 of Ezra Stiles Gannett's *Printed Sermons,* at Andover-Harvard Theological Library, shows how accurate she became.

50. Diary, 16 December 1849, 23 June 1854. Entries for 8 June, 6 August 1856 show her longing for an arduous task or for a trip to the West, such as is permitted to young men.

51. Diary, 7 June 1855, 16 February 1856.

52. Diary, 7 July 1854 (Mary Quincy), 12 September 1856 (Louise Slade), 1 October 1857 (Jenny Revere).

53. The letter, not fully dated, is in Paine Papers, box IV, folder 8.

54. Letters of 12 May, 4 August 1855, and others in Paine Papers, box IV, folders 11, 12, 13; diary, 31 December 1855.

55. Jenny's letters are in Paine Papers, box V, folders 10, 11, 12, 13, not all of them fully dated.

56. Diary, 15 September 1855.

57. Letter from Susie, Paine Papers, box IV, folder 13; and typed copy of Elizabeth's letter to her (undated, but about 15 September 1855), box XIII.

58. Letter of 21 September 1898, Paine Papers, box V, folder 13.

59. Letters from Marian Hovey are in Paine Papers, box XI, folders 4—12.

60. Paine Papers, box IX, folder 12; other letters are in box VIII, folder 7, and box IX, folders 1, 5, 6, 14. Some of Lizzie's letters have been printed in *Letters of Elizabeth Cabot,* 2 vols. (Boston, 1915), 2: *passim.*

61. Diary, 12 September 1856. Note also 10 August 1857, the scene at Beverly with girls talking as they worked on rugs. For wider discussion, see Carroll Smith-Rosenberg, "The Female World of Love and Ritual," in *Disorderly Conduct: Visions of Gender in Victorian America* (New York: Knopf, 1985); Nancy Cott, *The Bonds of Womanhood: "Women's Sphere" in New England, 1780—1835* (New Haven, Conn.: Yale University Press, 1977), esp. chap. 7; Anne Firor Scott, *The Southern Lady: From Pedestal to Politics, 1830—1930* (Chicago: University of Chicago Press, 1970), esp. chap. 2; Lee V. Chambers-Schiller, *Liberty, a Better Husband: Single Women in America, the Generation of*

1780—1840 (New Haven, Conn.: Yale University Press, 1984), chap. 7; Carl Degler, *At Odds: Women and the Family in America from the Revolution to the Present* (New York: Oxford University Press, 1980), chap. 7.

62. Diary, 29 September 1855, 10 April 1858, among many.

63. Diary, 1 March 1859.

64. Diary, 21 June 1857.

65. Diary, 31 March 1857. Earlier that day, she had found that Mrs. George Lyman knew that she had rejected Joe Gardner.

66. Ellen K. Rothman, *Hands and Hearts: A History of Courtship in America* (Cambridge, Mass.: Harvard University Press, 1987).

67. For example, diary, 7, 8, 11 October, 13, 14, 28 November, 18 December 1856, 31 March, 1 April 1857, 9, 17 April 1858.

68. Diary, 22 May, 4 December 1859.

69. Diary, 18 December 1856, 26 February 1857, 19 February 1859. An entry for 9 April 1858 shows that a man, too, could suffer embarrassment.

70. This may be what Josiah Quincy had in mind when he told Elizabeth that an engagement might enable him to win her affection, as thus far he had failed to do (diary, 31 March 1857).

71. Diary, 19 September 1856.

72. The description exists only in typed copy, Paine Papers, box XIII. The portrait forms the frontispiece to the second volume (1856—57) of the diary typescript.

73. Diary, 17 May 1849 (her responsibility), 28 October 1856 (she gives William Powell a lock of her hair as he leaves for Europe), 4 February, 13, 15, 20 March 1866 (she helps her father prepare the short section on Edward in Thomas W. Higginson, ed., *Harvard Memorial Biographies,* 2 vols. (Cambridge, Mass.: Francis & Sevier, 1866), 1:409—14.

74. Diary, 19 August 1849, 5 May, 3 October 1850, 31 May, 17 October 1857.

75. Diary, 16 December 1849, 7 September 1850, 27 January 1856, 31 May, 24 October 1857, 14 May, 19 October 1858. For wider studies of

parent-daughter relationships, see Barbara Welter, *Dimity Convictions: The American Woman in the Nineteenth Century* (Athens: Ohio University Press, 1976), chap. 1; Chambers-Schiller, *Liberty, a Better Husband,* chap. 6. Certainly Mrs. Mason had more than her share of misfortune and strain. She had taken care of three children of a sister who died young. Marrying in 1831, she had had twin daughters who died soon after birth. Then she had three children, who survived, in 1834, 1835, and 1837.

76. Diary, 3 March 1855. When Aunt Parkman died, Elizabeth remarked, "She had been almost a mother to me" (diary, 8 January 1874).

77. Diary, 3 June, 18 September 1855, 2 November 1856, 24 May 1857, 20 March 1859. Her references to séances seem to reflect no more than a momentary fashion within the Quincy family.

78. Diary, 6 December 1857, 8 May 1870.

79. Diary, 23 August 1869.

80. Diary, 11 June 1854.

81. Diary, 15 July 1849, 15 September 1850, 25 May 1854, 21 November 1855, 12 September, 3 October 1856, 6 June 1857 ("A woman's life is in others"), 1 March, 1 September 1858. See also 4 October 1862, in which Elizabeth defines women's role in the Civil War—to keep alive humane standards amid all the horrors and violence. She never concerned herself with women's legal disabilities.

82. Diary, 13 February 1858; Lizzie's letter is in Paine Papers, box V, folder 8. Elizabeth's ideal approximated to the "Christian gentleman" as defined in J. A. Mangan and James Walvin, eds., *Manliness and Morality: Middle-Class Masculinity in Britain and America, 1800–1940* (Manchester: Manchester University Press, 1987). Contrast her admiration for Edward Cabot, Sidney Coolidge, Greely Curtis, Henry Lee Higginson, Stephen Perkins, and Paul Revere with her disparagement of Richard Fay.

83. The advertisement is in diary, 26 January 1860. For his farming, see 10 July 1862, 17, 18 February, 15 August, 26 September 1865, 21 April, 13 September 1866.

84. See the *Brookline Press* and the *Brookline Chronicle,* both 14 May 1904. No portrait was found in any of Boston's great collections.

85. Letters from Walter are in Paine Papers, box VII, folders 12, 13. Elizabeth's to him, from Arques in Normandy and Magnolia, Florida, are in box VII, folder 18.

86. Diary, 5, 19 June 1857, and many examples from her married life. For a comparison, see Pamela Horn, *The Rise and Fall of the Victorian Servant* (Gloucester: Sutton, 1986). English staffs were much larger, especially in country houses.

87. Among many examples, diary, 6 October 1862, 1 March 1866, 6 April 1870, 16 June 1886.

88. Diary, 4 October 1862, 20 January 1864. Remember that one in six who enlisted in the Union Army perished, though casualties were uneven between regiments and, therefore, between districts. For a recent study, see Maris Vinovskis, "Have Social Historians Lost the Civil War? Some Preliminary Demographic Speculations," *Journal of American History* 76 (1989): 34–58.

89. Diary, 5 July 1863 (Walter's health kept him out of the army), 20 January, 27 August 1865, 24 August 1869.

90. Diary, 12 October 1862. In no other entry does she touch on this topic.

91. Deaths are recorded in the diary on 7–10 March 1855 (Marianne Sears), 31 May 1856 (Julia Robbins), 28 January 1859 (Charlotte Parker), 13 September 1869 (Isabella Appleton); the farewell is 11 August 1865. Statistics are in *Massachusetts Public Documents 1860, Doc. 1,* Registration Report for 1859, 72, and *1870, Doc. 1,* Registration Report for 1869, xc, xcv. The whole subject is treated by several modern writers: Carroll Smith-Rosenberg, "From Puberty to Menopause," in *Disorderly Conduct;* Welter, *Dimity Convictions,* chap. 4; Scott, *Southern Lady,* esp. 37–40; Degler, *At Odds,* chaps. 3, 8, 9, 10.

92. Diary, 28 May 1867, 3 July, 4, 23 August 1869, 2 April 1871, 15

December 1872, 19 January 1873, 6 March 1874 (when she was nearly forty). See Smith-Rosenberg, *Disorderly Conduct,* 193–95.

93. Diary, 12 September 1856. See Rothman, *Hands and Hearts,* 63–75, 98–102, 157–65; and Scott, *Southern Lady,* 27–28.

94. Diary, 4 July 1858.

95. Diary, 19 July 1857.

96. Diary, 17 August, 23 December 1856, 18 April 1857, 15 April, 19 July 1858.

97. Diary, 11 July 1851. For similar sentiments, see 16 December 1849, 3 February 1850.

98. Diary, 21 November 1859. For references to the diary as a friend, see 23 December, 24 April 1858.

99. Thomas D. Mallon, *A Book of One's Own: People and Their Diaries* (London: Pan, 1985).

100. Diary, 6 January 1858.

Chapter One

1. This is the very first entry. Elizabeth describes the journey, by train and steamboat, and introduces characters who will recur in the diary, e.g., the Baylies and Van Schaick families.

2. Probably the home of Dr. John C. Hayden, 131 Tremont Street, which all processions were likely to pass. See also the journal of Mary Josephine Faxon Forbush, 4 July 1846, Boston Athenaeum, noting the firemen with their engine brightly polished and an Irish temperance contingent in the procession of that year.

3. On Park Street, for an early view of which, see Jane H. Kay, *Lost Boston* (Boston: Houghton Mifflin, 1981), 112.

4. Alonzo Papanti had come to Boston in 1823, at age twenty-four, as a political refugee from Tuscany. At first a theater musician, he became a celebrated dancing instructor. In the late 1830s, he began to run classes and

exclusive assemblies (both mentioned in the diary, 16 November 1854). After his death in 1872, his son carried on the work. See Alexander Corbett's scrapbook, 17, Boston Athenaeum, "Papanti's is no more." There is a description of a cotillion, which appears to be synonymous with a "German," in Abigail A. Homans, *Education by Uncles* (Boston: Houghton Mifflin, 1966), 103–5.

5. For these and many family members mentioned later in the diary, see the Cast of Characters.

6. Almost certainly Elise Slade, Mrs. Schmidt, for the diary, 29 May 1845, shows her two children (twins?) christened. This, and Daniel Slade's presence at the deathbed, indicates that the dead girl was Ellen Slade, not the Rogers daughter of the same name. Daniel's gift to Elizabeth, 1 January 1856, of a watercolor by Ellen Slade further confirms this conclusion, as does the almost certain presence of Ellen Rogers, 25 December 1866.

7. Ezra Stiles Gannett (1801–71) was William Ellery Channing's assistant at the Federal Street Church, then minister until his death. A founder of the American Unitarian Association and of Boston's Benevolent Fraternity of Churches, he was regarded as a leading opponent of the Transcendentalist wing of the denomination, led by Theodore Parker. See William C. Gannett, *Ezra Stiles Gannett: Unitarian Minister in Boston, 1826–1871* (Boston: Roberts, 1871).

8. Theodore Lyman, Jr. (1792–1849), was the son of a merchant. Writer, collector of books, member of the state legislature, and founder of the Boston Farm School and the State Reformatory, he was mayor of Boston during 1834–35. He had an estate in Brookline, on which his son Colonel Theodore Lyman was Elizabeth's neighbor after the Civil War.

9. The episode suggests, in rather extreme form, Mr. Mason's isolation from family concerns, which Elizabeth will note later.

10. Aunt Isabella (Mrs. Jonathan Mason) will go to Europe in 1851, intending a long tour but dying a year later at Pau.

11. Thomas Gold Appleton (1812–84) was traveler, art collector, and essayist, famous for his conversation. See Emerson, *Early Years of the Saturday*

Club, 217–26; and Susan Hale, *Life and Letters of Thomas Gold Appleton* (New York: Appleton, 1885), esp. 258–66.

12. Fort Adams, a low-profile structure of earth reinforced with brick, stood near the end of the island where Newport is located and commanded one approach to Narragansett Bay.

13. Anna Cabot Jackson Lowell was the sister-in-law of the poet James Russell Lowell and mother of the Civil War hero Charles Russell Lowell.

14. Diary, 29 December 1850, claims that she has taken Latin to the point where she can easily read Sallust, an accomplishment sufficiently rare among girls to justify this second reference.

15. Elizabeth does not say so, but it seems unlikely that Boston had two mastodons, and the known one was in the private museum of her uncle, Dr. Warren.

16. William Cullen Bryant (1794–1878) was editor, translator of Homer, and poet. Volumes of his verse had appeared since 1821, the most recent edition in 1845. James Thomson (1700–1748) was an English poet, author of *The Seasons* (1730) and *The Castle of Indolence* (1748). Editions containing poems and biography appeared from the late eighteenth century (the *Life* sometimes by Dr. Johnson, sometimes by Patrick Murdoch), most recently in London in 1845. Henry Wadsworth Longfellow (1807–82) was both a poet and Harvard's Professor of Modern Languages. An edition of his verse had appeared in 1845, but no positive identification is possible. The anonymous volume was probably *The Gift: A Christmas and New Year's Present,* ed. Mrs. Leslie (Philadelphia: Carey & Hart, annually 1835–44), but possibly *The Gift for all Seasons: A Juvenile Manual* (Philadelphia: Anners, 1844). The only recent editions of *The Arabian Nights* in four volumes were both published in London: by Jolland in 1838 and by Washbourne in 1844.

17. The house was on Temple Place. Perkins also had an estate at Brookline. Seaburg and Paterson, *Merchant Prince of Boston,* 387–93.

18. "Circus" must mean the arena of her riding school. Mr. Mason's club may have been the Agricultural Society, positively mentioned in the diary on

8 February 1845 and 10 February 1855. As late as 31 May 1857, Elizabeth looks back to her childhood with Mary, "the ball and hoop delights, the tag on the State House steps."

19. Most probably John G. Lockhart, *Memoirs of the Life of Sir Walter Scott.* First published in seven volumes (Edinburgh, 1836–38), there were many other editions, including American in a single large volume, by 1846, though Lockhart's own abridgment appeared only in 1848.

20. Martha Frizzell, *A History of Walpole, New Hampshire,* 2 vols. (Walpole, N.H.: Historical Society, 1963), 1:216, shows that grandfather Jonathan Mason had bought the land, and built the house and the huge barn, in the 1820s.

21. The Philharmonic Society, founded in 1844, gave popular concerts, in reaction against the heavier programs of the Boston Academy of Music (1833).

22. See A. H. Saxon, *P. T. Barnum: The Legend and the Man* (New York: Columbia University Press, 1989), esp. 123–55.

23. By "Aunt Perkins" Elizabeth may mean Anna D. Perkins, wife of Uncle Henry B. Rogers and mother of Annette. Annie Webber was the daughter of a physician and a friend of the Mason family; she came to Walpole at the age of sixteen as a sort of governess. She is first mentioned in the diary on 8 August 1844. Treated as an equal, dining with the Masons, and paying frequent visits when working in another family, she was a close and admired friend of Elizabeth's; their association lasted for at least a quarter of a century.

Chapter Two

1. William H. Channing, *Memoir of William Ellery Channing,* 3 vols. (Boston: Crosby & Nicholls, 1848), a biography of a founding father of American Unitarianism (1780–1842). The preface claims, "This work is an autobiography, in so far as the materials at my command have enabled me to give it this character."

2. Jared Sparks (1789–1866) was Unitarian minister, historian, editor of Franklin's and Washington's writings, professor at Harvard, and its president, 1849–53. His *Library of American Biography* first appeared in ten volumes (Boston: Hilliard, Gray, 1836–40); by 1848, it was available in other editions with up to twenty-five volumes, a substantial proportion of them written by himself.

3. The forty-eight-page pamphlet *Celebration of the Introduction of the Water of Lake Cochituate into the City of Boston, October 25, 1848* (Boston: Eastburn, 1848) describes the early-morning artillery salutes and ringing of church bells and gives the order of the procession. Including as it did Harvard officers and students, officials from many towns, firemen, Masons, and temperance societies, it took about two hours to pass. Streets, and gateways into the Common, were decorated. From their press, the printers distributed a celebratory song. After a short service on the Common, and speeches from Water Commissioner Nathan Hale and Mayor Josiah Quincy, a fountain was turned on. In the evening, Bengal lights surrounded it, and the streets were illuminated. The Boston Athenaeum has two admirable prints. See also the journal of Mary Josephine Faxon Forbush, 25 October 1848; and for the background, Nelson M. Blake, *Water for the Cities: A History of the Urban Water Supply in the United States* (Syracuse, N.Y.: Syracuse University Press, 1956), chaps. 9, 10. Oak Hall was a clothing establishment, housed from 1840 to the 1890s in a wooden building, of fanciful Gothic design, on North Street (Kay, *Lost Boston*, 80–81).

4. The Rev. Tilden was Unitarian minister at Walpole, 1848–55. Elizabeth had been required by Mrs. Lowell to make regular summaries of sermons (diary, 30 November 1845), and she retained her skill.

5. "Cry out that" means "exclaim in horror when" girls learn at school.

6. Although there were exceptions, including John D. Long and Charles W. Eliot, few boys of fourteen and fifteen were entering Harvard in the

1850s. But the difference in age between these girls and Harvard men may not have been as great as would be the case today.

7. This is the first mention of Walter in the diary. He was a Harvard senior, nearly twenty-one.

8. Elizabeth must have been reading a serial version, either one brought from England or the one issued by Wiley of New York City. Publication in book form took place only in November 1850. She also read *Barnaby Rudge* to herself and *Bleak House* aloud to her mother, both in 1856; but Mr. Mason had been reading *Pickwick Papers* aloud at Walpole as early as 27 July 1844.

9. The most recent monograph on West Point is James L. Morrison, Jr., *"The Best School in the World": West Point, the Pre–Civil War Years, 1833–1860* (Kent, Ohio: Kent State University Press, 1986); but its preeminence over other American technical training would not have been apparent to the young visitor. In view of Elizabeth's final point, see also Sandra L. Myres, "Romance and Reality on the American Frontier: Views of Army Wives," *Western Historical Quarterly* 13 (1982): 409–27, though the women's testimony is somewhat later than 1851.

10. In 1860, Massachusetts had 44,000 people who had been born in New Hampshire, Vermont had 17,000, Maine and New York 12,000 each. Unfortunately, the federal censuses do not show rural to urban migration within a state. The Massachusetts census of 1885 shows Boston with 10,000 (in round numbers) born in New Hampshire, Lowell and Haverhill 4,000 each, Lynn 3,000, Lawrence 2,000, Cambridge and Worcester 1,500 each.

11. Edward George Earle Bulwer (1803–73), Baron Lytton in 1866. A political career gave him his title, but earlier he had been a prolific writer (novelist, playwright, and translator from German), an edition of his works, a decade before his death, running to forty-three volumes. *Pelham* and *The Disowned* appeared in 1828, *The Last Days of Pompeii* in 1834, and his famous play (often performed in Boston) *The Lady of Lyons* in 1838.

12. Sir Walter Scott (1771–1832) was a successful lawyer and poet before

he published the novel *Waverley* in 1814. Many of his later novels were set in other countries or in the Middle Ages, but his reputation rests more securely on his stories set in Scotland in the century and a half before he wrote, to which the name "Waverley novels" is commonly applied. *Old Mortality* appeared in 1816.

13. *Memoir and Writings of James Handasyd Perkins,* ed. William H. Channing (Boston: Crosby & Nicholls, 1851). A Unitarian minister, Perkins also wrote *Annals of the West.* His relationship to Thomas Handasyd Perkins remains unclear.

14. A diary entry for 2 May 1852, while respectful toward Mrs. Hodges, proclaims Mrs. Lowell's special influence: "I fly towards the heavens, looking at earth and its creatures, but from a position high above it." An entry on 9 May adds, "She is a bright star on this earth."

15. The French teacher was Émile Arnoult, 12 Oxford Street.

16. Signor Corelli sometimes sang at Music Fund Society concerts, but no biographical data have been found.

17. George Ticknor's daughters were Anna Eliot, later prominent in adult education (the Society to Encourage Studies at Home), and Eliza Sullivan. For the family's life, see *Life, Letters and Journals of George Ticknor,* 2 vols. (Boston: Osgood, 1876), esp. 1:397, 2:327–29, 335–37; (the volume was produced by George S. Hillard, Mrs. Ticknor and Anna); and David B. Tyack, *George Ticknor and the Boston Brahmins* (Cambridge, Mass.: Harvard University Press, 1967), chap. 5.

18. August Fries was a violinist and also a member of the Mendelssohn Quintette Club (1849–58). The Music Fund Society (1847–55) was organized by local musicians and held concerts at Tremont Temple as well as the rehearsals mentioned shortly.

19. I know of other references to the Germania Band, as playing at social functions, e.g., in Newport hotels, 22 August 1854; and small groups played in private homes. There was an orchestra of that name, which toured the United States during 1848–54 and spent much time in Boston, performing

chamber music as well as larger works, using the Melodeon or Music Hall. I am not wholly convinced that this was all one organization.

20. This is the ball that in the introduction is related to the interior arrangements of 63 Mount Vernon Street. The "flower room" cannot be identified, though it may have been the small room on the "principal floor" and over the vestibule. Nor can one bedroom be distinguished from another. The parlor may have been used for receiving guests, who could have used the staircase to reach the dressing rooms, then descended when ready; afterward they could have moved next door to the "center room" and dining room to begin dancing.

Chapter Three

1. *Galignani's New Paris Guide for 1852* (an English-language version of a work that had gone through twenty-three editions since 1814), 311–12. A much later Baedeker *Guide* insists that the column was made of bronze. The "belts" had the effect of dividing the surface into sections.

2. The Arc de l'Étoile is more commonly known as the Arc de Triomphe, which stands in the Place de l'Étoile.

3. The "Boulevards," sometimes called "the inner" or "the great," dated from Louis XIV's time, stood on the line of older fortifications, and extended from the Place de la Bastille to the Madeleine. The *barrières* were a ring of collecting posts for the levying of the *octroi*, a duty on goods brought into the city. The cemetery was founded in 1804, on the site of a country estate once owned by Père Lachaise, confessor to Louis XIV. See *Galignani*, 44–46, 300–5; and Anthony Sutcliffe, *The Autumn of Central Paris: The Defeat of Town Planning* (London: Arnold, 1970), esp. 4, 12–15, 20–42. Elizabeth was seeing Paris, whose population had just topped the million mark, before Baron Haussmann began redesigning the streets.

4. Casimir Périer (1797–1832) was a banker, then a politician, one of those instrumental in putting Louis Philippe on the French throne in 1830. Appointed premier, he died in the cholera epidemic of 1832. His monument

was a landmark because it stood at the center of the Grand Rond, from which five avenues radiated.

5. The parade marked the return of Louis Napoleon (president, with prolonged tenure and extended powers since 1851) after a carefully planned provincial tour, designed to demonstrate popular support for his becoming emperor. Despite Elizabeth's comment on the Parisian crowd's limited response, the decision was taken, and ratified by plebiscite, within a few weeks. Louis Girard, *La Deuxième République et le Second Empire, 1848−1870* (Paris: Association pour la Publication d'une Histoire de Paris, 1981), 80, 86−87, has photographs of some of the scenes. The rue de la Paix runs from the Place Vendôme to the Boulevards.

6. Mrs. Edward Brooks's husband was a son of Peter Chardon Brooks (reputed the richest man in New England), managed his Boston real estate, and was himself thought to be worth $200,000. Franklin Dexter was probably half as rich.

7. Elizabeth's earlier impression of *vivandières* was probably derived from popular fiction or from Donizetti's opera *La Fille du Régiment* (1840).

8. Elizabeth had been in Milan on 13 September 1852, but her detailed diary volumes do not cover that episode, so we have no strictly contemporary record of her impressions. The St. Paul's mentioned is, of course, Christopher Wren's seventeenth-century cathedral in London.

Chapter Four

1. Charlotte M. Yonge (1823−1901), *The Heir of Redclyffe* (London: Parker, 1853), a long novel of inheritance, family division, love fulfilled and love renounced, and premature death. As so often, Elizabeth is up to date in her reading.

2. John Ruskin (1819−1900), *Modern Painters,* 5 vols. (London: Smith, Elder, 1843−60).

3. Sir Thomas Noon Talfourd (1795−1854). His *Ion* was a five-act trag-

edy, published in London in 1835, acted there the following year, and published in New York in 1837. Anna C. O. Mowatt (1819–70) very early in life wrote verse. When her husband lost his money and became an invalid, she turned to public poetry readings, then to writing novels, books on household management, and in 1845 a successful play, *Fashion.* In that year she took her first stage part, in Bulwer Lytton's *The Lady of Lyons,* and went on to Shakespearean roles. Leaving the stage in 1854, she married William F. Ritchie, editor of the *Richmond Enquirer,* moved to Virginia, and became interested in the campaign to restore Mount Vernon. Leaving her husband, during the Civil War she went to Europe, and died in England.

4. The diary, 6 June 1845, records seeing Verdi's *Ernani* (1844); and she had already seen, she says, *Romeo and Juliet,* which *Memorial History of Boston,* 4:433–34, makes clear must have been Bellini's *I Capuleti ed i Montecchi* (1830). After that, for several years Elizabeth is uninformative about operas. Not all her listed singers can be found in reference works. One, Steffenone, she misspells. The Howard Athenaeum opened in 1845, but after a few years it went over to lighter entertainment, superseded, probably, for opera by the huge Boston Theatre, which opened 11 September 1854.

5. "Relation of the North to Slavery," in Ezra Stiles Gannett, *Printed Sermons,* vol. 3, Andover-Harvard Theological Library. It was a commentary on the return of Anthony Burns to slavery under the law of 1850, despite a struggle to set him free—Elizabeth was an eyewitness to one of the less violent episodes. Her summary is a fair one, both as to Gannett's conclusion and the reluctance with which he reached it. The volume contains three other sermons on the fugitive slave issue, and they show how Gannett moved away from a passive resistance position. Attached press cuttings show how widespread was Mr. Mason's reaction. Then, after Brooks's attack on Sumner, Gannett, 8 June 1856, preached a sermon in which he openly discussed the possibility of war.

6. Probably Samuel K. Lothrop (1804–86), minister of Brattle Square Unitarian Church.

7. The Suffolk County jail stands near Massachusetts General Hospital and therefore was on the way from Beacon Hill to the railroad depots, three of which then stood on Causeway Street. It was chiefly used for people remanded before trial and other short-term prisoners.

8. Charles Russell Lowell was a brilliant Harvard student who traveled widely in Europe and whose work on railroads in the West impressed John Murray Forbes. He became a cavalryman in the Civil War. Within three years he was a brigadier-general (at the age of twenty-eight), and it seems that Sheridan planned a further promotion. During the summer of 1864, he had thirteen horses killed under him, though he emerged unscathed. Then, already wounded at Cedar Creek, near Front Royal in the Shenandoah Valley, he was killed the same day leading a charge against a Confederate position. See Edward W. Emerson, *Life and Letters of Charles Russell Lowell* (Boston: Houghton Mifflin, 1907). His brother James Jackson Lowell had died of wounds in the Peninsula in 1862.

9. Henry Lee Higginson (1834–1919) longed to pursue a career in music and underwent considerable training in Europe. Deciding that his talent was too limited, he joined the Lee, Higginson financial house and became a millionaire. He married Ida, daughter of scientist Louis Agassiz.

10. For Joe Gardner, later a suitor, see the Cast of Characters.

11. The visit to Newport was a break within the usual summer at Walpole. "Polking" refers to dancing the polka. Compare Thomas Gold Appleton's remark, ca. 1852, on Newport: "The same scheming mammas, and polking daughters, the same roaring table d'hôte, the same Bloomer bathing" (Hale, *Appleton,* 277).

12. As one of Elizabeth's heroes, Henry Whitney Bellows (1814–82) deserves a rather full note. Minister of First Church, later All Souls', New York City, he was a leader in the U.S. Sanitary Commission during the Civil War and a promoter of Antioch College and of the National Council of Unitarian Churches. Although born in Boston and working in New York, he spent much time at Walpole, for his family had been its founders. The diary

(5 October 1854), records a celebration, with fifty residents and as many visitors, centered on a new obelisk, to Benjamin Bellows, in the burying ground. His parents settled there; he had honeymoons there after both his marriages; one child was born there; in 1854 he bought the family farm; and, with his first wife, three children who died young, and other family members, he is buried there. See Walter D. Kring, *Henry Whitney Bellows* (Boston: Skinner, 1979). Bellows often preached at Walpole in the summer: the diary refers to him as early as 28 July 1844.

13. She had been enlisted as a teacher a week earlier.

14. This blank-verse dramatic poem (Boston: Ticknor & Fields, 1854), written by Mary Quincy's brother Josiah, is a story of duty and self-sacrifice, set in Republican Rome; contemporaries compared it with Talfourd's *Ion*. See Mark A. DeWolfe Howe, *Josiah Phillips Quincy* (an offprint from the *Proceedings of the Massachusetts Historical Society,* December 1911). William Cullen Bryant's New York newspaper was the *Evening Post*.

15. John Gorham Palfrey (1796–1881) was minister of Brattle Square Church, professor at Harvard Divinity School, lecturer, officeholder, and writer, especially of a *History of New England*. Elizabeth is referring to his *Harmony of the Gospels* (Boston: Gray & Bowen, 1831).

16. Otto Dresel, a pupil of Liszt's, had arrived in Boston in 1852. Pianist and teacher, he organized several instrumental and choral groups to perform German music. He played concertos with the Germania and joined the Mendelssohn Quintette whenever a pianist was needed. *Midsummer Night's Dream* was incidental music for Shakespeare's play, composed in 1843 by Felix Mendelssohn-Bartholdy (1809–47), after an earlier overture.

17. Diary, 16 February 1858, also mentions performances, at the Cabots'. The Agassiz family deserves comment. Ida, Pauline, and Alexander were the children of Louis Agassiz's first marriage and came to the United States after their mother's death in Europe. Ida has already been mentioned. Pauline married millionaire Quincy Shaw and later became a pioneer in Boston of the kindergarten movement. Alexander, a pioneer with Shaw in the Calumet and

Hecla copper mine in peninsular Michigan, millionaire, but also eminent zoologist, married Anna Russell, sister-in-law of his close friend Theodore Lyman III.

18. Charles Follen was probably the son of the refugee and professor of the same name (1796–1840), who had married Eliza Lee Cabot. Catharine Sedgwick (1789–1867) was a novelist from the 1830s, living first at Stockbridge, then at Lenox.

19. *Lucrezia Borgia* (1833) and *La Favorita* (1840) were by Gaetano Donizetti (1793–1848). The prologue of *Lucrezia* is set in Venice; the remainder of the action takes place in Ferrara. *Norma* (1831) was by Vincenzo Bellini (1801–35), and the title role was later to be one of Maria Callas's triumphs. Giovanni Mario (1810–83) became an opera star only after a brief military career; in 1844, he married Giulia Grisi (1811–69), a soprano who retired in 1861 after thirty-three years of performances.

20. Albertina Shelton, daughter of merchant Philip Shelton of Pemberton Square, was the acknowledged star of this circle of amateur singers. Note, e.g., her six solos, duets, and trios in the program of Bendelari's concert, attached to diary, 26 April 1855.

21. The Thayers were not intimate friends of the Masons, but visits were quite often exchanged—diary entries mention a ball on 5 December 1854 and a dinner party on 20 February 1856. Nathaniel and John E. were partners in banking, financing factories, and railroads. By the 1860s Nathaniel was a millionaire. The next generation, bearing the same names, were both millionaires by 1892.

22. Horatio Greenough (1805–52), a protégé of Washington Allston, spent much of his career in Italy and France. He worked on sculptures of Lafayette and Washington and on groups for the Capitol. The Franklin statue was placed the next year in front of City Hall on School Street.

23. Randolph Rogers (1825–92) was partly self-taught and partly trained in Italy. Among his works were bronze doors for the Capitol at Washington, D.C.

24. The program, attached to the diary, shows that almost all the items were by Rossini, Donizetti, and Bellini. Elizabeth was correct in reporting fifty-four singers (most of them only in the chorus); and five ladies accompanied. Although the program lacks the modern degree of detail, it is possible to be almost certain that Elizabeth sang, as solo, "Com'è bello," the first aria (then commonly termed the *cavitina*) in *Lucrezia Borgia,* when Lucrezia finds her son asleep during an evening entertainment; and, with Tina Shelton, the duet for Anne and Jane Seymour, who had supplanted her, in act 2, scene 1, of Donizetti's *Anna Bolena* (1830). It is the only duet for two women in that opera. She had been practicing the former with Corelli, 19 March 1855. *L'Elisir d'Amore* (1832) was a comic opera by Donizetti.

25. Covenants of Federal Street Church, in Arlington Street Church Records, 449/9 (4), Andover-Harvard Theological Library. Although some detail of the ceremony may have been omitted there, the main point is clear: that the candidate subscribed to a covenant, which professed belief in God, in Scripture as the record of His revelation, in Jesus Christ as "Teacher, Saviour, and Lord," and in His resurrection. It expressed a desire to live according to God's will, acknowledged sin, and promised obedience to Christ's teaching in the hope of "forgiveness of sin and life everlasting." This is much more positively doctrinal than later Unitarian statements, but still very far from the Congregationalist (and Baptist) requirements, which included a convincing description of a conversion experience.

26. Lucy Lyman Paine Sturgis later married Charles R. Codman, who became one of the lay leaders at Trinity Church. Russell was her brother, at least the third generation with the name. Their father was a partner in Baring's, international bankers.

27. Annie Loring was the daughter of lawyer Charles G. Loring, who is found (diary, 20, 21 January 1857) arguing before the U.S. Supreme Court. *Evelina* (1778) is a novel by Fanny Burney (Mme. d'Arblay, 1754–1840), daughter of Dr. Charles Burney, musical scholar and friend of Dr. Johnson's.

28. *Marie Stuart* (1820) was a verse tragedy by Pierre Antoine Lebrun

(1785–1873). It was one of the few modern plays in the repertoire of Élise Rachel Félix (1821–58); her fame depended chiefly on such classic French tragedies as Racine's *Athalie.*

29. See Introduction and its note 47. Diary, 2 June 1854, shows that Mrs. Lowell had given up her school because of ill health.

30. Dr. George Derby, 11 West Street, and perhaps a relation, since Uncle John Rogers had married Ellen Derby.

31. The diary does not follow up this episode. There may be some reference to the fact that the younger woman had been divorced in 1840, but perhaps no more was involved than curiosity about the element of secrecy and surprise.

32. Orville Dewey (1794–1882) was a minister at Federal Street Church under Channing, then at New Bedford, in New York City, then in Boston again, 1857–61, at New South.

33. Her brother William Powell Mason, Jr., not her cousin Powell Parkman.

34. The old Trinity Church on Summer Street, then a high-class residential district. For a photograph, see Kay, *Lost Boston,* 12; for residents and atmosphere, see *New England Magazine,* n.s., 19 (1898–99): 333–56. Note the distinction between dress deemed suitable for church and that appropriate to an evening reception.

35. A "cricket" was a low stool.

36. *Oberon* was an opera by Carl Maria von Weber (1781–1825). Robert Franz (1815–92) was a German organist, choirmaster, and composer of songs, the first series published in 1843. *Orpheus,* however, cannot be identified with confidence. Elizabeth's phrasing suggests a piece she thought well known. The context suggests that there is a firm statement about a "selection," which rules out a single song. The club's purpose was to perform *German* music. Every candidate proves in some way wrong. Monteverdi's Italian opera was unknown. Offenbach's (French) had not yet been written. Liszt's work (1856), even if so quickly known in Boston, was a symphonic poem for

orchestra or arranged for four hands at the piano. Why should the great work of Christoph Willibald Gluck (1714–87) be chosen, when the Vienna version (1762) was in Italian and the Paris version (1774) in French? Yet it seems the most likely. It was known in Boston, and a single voice is certainly dominant, selections being wholly appropriate.

37. Elizabeth told her father two days later.

38. Henry David Thoreau (1817–62) had published *Walden* (Boston: Ticknor & Fields) two years earlier.

39. Georgina Lowell was the younger daughter of Francis Cabot Lowell II, 56 Beacon Street, and a lifelong friend of Ida Agassiz. Her elder sister, Mary, who married Dr. Algernon Coolidge, is occasionally mentioned in the diary.

40. Henry David Thoreau, *A Week on the Concord and Merrimack Rivers* (Boston: Monroe, 1849).

41. Cousin Daniel Slade and his wife. Elizabeth never calls her anything but Louise and states that she had no relations. The word *foreigner* may provide the clue. And Tompkins, *History of the Boston Theatre*, 41–43, tells us that the only sister of opera singer Elise Hensler married a Dr. Daniel Slade and assigns him to a Harvard class that neatly fits his age, recorded with his death in the diary on 11 February 1896. This is somewhat reinforced by the appearance in the 23 March 1855 concert program, among other girls who were Elizabeth's friends, of "Miss L. Hensler." Perhaps opera singers were to be admired on the stage but not welcomed as members of the family.

42. Stephen Perkins, born in 1835, was a merchant's son. He left Harvard because of eye trouble, toured Europe, spent a year at Harvard Law School, then turned to mathematics at the Lawrence Scientific School. He was also known as an oarsman. Joining the Second Massachusetts, he was killed in 1862 at Cedar Mountain, Virginia, on a day when fourteen of his twenty-two fellow officers became casualties. *Harvard Memorial Biographies*, 1:349–57.

43. In fact, the *Boston Daily Advertiser*. Hale succeeded his father as proprietor and editor in 1854, though he also had a political career.

44. Diary, 8 October 1856, records hearing a pacing overhead, at Quincy,

in what she thought was Josiah's room. Four days later she writes, "I can think of little else but Joe Quincy"; diary, 28 November 1856, shows her reading and rereading his verse dramas, and she continued to think about him until his marriage in 1859. John C. Fremont (1813–90) was an army officer in the Corps of Topographical Engineers, a famous explorer of the West in the 1840s, the husband of Jessie the daughter of Senator Benton of Missouri, and the Republican party's first presidential candidate. Later, he was an unsuccessful general in the Civil War.

45. Theodore Parker (1810–60) was a Unitarian minister who, in his theology, went far beyond Channing and Gannett and who was also radical in his views on capitalism and slavery. His ideas are made particularly clear in "Theodore Parker's Experiences as a Minister," a long letter to his congregation written when he was already mortally ill; it is printed in John Weiss, *Life and Correspondence of Theodore Parker,* 2 vols. (London: Longmans, Green, 1863; New York: Appleton, 1864), 2:447–513. Elizabeth is probably referring to *Sermons of Religion* (Boston: Crosby, Nichols, 1853), but possibly to *A Discourse on Matters Pertaining to Religion* (Boston: Little, Brown, 1842).

46. James Savage (born 1832) traveled and studied in Europe after an undistinguished career at Harvard. He joined a drill club as soon as John Brown had been executed. As soon as war broke out, he volunteered, and in October 1862 he died, from the effects of amputation, two and a half months after receiving three wounds at Cedar Mountain. See *Harvard Memorial Biographies,* 1:305–26.

47. Thomas Jefferson Coolidge (1831–1920) married an Appleton, worked in cotton manufacturing, banking, and railroads, and from 1892 to 1896 was U.S. minister to France. The Baylies family, apparently New Yorkers, were an occasional part of Elizabeth's social circle for many years, both in America and in France.

48. Diary, 28 February 1857, describes Joe Gardner's face, seen by gaslight, as "deathly pale and miserable." Yet she cannot refrain from the sharp phrase, about Gardner's "fears, aspirations however few. . . ." On 7 April,

Joe Quincy was still in her thoughts. Even when both men sailed for Europe (in the same ship) and when Henry Van Schaick married, Elizabeth did not attain peace of mind.

49. William Page (1811–85) was a painter of portraits and of religious and mythological subjects, resident in Italy 1849–60.

50. Despite her doubts, Dr. Gannett's Sunday School Record Book, 1858–59, in Arlington Street Church Records, 449/10 (18), shows "Miss Mason" still responsible for a class of four children. The last diary reference is 1 January 1860.

51. In other words, contact with the Cabot family, though not close, was quite independent of Walter's presence or absence. A birthday party at "Sarah Cabot's" had been mentioned in the diary as early as 6 March 1846.

52. Fanny Huntington would marry Josiah Quincy in 1859.

53. There is a curious contradiction between her saying that his face was new to her and her remark in the diary, 6 November 1857, that he was a "very warm friend." The friendship, if it existed, could not have been of long duration.

Chapter Five

1. The same fate overtook Frances Elizabeth Appleton, the second Mrs. Longfellow, in 1861, though it took her longer to die.

2. "The Lancers"—a form of dance popular in the nineteenth century. Webster defines as a set of five quadrilles, each in a different meter.

3. Diary, 18 October 1858, shows Elizabeth taking over the housekeeping; 21 October will reveal her continuing anxiety about her duties, as a boy puts down carpets and a black woman washes paint, to put the library in good order.

4. The engagement had been noted in the diary on 13, 14 September 1858, with doubts as to whether the match was suitable.

5. Elizabeth's letter to old Mrs. Cabot, 15 February 1869, written from

Pau, treats Walter's health, mentions horseback riding, and stresses his "passion" for fencing (Paine Papers, box VIII, folder 8).

6. Parish records (Andover-Harvard Theological Library) are dominated from 1855 through 1861 by discussion of, and preparation for, abandoning the Federal Street site. After occupying temporary quarters and making new arrangements for pewholding, Arlington Street Church was completed and occupied, on the edge of what would become the fashionable Back Bay. A plan attached to a report at the end of 1861, duplicated in 449/24 (4), shows Mr. Mason holding a pew valued at $525, in a church whose average was $436, with a range from $125 to $850. Some familiar names appear, but the mention of a J. P. Gardner does not, unfortunately, help us in solving the mystery of Joe's identity.

7. Paul Revere was wounded at Antietam, where his brother Edward was killed. He himself died in 1863 of Gettysburg wounds (*Harvard Memorial Biographies,* 1 : 204–20).

8. Her brother had been in Europe since November 1856.

9. The former Jenny Revere, now Mrs. Reynolds.

10. The reference to meeting Loulie and Joe is inconclusive. She encountered them separately. Worse, a Gardner and a Gardiner estate would fit the narrative equally well.

11. Unprinted diary entries show that Walter called twice after the Brookline encounter.

12. Greely Curtis was a man Elizabeth admired, but he was never a suitor. The *City Directory* shows him an engineer, living at 9 Pinckney Street.

13. Frederick E. Church (1826–1900) was a painter, settled in New York City, who undertook extensive travel to the Caribbean, South America, and the Near East, making sketches for future work. *The Heart of the Andes* was a new painting, which, with *Niagara* (1867), remained his most famous.

14. James Freeman Clarke (1810–88) was a Unitarian minister, an early associate of the Transcendentalists though less adventurous in his theology. He was a translator of German literature, a prolific writer on religious topics,

and a supporter of women's education. His Church of the Disciples (1841) was noted for congregational participation in services, for flexibility in timing celebration of the Lord's Supper, and for innovation in philanthropy, e.g., the Home for Aged Colored Women, which Clarke's mother helped found. See James Freeman Clarke, *Autobiography, Diary and Correspondence,* ed. Edward Everett Hale (Boston: Houghton Mifflin, 1891); and John W. Thomas, *James Freeman Clarke, Apostle of German Culture to America* (Boston: Luce, 1949).

15. Paine Papers, box VII, folder 17, provides the evidence: letters from Sadie to Walter while he was studying in Paris, expressing warm affection, with terms of endearment, comic drawings, and once a complaint that he does not write as well as he talks. Sadie was six years younger than Walter, sixteen to twenty-two while he was away, and a year younger than Elizabeth.

16. Samuel Cabot is rarely mentioned in the diary. His few letters to Walter (Paine Papers, box VII, folder 8) are straightforward, businesslike, unrevealing. A glimpse of his personality, consistent with Elizabeth's impression here, is given many years later by James Elliot Cabot: "He was a silent man, rather a dyspeptic, always kind, but not very much occupied about us children" (*Autobiographical Sketch, Family Reminiscences, Sedge Birds* [Boston: Ellis, 1904], 9). He had three more years to live.

17. Quite possibly Harriet Sears Amory, who on 14 November 1860 married Joseph P. Gardner (Louise Tharp, *Mrs. Jack: A Biography of Isabella Stewart Gardner* [Boston: Little, Brown, 1965], 21).

Chapter Six

1. Perhaps Nathan Bangs, *A History of the Methodist Episcopal Church,* 4 vols. (New York: Mason & Lane, 1839–41), but more probably John Lednum, *History of the Rise of Methodism in America* (Philadelphia, 1859). At least eight American editions of Emerson's *Essays* existed, so no identification is possible.

2. Readers are again reminded of the short sketches in *Harvard Memorial Biographies*.

3. Edward Everett Hale (1822–1909) was Unitarian minister at Worcester, then at Boston's South Congregational, 1856–1900. He was also an editor, writer of utopian and other fiction and of history, and a social reformer. His sermons (more than sixteen hundred of them) are in Andover-Harvard Theological Library, and his enormous journal is in the New York State Archives, Albany. In those days, an employment office usually dealt with domestic servants.

4. This must be the Woman's Loyal National League, which existed from May 1863 to August 1864. It was founded by Susan B. Anthony, Elizabeth Cady Stanton, and others, and its male allies included Senator Sumner. Its aim was to exert pressure upon Congress, by petition, to make Emancipation nationwide by constitutional amendment, and to include the vote for women as well as blacks, all in the cause of the national tradition of freedom and equal rights. The diary does not tell us how Elizabeth weighed the two issues of abolitionism and women's rights. See Elizabeth Cady Stanton, *Eighty Years and More: Reminiscence 1815–1897* (New York: Schocken, 1971; 1st ed. 1898), 235–40, including one of the foundation documents. There is some further clarification in Lois Banner, *Elizabeth Cady Stanton: A Radical for Women's Rights* (Boston: Little, Brown, 1980), 93–94. Hannah was presumably Dr. Sam Cabot's wife.

5. Guy and Godfrey were two of Dr. Sam Cabot's children. Eddie Reynolds was a child of the former Jenny Revere. Lucy Codman was the former Lucy Sturgis.

6. Founded in 1861, standing first on Southac Street, then, from 1865, on Myrtle, the Home for Aged Colored Women never had more than about twenty residents; but many prominent Bostonians sat on its governing body or subscribed, including Anna Loring and Mrs. Samuel Cabot (Hannah?). Later officeholders included Charles R. Codman, Edward W. Hooper (later

treasurer of Harvard), and Thomas Wentworth Higginson. An incomplete set of *Reports,* 1861–97, may be found in the Boston Athenaeum.

7. Probably Dr. Sam Cabot was at his country home, which was conveniently at Milton. It is much described in the early sections of the Godfrey Lowell Cabot diary, typed copy, Godfrey Lowell Cabot Papers, boxes 65–70, Massachusetts Historical Society.

8. Ponkapog and Great Ponds lie a little to the south of the Blue Hills, so quite close to the Cabots' house.

9. The oratorio (1846) by Felix Mendelssohn-Bartholdy, which with Handel's *Messiah* and Haydn's *Creation* were Boston's favorite choral works.

10. The "chair" was the *sedes gestatoria,* attached to poles so that twelve men could carry the Pope shoulder high. The reigning pontiff was still Pius IX. The Cabots' visit took place before the occupation of Rome by Italian troops, which put an end to the Papal States and completed the unification of Italy.

11. Early in Elizabeth's European tour, Mr. Mason died. See letters from Mrs. Mason, 3, 10 December 1867, Paine Papers, box VI, folder 11. Her brother Powell has been explaining the immediate effects of the will.

12. William Wetmore Story (1819–95) was a lawyer, writer on law, and poet, but he was best known as a sculptor. He lived for many years in Italy and was the most prominent member of the American community in Rome. Henry James wrote *William Wetmore Story and His Friends,* 2 vols. (Boston: Houghton Mifflin, 1903). Aurora strewing flowers before Apollo's chariot was the subject of a painted ceiling (1613) by Guido Reni. Guidebooks published early in the present century were still full of admiration. The Cabots visited the Palazzo Rospigliosi and the more numerous art treasures in the Casino Rospigliosi-Pallavicini, both near their apartment on via Gregoriana.

13. This may be elucidated by diary, 12 June 1869. Then it was Elizabeth, with most of the money, indeed a very large fortune, who dreaded extravagance.

14. Lynton, Lynmouth, and Watersmeet are in the extreme northeast of Devonshire, Lynton having a view across the Bristol Channel to South Wales. Railroad access from the outside world existed only from 1898 to 1935. Their hotel, the Valley of Rocks, was named after a natural feature a mile away. Elizabeth's interest in her symptoms reflects her pregnancy.

15. Pau, close to the Pyrenees, was a spa and holiday resort, with a climate some doctors praised as particularly favorable. The church mentioned was Holy Trinity: there were two other Church of England buildings, one Church of Scotland, and one French Protestant. For an encyclopoedic account, see Joseph Duloum, *Les Anglais dans les Pyrénées et le début du tourisme pyrénéen, 1739–1896* (Lourdes: Les Amis du Musée Pyrénéen, 1979), esp. pt. 3.

16. "Have no tongues" means that they spoke no French or other foreign languages. Mrs. Mason had joined them in England, June 1868.

17. Dr. Irving Bagnell practiced at Pau from 1856 until his death in 1905.

18. St. Martin's was one of the Catholic churches.

19. Steeplechasing had started as early as 1841, fox hunting in 1842.

20. Arques and Varengeville are both near Dieppe in Normandy, the castle at Arques being a particularly impressive Norman ruin.

21. George Eliot's (Mary Anne Evans, 1819–81) *The Spanish Gypsy* is a verse drama completed in 1868. It took her four years to write since she was also busy with her novel *Felix Holt.* In preparation, she read widely both in Greek drama and in Spanish history and traveled in Spain, in 1867 passing through Biarritz and Pau. See Gordon Haight, *George Eliot: A Biography* (London: Penguin, 1985), 376–406.

22. Diary, 23 August 1869, explains that Walter has planned "a little tour" of Holland and the German states.

23. Bagnères-de-Bigorre was cooler than Pau, being in the mountains. See Duloum, *Les Anglais dans les Pyrénées,* 434–41, and a romantic sketch on 247.

24. Biarritz is on the French Biscay coast not far from the Spanish border.

It was to become even more fashionable, Edward VII sometimes staying for several weeks. The Cabots were on their way to Spain for a few days, and they went as far as Madrid and Toledo.

25. Charles Spurgeon (1834–92) eventually became a Baptist preacher after earlier connections with Independents and Methodists. After he had settled in London in 1854, the Metropolitan Tabernacle, seating 6,000 people, was built for him in Southwark, not far from the Elephant and Castle. He had no formal ordination, wore no clerical dress, and permitted neither choir nor musical instruments. In 1877, he left the Baptist Union, deeming his fellow ministers lax in their devotion to Calvinist theology. See William O. Chadwick, *The Victorian Church,* 2 vols. (London: Black, 1966–70), 1 : 417–21. With the single exception of the divinity of Christ, it was the Atonement, the place of Christ's death in the plan of salvation, that most clearly separated liberal from orthodox Christian doctrine.

26. West Beach was where old Mrs. Cabot's Beverly Farms summer home was located.

27. The family and Mlle. Rhode were in old Mrs. Cabot's house, Elizabeth and Walter not yet owning a Brookline home of their own.

28. The last entry in the diaries of Hannah Rogers Mason is dated 26 May 1872. It is followed by an account of her mother's death by Elizabeth, a little fuller than in *her* diary.

29. Her memory was playing her false: she had been to Walpole for the summer of 1856, then on a visit with Powell and Fanny in 1863, as well as very briefly with Walter during her 1860 honeymoon.

30. The Woman's Education Association of Boston was founded in 1872; the Boston Athenaeum holds an incomplete set of its *Reports,* 1873–1903. Mrs. Samuel Cabot, Mrs. J. Elliot Cabot, and Kate Gannett Wells (daughter of the Federal Street minister) appear at various times as officers. Despite the diary entry, the reports first show Elizabeth as a member of the executive committee in 1873 and again in 1895, an ordinary member from 1883. Her daughter Elise was a member by 1895. "Parlor meetings" were held to discuss

and launch a variety of projects: chemistry classes for young women, help for girls pursuing an advanced course at the Normal School, training for nurses, kindergarten, a diet kitchen, a cooking school, gymnastics classes, a country vacation home, pictures in the public schools, and traveling libraries. One concern was support for the Society for Encouraging Studies at Home, founded by Anna, Lizzie Ticknor's elder sister. Another was the promotion of what became Radcliffe College (see below, n. 45). The association's mode of operation was to explore a topic, find capable people, provide modest funds for initial development, then let projects proceed independently.

31. "Mimi" was Elizabeth Russell, wife of Theodore Lyman III, their immediate neighbor in Brookline. Her husband often used the nickname in his private notebooks.

32. Complications following Mabel's fall in October 1880 led Dr. John Homans, four months later, to diagnose a "hopeless" case of sarcoma. Doctors were divided about the usefulness of taking the girl to Europe, though Sam Cabot's doctor son Arthur had recently studied in England and could arrange introductions. On 31 August 1898, when Marian Hovey died, Elizabeth credited her with exerting the decisive influence. When the Cabots reached London, Mr. Meredith (British usage styles a surgeon "Mr." and a physician "Dr.") put them in touch with far more eminent men. We do not know the scale of the fees. Sir James Paget (1814−99) was elected fellow of the Royal Society in 1851 and was created baronet twenty years later. He was prominent in the Royal College of Surgeons and London University, and in 1881 he presided over the International Congress of Medicine, held that year in London. In some ways, Thomas Spencer Wells (1818−97) was even more impressive. He too became president of the Royal College of Surgeons and in 1883 baronet. Starting with a practice in ophthalmic surgery, he moved to midwifery and thence to ovariotomy; by 1880, he had performed a thousand such operations, many of them before Lister's reforms. *Dictionary of National Biography,* 20:1144, goes so far as to call him "the originator of modern abdominal surgery." He wrote several books, which were translated into Eu-

ropean languages, and his honorary degrees came from Leyden, Bologna, and Kharkov.

33. The Cabots were now in Manchester Street, near Manchester Square, occupying two floors of a house and part of a third.

34. A brougham was a four-wheeled carriage, enclosed, carrying two to four passengers, the driver sitting outside and in front.

35. After the first night, Elizabeth was not allowed to remain with Mabel because any excitement at once raised the girl's temperature. From 19 April, the parents felt able to resume shopping, sightseeing, and theater going. On 16 April, Walter thought it safe to send a cable to Brookline, announcing the operation's success. Paine Papers, box IX, folder 14, has letters from Lizzie Cabot, with whom three of the children had been left. One, dated 25 April, underlines the anxiety and tension felt, especially by Harry. Another, 1 May, records the arrival of news (presumably by letter) of Mabel's convalescence: "It seems like being in heaven. I could not sleep last night for very happiness. Mrs. Cabot glows all over. . . . Harry looks as if a mountain had fallen from his back, and goes singing and whistling about the house." Note that, one day, Elliot Cabot sent a cable to Mr. Meredith, at 11 A.M., and received a reply at 6 P.M.

36. Stopford A. Brooke (1832–1916) was at first a clergyman in the Church of England, then from 1880 an independent preacher who often spoke in Unitarian chapels. Early in life, he had published a celebrated biography, *Life and Letters of Frederick W. Robertson* (London, 1865), of a man who was one of the early leaders of the Broad Church movement in Anglicanism and was much admired by Phillips Brooks.

37. Henry P. Liddon (1829–90), a Church of England clergyman, was a follower of Pusey, whose *Life* he wrote, in the Oxford Movement. He was an Oxford professor and from 1870 also a canon of St. Paul's Cathedral, traveling to London when his duties required. He promoted improved music and organized daily celebration of Holy Communion and daily sermons during Lent. An opponent of German biblical criticism, he thought that Christ's literal

acceptance of the Old Testament was binding on believers. A student of the great French pulpit orators, he was often heard by 2,000 people at St. Paul's, and Chadwick rates him the greatest preacher of his time (*The Victorian Church,* esp. 2:75, 100–3, 150, 181, 386–87).

38. Lord Beaconsfield (Benjamin Disraeli, 1804–81), a former prime minister, who had died on 19 April and was to be buried on 26 April.

39. Mabel's recovery had been rapid: from light diet, with laudanum "to keep the bowels quiet," to a walk from bed to sofa on 1 May, a carriage ride to Westminster Abbey on 13 May, and so to embarkation a week later. From 2 to 7 May, Elizabeth and Walter felt able to be in Paris. They also found time to hear Mr. Gladstone handle questions, as prime minister, in the House of Commons and to meet housing reformer Octavia Hill.

40. Elizabeth's birthday came during the westward crossing, and letters and cards, stored since embarkation, were delivered to her.

41. The Cabots had disembarked at Queenstown instead of Liverpool and, after touring Ireland, had moved on to North Wales and the Lake District. They traveled through Scotland as far as Inverness. After some time in London, they visited Yorkshire and the Midlands, then, moving through London and Paris, settled first at Cannes, then at Grasse, with side trips to Florence and Rome. After that, they went to Bavaria (hearing Wagner's *Parsiphal* at Bayreuth), Switzerland, Paris, and back to London, before sailing from Liverpool. During this tour, they were in touch with Sir James Paget—diary, 17 October 1885, shows them giving him a photograph of Niagara—and Mr. Meredith. Scarborough, on the North Sea coast of Yorkshire, had been a spa and resort since the eighteenth century—Sheridan wrote a comedy with the town as its setting. In the mid-nineteenth century, rail links with Hull and York opened it to people from industrial cities, even for single-day excursions.

42. The most famous of the light operas of William S. Gilbert (1836–1911) and Arthur Sullivan (1842–1900). First performed in 1885, *Mikado* ran for two years.

43. A spectacular play, by William G. Wills (1828–91), loosely based on Goethe's *Faust,* but chiefly designed, at the great actor's instance, to exhibit Irving's talents as Mephistopheles and Ellen Terry's as Margaret. It was also a means of exploiting new effects produced by electricity. It ran for sixteen months, 1885–87. Henry Irving (1838–1905) and Ellen Terry (1847–1928) regularly acted together between 1878 and 1902. See Bram Stoker, *Personal Reminiscences of Henry Irving,* 2 vols. (London: Heinemann, 1906), 1 : 146–47, 175–83; and Ellen Terry, *The Story of My Life* (London: Hutchinson, 1908), 239–45 and photographs facing 141, 238, 239.

44. Once again, one regrets the absence (even at the National Maritime Museum, Greenwich) of any deck plans that would permit us to visualize the vessel's accommodation for its 200 cabin passengers. We know that the *Cephalonia* could also carry 1,500 emigrants in dormitory-style steerage, but they are never mentioned in the diary.

45. The Boston Children's Aid Society was founded in 1864. The Boston Athenaeum has most of its *Reports* from 1887–88 through 1903. Wayward boys who had been through the courts were placed on three farms. Those destitute or in danger, rather than delinquent, might apply; and they were then given advice, supervised in their own homes, or placed with other families, as were a few wayward girls. An interesting additional project was the placing of small collections of books in children's homes, to be used by neighbors. Throughout, careful visiting was essential. Although some parents made contributions, most of the $40,000 or $50,000 a year came from members' subscriptions or occasional donations or bequests.

46. The story had begun in 1873, when Harvard entrance-type examinations were set for girls and when, at the Social Science Convention, Thomas Wentworth Higginson, James Freeman Clarke, and Wendell Phillips argued against President Eliot for the admission of women to Harvard. Three years later, with his own daughter's needs in mind, Arthur Gilman of Cambridge began canvassing opinions on some separate but equal education plan. In 1879 a circular was issued, a committee of ladies (including Mrs. Agassiz)

promised aid, and several professors agreed to lecture to women. In 1882, the Society for the Collegiate Instruction of Women was incorporated, with Mrs. Agassiz president, Gilman secretary, and Joseph B. Warner of Boston treasurer. The full organization came in 1893–94, after much discussion, of which Elizabeth provides only a glimpse. The principles were the handing over of property to Harvard, the maintenance of independent management, and the approving of teachers and countersigning of degrees by Harvard. Academic credibility was guaranteed, the women handled their own affairs, and the dreaded prospect of coeducation at Harvard was avoided. The name Radcliffe was adopted, from the maiden name of Lady Mowlson, a seventeenth-century English benefactress of Harvard. Mrs. Agassiz continued as president. See Lucy A. Paton, *Elizabeth Cary Agassiz: A Biography* (Boston: Houghton Mifflin, 1919), esp. chaps. 9, 10; Dorothy E. Howells, *A Century to Celebrate: Radcliffe College, 1879–1979* (Cambridge, Mass.: Radcliffe College, 1978). A summary is in Helen L. Horowitz, *Alma Mater: Design and Experience in the Women's Colleges from Their Nineteenth-Century Beginning to the 1930s* (New York: Knopf, 1984), 98–104, 237–47, with emphasis on the desire of alumnae for a full Harvard diploma and on the development of a teaching campus and halls of residence during Agnes Irwin's deanship.

47. Not quite all these people can be identified; but an effort is worth while since this was arguably the most important project in which Elizabeth was ever engaged, even though in a subordinate capacity. Charles W. Eliot (1834–1926) was president of Harvard 1869–1909; for a full and highly favorable account, see Henry James, *Charles W. Eliot, President of Harvard University, 1869–1909*, 2 vols. (Boston: Houghton Mifflin, 1930). William W. Goodwin (1831–1912) became professor of Greek at Harvard at the age of twenty-nine, after study in Germany. He was one of the incorporators in 1882 and remained on the governing body until his death. Elizabeth Cary Agassiz (1822–1907) was a granddaughter of Thomas Handasyd Perkins. In 1850, she married the widowed scientist Louis Agassiz and brought up the three children of his first marriage. She ran a school, accompanied him on his

Brazilian expedition (including the Amazon valley) and helped him write his report (1867), then went on the *Hassler* expedition to South America (including the Strait of Magellan) and wrote articles about it. After Louis died in 1873, she spent years in writing his biography (published in 1885), at the same time bringing up the children of her widowed stepson Alexander. She was involved in the Annex project from the beginning. William E. Byerly (1849–1935) was professor of mathematics and for a long time a lecturer at the Annex and Radcliffe. Joseph B. Warner (1848–1923) was a Boston lawyer and for many years treasurer, being succeeded by Henry Lee Higginson. Mrs. Palmer (Alice Elvira Freeman Palmer, 1835–1902) was a teacher, a professor, and then president at Wellesley; she resigned in 1885 on her marriage to Professor George H. Palmer of Harvard but served as trustee of Wellesley and, briefly, as dean of women at the University of Chicago. She also sat on the State Board of Education, was president of the Woman's Education Association, and was a leading figure in both the Association of College Alumni and the Congregational church.

48. In 1893, a depression had begun, perhaps the most severe in nineteenth-century America. Very much was left to voluntary relief organizations.

49. *Lohengrin* (1850) by Richard Wagner (1813–83) and *Carmen* (1875) by Georges Bizet (1838–75) were performed in Mechanics' Building (see Kay, *Lost Boston*, 203). The Polish singer Jean de Reszke (1850–1925) made his operatic debut as a baritone but soon turned tenor, specializing first in French, then in Wagnerian roles. His brother Edouard was a famous bass and his sister Josephine a successful soprano. Nellie Melba (1859–1931) was an Australian soprano active from 1887 to 1926. Emma Calvé (1858–1942) was a soprano especially famous as Carmen (see the photograph in Orrey's *Encyclopoedia of Opera*, 69). Pol Henri Plançon (1854–1914) was a bass who performed from 1877 to 1908. The other opera was almost certainly *Roméo et Juliette* (1867) by Charles François Gounod (1818–93), for the de Reszkes and Melba appeared elsewhere in the version revised in 1888.

50. The Cabots had taken a quick trip to Europe, particularly to see Venice.

51. Massachusetts Institute of Technology, then on Boylston Street—see the photograph in Kay, *Lost Boston,* 17.

52. Frederick C. Shattuck (1847–1929) was physician, medical writer, and teacher, deeply interested in the Massachusetts Historical Society. He married Elizabeth Perkins Lee, daughter of Henry Lee and Elizabeth P. Cabot, of Brookline, so, like Sam Cabot, he was both a relation and a professional adviser.

53. Agnes Irwin's (1841–1914) father was a mayor of Pittsburgh and a congressman. She taught, became head of a school, and was dean of Radcliffe from 1894 to 1909. She was also president both of the Woman's Education Association of Boston, 1901–7, and of the first association of private school headmistresses.

54. The Venezuela crisis, involving danger of war between Britain and the United States, had as its substance a boundary dispute between a European state and one in Latin America, with the United States invoking the Monroe Doctrine and threatening to decide the issue unilaterally. In the end, arbitration was resorted to, between Britain and Venezuela.

55. Karr, "Evolution of an Elite Suburb," 350–54.

56. Walter J. Damrosch (1862–1950) was the son of an equally famous musician, Leopold Damrosch, an immigrant from Germany. Both men were pioneers in the performing of Wagner's operas in the United States. Walter had his own opera company from 1895. Then he turned to symphonies. His distinguished career ended with activity on radio. *Fidelio* (1805) was the only opera composed by Ludwig van Beethoven (1770–1827).

Chapter Seven

1. Diary, 18 February, 1904.
2. Diary, 7 February 1902.

3. Diary, 11 May 1904.

4. Diary, 1 April 1905.

5. In addition to the passage quoted, see diary, 7 May 1898, 21 April 1901, 29 August 1903.

6. Diary, 3 March 1902.

7. The volume for 1921, 10.

8. Mabel was to marry, 24 September 1904.

INDEX

...em him. Does he love one. I cannot know, I dare
not hope, I cannot despair. I try to wait with
Patience & faith, but oh how hard it is. If he
does not. and I cannot but feel that I have
too many Blessings to receive this also, if he does—
it may become a more precious & blessed thing to
me, for I know that this is the crisis of my
life, after this I shall no longer search for what
I know I cannot find on earth. no more tie
to earthly things will be severed.— Oh what a
wonderful, what a blessed thing is life, Sorrow is
but an aid, and leaves a Happiness which is
divine, a happiness of heaven which one can never
even imagine until earthly pleasures begin to
fail & please. I write as if tired of earth, as
if a long life of suffering had deprived me of
every worldly blessing. and in fact I have every
good gift, but thanks be to God, and his
blessed influences. I have still more, I begin to
see also the heavens. and before their glory, earth
pales. On the contrary I can enter upon life now
with tenfold vigor & interest. It is our present
sphere, rich with opportunities gifts, pleasures
discipline. to be developed by never ceasing